Public Goods and Public Allocation Policy

STAATLICHE ALLOKATIONSPOLITIK IM MARKTWIRTSCHAFTLICHEN SYSTEM

Herausgegeben von
Klaus Conrad, Heinz König, Hans-Heinrich Nachtkamp,
Rüdiger Pethig, Ulrich Schlieper, Horst Siebert, Eberhard Wille

Band 14

Verlag Peter Lang
Frankfurt am Main · Bern · New York

RÜDIGER PETHIG (Ed.)

PUBLIC GOODS AND PUBLIC ALLOCATION POLICY

Verlag Peter Lang
Frankfurt am Main · Bern · New York

CIP-Kurztitelaufnahme der Deutschen Bibliothek

Public goods and public allocation policy /

Rüdiger Pethig (ed.). – Frankfurt am Main ;
Bern ; New York : Lang, 1985.
(Staatliche Allokationspolitik im markt-
wirtschaftlichen System ; Bd. 14)
ISBN 3-8204-8508-2
NE: Pethig, Rüdiger [Hrsg.]; GT

Diese Arbeit ist im Sonderforschungsbereich 5,
"Staatliche Allokationspolitik" Mannheim ent-
standen und wurde auf seine Veranlassung unter
Verwendung der ihm von der
Deutschen Forschungsgemeinschaft
zur Verfügung gestellten Mittel gedruckt.

ISSN 0721-2860
ISBN 3-8204-8508-2

Druck und Bindung: Weihert-Druck GmbH, Darmstadt

Preface

In the Musgravean tradition the concept of public goods has become a central element of the theory of public allocation policy. The basic argument for this prominent role of public goods is that jointness in consumption - and possibly also nonexcludability of consumers who are unwilling to pay - renders market provision inefficient ('*market failure*'). Hence public intervention was called for to enhance allocative efficiency. In recent years, however, quite a different research program, namely the economic theory of policy (or public choice), provided explanations for the working of *public* allocation procedures for public goods. The thrust of this theory is that it is not at all clear whether the public provision of public goods, per se, is apt to improve upon the market allocation. Public choice economists rather identified various inefficiencies in public allocation procedures which are sometimes paraphrased as '*policy failure*'.

Most contributions to the modern theory of public goods are somewhere located in the wide ranges of 'market failures' and/or 'policy failures'.[1] This wide spectrum is also characteristic for the eight contributions of the present volume: The first two papers, i.e. that of M.E. Burns and C. Walsh and that of B.-A. Wickström, study 'market' allocation procedures in the absence of public intervention - for either costlessly excludable or nonexcludable public goods. The next two investigations of R. Pethig and O. von dem Hagen focus attention not only on 'exit' but also on 'voice' (Hirschman), that is, on voluntary or market activities broadly conceived as well as on participation in political allocation procedures. Political allocation procedures (voice) are studied in the subsequent contributions by H. Hanusch and P. Biene and by F. Dudenhöffer who focus attention on elections. A. Endres assesses the impact and efficiency of alternative policy tools for environmental protection. Giving policy advice presupposes a normative, comparative analysis of policy instruments and allocation procedures. Scope and limits of such an analysis are discussed by W. Blümel in the last paper of this volume.

----

1) Blümel, W., Pethig, R., and von dem Hagen, O. (1985), The Theory of Public Goods: A Survey of Recent Issues, Discussion Paper 80-84, Economics Department, University of Oldenburg.

These brief remarks demonstrate how closely this volume reflects the wide scope of public-goods theory. But clearly, the reader deserves some more information and guidance. Therefore, in what follows, the individual contributions will be characterized in more detail.

Burns and Walsh contribute a piece of research to what might be adequately called the 'price theory of (excludable) public goods'. This theory emerged gradually in recent years and is not yet fully developed. A monopolist is given various possibilities of price setting, price discrimination and market separation. According to a wide-spead intuition that is also shared by legislative bodies, price discrimination and market separation should not be politically supported. It is shown, however, that those strategies may be efficiency enhancing, because under some qualifications they reduce both underprovision and rationing by prices.

Wickström presupposes non-excludability, that is, the impossibility to secure positive revenues from market sales. In case of non-cooperative behavior it then follows that only voluntary contributions can be expected to finance the public good under consideration. This leads to a Nash equilibrium of independent adjustments in which the public good is under-provided. However, if one assumes - as does Wickström - that each individual relates his own contribution to the average payment of the others, then one obtains an allocative improvement or even a Pareto efficient provision. In this way Wickström demonstrates that the discrepancy between individual incentives and group interest might not be as severe as suggested by Olson's theory of group formation.

Pethig's paper deals with the related issue of mobilizing latent interest groups. There is a lobbying organization for each of two groups that is engaged in competitive lobbying for group-specific public goods. In order to finance its costly lobbying activity, it has to generate negative selective incentives for membership recruitment. Since each group competes for limited public funds, a 'tug of war' results that is modelled in the paper as a non-cooperative game. The use of parametric functions allows for a complete characterization of the model and offers specific results in comparative-static analysis.

Voluntary transactions are also the basic feature of allocation procedures for local public goods, because there is freedom of 'exit' for each agent. The rapidly growing literature on the theory of local public goods was preoccupied with the exit option but so far there are only a few papers that consider 'voice', i.e. the participation of citizens in the communal political decision process, in addition to the exit option. Von dem Hagen gives an introduction into this complex theoretical issue and then tackles it by means of a model in which the political process in each community is described by the MDP-procedure. Using some suitable simplifications he succeeds in deriving some economically interesting conditions for the existence of Tiebout equilibria.

In the model developed by Hanusch and Biene the agents have a simultaneous vote on the public-good provision, the income-tax rate and on transfer payments. The working time is determined endogeneously and the individuals differ with respect to their productivity (ability). The greater an agent's ability the lower is his most preferred tax-transfer combination. If the distribution of individual abilities is skewed to the right the median voter desires a positive tax rate and a positive amount of the public good but his most preferred transfer payment is not necessarily positive. The inclusion of the labor-leisure decision implies that the voters implicitly also 'solve' the equity-efficiency trade-off.

Dudenhöffer investigates the problem of unilateral transfrontier environmental pollution. In an interregional setting the citizens of two regions have a majority vote on the public good 'environmental quality' of their respective region. A supraregional environmental protection agency then implements these regional quality standards by imposing suitable emission taxes. Among other things Dudenhöffer's model explains the interregional allocation of environmental qualities and productive activities and how this allocation is determined by the interregional distribution of wealth and population.

Endres also focusses attention on environmental economics. But in contrast to Dudenhöffer he presupposes that ambient quality standards are already 'somehow' politically determined. On this basis he investigates the empirically relevant but so far theoretically rather neglected case that the pollution damage might be increased by the interaction of several harmful ambient pollutants. For various types of pollutant interaction Endres then investigates how an environmental protection agency might implement predetermined quality standards at minimum cost if it operates under incomplete information. The author compares the relative efficiency of emission taxes and transferable discharge permits.

The final paper by Blümel differs from the others in that it does not aim at contributing to the (positive) theory of public goods. It rather assesses and evaluates the state of arts of the normative analysis of allocating public goods. Central for normative comparisons of allocation procedures is the concept of allocative efficiency, i.e. the Pareto criterion. Additional criteria are informational efficiency and incentive compatibility. Blümel argues that in many cases theoretical efficiency comparisons are inconclusive because deviations from Pareto efficiency are derived in just about any informationally feasible allocation procedure for public goods. The options available are those between different types of 'failures' which cannot be easily ranked and compared without turning to the elusive concept of welfare functions. More recent developments such as the transaction-costs economics, the property-rights analysis and the new economic institutionalism certainly provided valuable new insights. But a comprehensive comparative analysis of allocation procedures for public goods that is useful for policy advice does not yet seem to be in sight.

I would like to thank Erika Dreyer for typing the manuscript with great care and also Alice Peschla for preparing most of the diagrams. Both fighted successfully not only against the usual intricacies of professional papers but also against the hazards of a stubborn high-tech word processor.

Rüdiger Pethig

Contents

Public Goods with Price Exclusion: Market Segmentation and Allocative Efficiency

by

Michael E. Burns and Cliff Walsh*

1. Introduction

Although analysis of public goods has a very long tradition in the Continental European economics literature,[1] it was largely through the publication of Paul Samuelson's (1954, 1955) seminal articles and Richard Musgrave's (1959) equally seminal treatise on Public Finance that the concept became a central element in the modern microeconomics and public finance literature. Since then, the nature of public goods, their contribution to theories of market failure and their role in models of political activity have been examined in great detail.

As Samuelson noted, of the two fundamental (polar) characteristics of pure public goods, it is their "jointness, or non-rivalness in consumption" characteristic, rather than their "impossibility of exclusion" characteristic, that gives rise to the important change in the conditions for optimality in the presence of public goods.[2] He also observed that, even if price exclusion were feasible, fulfillment of those optimal conditions was unlikely to be achieved by decentralised markets.

---

* Professor of Economics, The Flinders University of South Australia, and Professor of Economics, University of Adelaide, Australia, respectively. This paper, prepared while Burns held a visiting appointment at the University of Adelaide, draws on and extends some of the results developed in a recent Working Paper, Burns and Walsh (1984). It is part of a continuing research programme developing the use of the demand distribution approach as a tool of microeconomic analysis.

1) See, for example, many of the contributions reproduced in Musgrave and Peacock (1958).

2) We refer, of course, to the now familiar requirement for efficient public goods provision, that the *sum* of marginal rates of substitution be equated with the marginal rate of transformation ($\Sigma MRS = MRT$).

It is with this latter case that we are concerned - the case of what we term price excludable (or, more simply, excludable) public goods. That is, we are concerned with goods which exhibit Samuelsonian jointness, in the sense that each unit produced could be fully and equally consumed by all members of the relevant consumption group, but for which price exclusion is feasible (and in the limit costless) so that access to consumption of any or all units produced can be denied to those unwilling to pay the required price. Although these goods (or services) may appear to simply combine elements of polar public goods and private goods cases, in reality they represent a third, separate polar case, with important and distinctive features of their own.

Examples of goods or services which exhibit these characteristics, with varying degrees of purity, include TV broadcasts available only on payment of cable or metered charges; information accessible only on payment of a fee; theatrical performances, or access to parks, museums and art galleries available on payment of single entrance or season ticket charges; plane trips or bus trips for which varying pricing arrangements exist; and access to roads or bridges only on payment of the required toll.

As the examples cited indicate, excludable public goods both are an important class of commodities which frequently arise in public policy discussion,and are associated with application of a rich variety of pricing strategies, reflecting the possibility of applying "discriminatory" pricing as a result of their characteristically "service" nature. Surprisingly, the literature dealing with their provision through private markets is, at best, slender. And where they have been discusssed in the policy literature, analysis has often focussed on what are arguably "peripheral" (though not unimportant) features of their provision (e.g. cultural externalities associated with theatrical performances; or conventional "decreasing cost with respect to output" problems) rather than on their more fundamental characteristic of "jointness with excludability".

There is, nonetheless, a growing literature on market provision of excludable public goods. It has its origins in the work of Earl Thompson (1968), who presented a model of competitive provision under the extreme assumption of perfect knowledge on the part of both producers and consumers and demonstrated that, in these circumstances, market output of excludable public goods would exceed the efficient output level. William Oakland (1974), on the other hand, provided a more conventional treatment of the competitive model, with consumers and producers being assumed to have no more knowledge than market processes would normally be expected to generate, and demonstrated that, in general, market output would be inefficiently low and that, whatever the output, it would be inefficiently price-rationed among consumers.

Although Thompson dealt with the case of perfectly discriminating monopoly provision as a fairly natural by-product of his competitive analysis, general models of monopoly provision of excludable public goods have been a more recent development. Brito and Oakland (1980), Burns and Walsh (1981) and Brennan and Walsh (1981) analysed a variety of monopoly pricing strategies in different analytical frameworks but produced a core set of essentially similar conclusions. Most notably: monopoly provision is characterised by high demand consumers being rationed by output rather than by price; and, where pricing strategies are applied uniformly across consumers (though not necessarily uniformly across different units of output), market output would invariably be inefficiently low and that output would inevitably be inefficiently price-rationed among consumers.

This brief statement of the extant results of models of market provision of excludable public goods makes clear at least two important facts. First, Samuelson's conjecture about the likely inefficiency of decentralised market provision of public goods, even where exclusion is possible, seems to be strongly supported: even competitive provision with exclusion does not generate efficient outcomes analogous to those achieved in competitive private goods markets. Second, the nature of market outcomes for excludable public goods pose different, and arguably more severe, problems for public policies designed to correct for market failure than arise with either pure public or pure private goods. In the case of excludable public goods, the problem is not merely to obtain "correct" levels of output from the market, but also to eliminate inefficient rationing of output among consumers.

The jointness property of public goods (whether excludable or not) implies that efficiency requires not merely that output be such as to satisfy the $\Sigma MRS = MRT$ rule, but also that the entire output be available for consumption by all (i.e. that there be no effective price-rationing) since the (social) cost of admitting an additional consumer to any unit produced is, by definition, zero. For private producers, where exclusion is possible and practiced, this second requirement would seem capable of fulfillment only under the unlikely situation where all consumers are faced with different (marginal) prices corresponding to their different valuations of the marginal unit produced. For pure public goods, this "inefficiency of price-rationing" problem simply does not arise since exclusion (and hence price-rationing) is infeasible or prohibitively expensive: whatever is produced will automatically be available for consumption by all, and hence public policy can focus "simply" on the problem of securing more efficient output levels. For pure private goods, the problem may not arise either, but for different reasons. Price-rationing is efficient in this case since each unit is separately, not jointly, consumed, and the appropriate pattern of consumption is secured with the uniform (marginal) pricing that profit-maximisation also usually requires: again, public policy can focus largely on securing more efficient outputs, usually leaving it to the market to efficiently allocate that output among consumers.[3]

In this paper we do not directly tackle the question of formulating public policies which address this problem of inefficient price-rationing of excludable public goods. Rather we consider the possibility, not so far explicitly analysed in the relevant literature, that pricing strategies involving segmentation of consumers into groups which are charged different prices may be possible, profitable and efficiency-improving relative to uniform pricing arrangements.[4]

Interest in these strategies (defined in more detail below) stems from several sources. For one thing, segmentation does seem to be involved, explicitly or implicitly, in pricing strategies utilised by excludable public goods producers. It is explicitly (if often imperfectly) practiced, for example, where prices for access to movies, theatrical performances or art galleries are varied according to time-of-day of consumption, or some identifiable characteristic (e.g. age or sex) of the

3) In private goods markets, inefficient price rationing *can* occur - for example where lump sum "entrance fees" are imposed which completely exclude some consumers who would willingly purchase units at per-unit prices equal to marginal cost.

4) By "uniform pricing" we mean, here, "uniform across consumers". This is consistent with discrimination across units of output where all consumers face an identical price *schedule* for access to units.

consumers. It is also at least implicitly practiced where access to consumption units is offered (on an either/or basis) through both single entrance charges and multiple entrance charges ("season tickets"). For another thing, the question arises how far this pricing stragegy might go towards eliminating the potential consumption inefficiencies that arise in the market provision of excludable public goods: contrary to a not uncommon presumption in popular thinking, and even sometimes embodied in anti-trust laws, public policies which facilitate and encourage the practice of market segmentation and price discrimination by monopoly producers may be efficiency improving in the excludable public goods context, since they may serve to both expand output towards more efficient levels *and* reduce the severity of price-rationing of consumption.

The framework of analysis we employ is based on the concept of a *demand distribution* developed in our 1981 paper (and explained in detail later) as a replacement for the more familiar construct of the aggregate demand function. It needs to be emphasised that use of this distributional approach is not simply an optional extra. As indicated in different ways by a number of authors - Spence (1978), Burns (1979), Brito and Oakland (1980) and Burns and Walsh (1981, 1984) for example - the analysis of both excludable public goods provision and of the provision of private goods where price discrimination is practiced require a framework that specifies or parameterises the intensity of demand across individuals.

In its most general form, analysis using the demand distribution is highly technical and dauntingly complex in comparison to the traditional two-dimensional methods of demand analysis. Some of this complexity must always remain if results of the greatest possible generality are to be derived. However, as in traditional demand analysis where useful insights have been derived through use of the linear demand function as an expository tool, there is a place for use of a linear demand distribution as an expository device in distributional analysis. The use of this device in the present paper serves not only to conveniently illustrate the pricing strategies we intend to analyse, but also to clarify the methodological approach essential to the proper comparison of the profitability and efficiency of those strategies.

Accordingly, our paper has a number of general aims: to illustrate and clarify important issues in the provision of excludable public goods; to generate further insights into the new frameworks of analysis that embody distributional information; and to generate new results on the implications of pricing strategies involving market segmentation.[5] In Section 2, we make some fairly general observations suggesting that segmentation may be able to generate both profitability and efficiency gains. In Section 3, the linear demand distribution is defined and used to identify characteristic features of a variety of pricing strategies with particular emphasis on those involving segmentation. This information is utilised in Section 4 to compare the profitability, output and (social) efficiency of the alternative strategies. Section 5 summarizes our conclusions.

2. Market Segmentation: Some General Results

It is appropriate that we briefly consider the major identifying characteristics of the class of problems we are concerned with - exemplified by (but not exclusive to) sale of theatre tickets. First, observation of common business practice reveals the use of marketing strategies involving uniform pricing, market segmentation and opportunities for individuals to self-select between individual and bulk purchasing (at discounted rates) of units of output (plays or whatever). Second, the actual product (e.g., an individual play) clearly has public goods characteristics, at least as long as relevant facilities (e.g. theatres) are utilised at less than full capacity. As is now well understood, both of these characteristics demand a framework of analysis that incorporates information about the intensity, or distribution, of demand across individuals. Not surprisingly, we will satisfy this informational requirement by drawing on the distributional framework developed in our own earlier work. However, before we briefly (re)define this approach, some attention must be paid to a further characteristic of the class of problems under consideration.

5) See, however, Burns and Walsh (1984) for a preliminary analysis of strategies similar to those considered here.

This matter relates to the question of homogeneity of output. Clearly, if we are thinking, for example, of a season of different plays, then output is not homogeneous. Even the same play shown on different nights would not reflect a homogeneous output. What should be realised here is that even in the absence of homogeneity, some questions will still yield a legitimate price-theoretic answer. Thus, suppose seven different plays were shown on seven different nights: individuals would be quite able to answer the question "how many plays would you attend if the price per play was such and such?" Indeed, for all the normal reasons we might expect individual responses to reflect the standard, downward-sloping demand relation:

$$q_i = q(p), \frac{\partial q_i}{\partial p} < 0 \qquad (1)$$

However this notion of a 'demand relation' is clearly somewhat different from the usual concept, not least because, in a sense, such a relation is not independent of supply. Thus the question of how many different plays may be produced during a season would be expected to affect how many different plays separate individuals would be willing to watch at various prices. The interestingly more complex questions raised due to heterogeneity of output are certainly not intractable, but for expositional purposes we think it useful to make our initial comparison of different pricing strategies under the assumption that individuals do not distinguish between plays - that is, output is homogeneous.

Let us now consider the details of our basic framework. We shall assume that a sufficiently large number of output units are provided (each consumed only once) to justify the assumption of continuous, differentiable demand relations of the form (1) above. Further (and this involves a restriction not enforced in much of our 1981 analysis) we shall assume that individual demand curves do not intersect and that income effects are negligible. Strictly speaking, these latter assumptions are necessary to justify analyses of complex pricing strategies based upon consideration of a single demand distribution. The assumptions taken together lead us to define a demand distribution

$$n = n(q, p) \qquad (2)$$

where n represents the number of individuals who would be prepared to consume at least q units of output should each unit be available at a uniform price p. An additional assumption made is that:

$$\frac{\partial n}{\partial p}, \frac{\partial n}{\partial q} < 0 \tag{3}$$

both the interpretation and plausibility of this assumption being discussed in our earlier work.[6] As a consequence of the assumptions made, it follows that a cross-section through the distribution at some particular (constant) value of n defines the demand curve of a particular individual, which in the absence of income effects also reflects individual valuations of specific consumption units. The fact that for any given uniform price more individuals appear to wish to watch the 'first' play than any other play need not be regarded as an indicator of actual attendances at the first or later plays. Indeed, we are unable to say precisely how large the consumption will be for any individual unit. At most, for a given uniform price level, we can only say that the largest consumption will be equal to or less than the number of individuals who want to consume at least one unit. Similarly, the smallest consumption of any unit must be equal to or greater than the number of individuals wishing to consume all units.

Bearing all of this in mind, the strategy of finding the optimal uniform price (OUP) for any given output (number of plays) will remain exactly as described in our 1981 paper and as illustrated in Figure 1. Thus, still valid are the important results that 'rationing' of some individuals will always be optimal and, that marginal revenue for this strategy will be the product of price and the number of individuals consuming the entire output. Of course, from what we have said above, the number of such consumers need not be the same as the number of consumers of any particular unit of output.

Against this familiar background of the well-known uniform pricing analysis let us now consider, at as general a level as possible, what can be said regarding the

6) Burns and Walsh (1981), pp. 169-170.

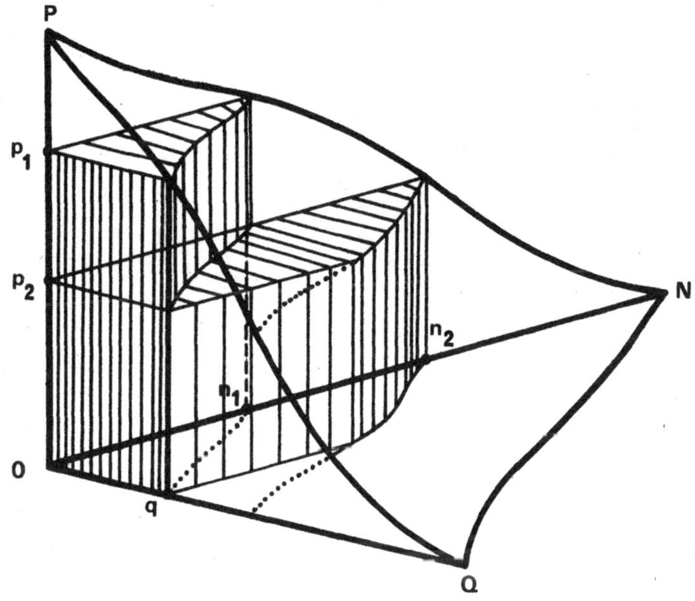

Figure 1: Optimal uniform pricing

implications of segmentation. Clearly, random segmentation will generate no expected revenue gains to the producer. In terms of the distributional approach offered here, suppose for simplicity that such segmentation of an initial distribution is achieved with equally sized sub-populations. The expectation would clearly be that the number of individuals with any particular demand characteristic in each of the sub-distributions would be half that in the initial distribution. Since the effect is analogous to a simple rescaling of the N variable, all optimal solutions will leave P and Q variables unchanged, optimal expected revenues in each sub-distribution being half the original amount. Clearly this is equivalent to the traditional demand analysis result that segmentation will increase revenue only where, at the initital simple profit-maximising price, elasticities differ between market segments.

Obviously the success of segmentation depends on achieving 'differentness'. As far as we know, the first attempts to derive 'optimal segmentation' properties appeared in our own earlier work [e.g. Burns and Walsh, (1982)], some of our initial results for a linear distribution being independently re-derived in Varian (1984). In fact, in both our own work and that of Varian it was assumed that optimal segmentation would be on a strict 'high-low' demand basis. It seems that some justification should be offered for such an assumption. To see that the result is indeed correct, consider a simple case where individuals each only consume one unit of the good in question. Consider further the optimal strict 'high-low' segmentation, illustrated for the linear case in Figure 2. Here the q_1 highest demand individuals have been segmented out, it being trivial to show for the linear case that maximum revenue requires:

$$p_1 = 2p_2 \qquad q_1 = q_2 - q_1 = Q - q_2 \tag{4}$$

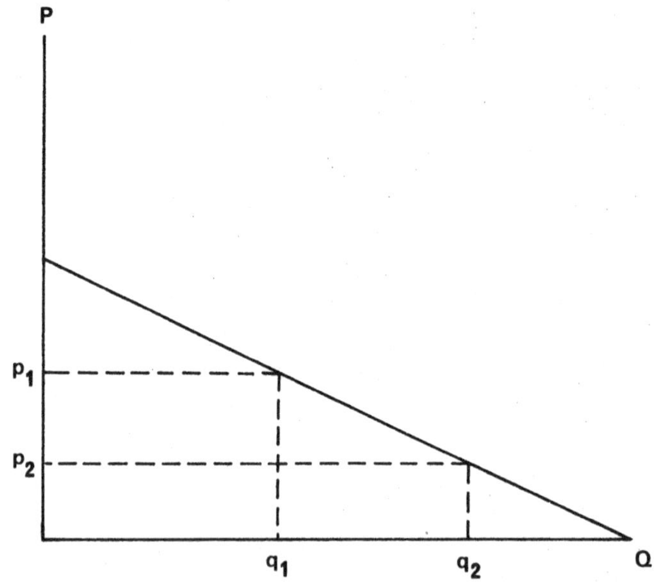

Figure 2: "High-low" segmentation

Whether we restrict consideration to the linear case or not, moving a marginal individual from one segment to the other can, by definition, have no effect on overall revenue. This result can be obtained alternatively by noting that p_1 must be set to maximise revenue in the "area" above p_2, while p_2 must be set to maximise revenue in the "area" to the right of q_1. Thus, moving the marginal high demand individual to the low demand segment reduces revenue by p_2 in the 'high' segment, raising it by the same amount in the 'low' segment.

Suppose we now consider moving a non-marginal individual from the 'high' to the 'low' segment, for simplicity considering the highest demand individual of all. Clearly we now lose p_1 in revenue from the 'high' segment but still gain (only) p_2 in the 'low' segment, a net loss of $p_1 - p_2$. These arguments can easily be made more general and completely rigorous. As they stand they clearly provide some rationale for the earlier approaches of ourselves and Varian.

Bearing in mind that perfect 'high-low' segmentation is unlikely to be feasible in practise, our initial approach will be to investigate this polar case so as to obtain some insights as to the potential gains in profitability (and gains or losses in social welfare) converged to in the limiting case. Consideration of how one might approach these solutions in practise is dealt with at a later stage. As for optimal segmentation, some general comments should be made before we proceed with the illustrative analysis making use of a linear distribution.

First, starting with a non-segmented distribution and the associated optimal uniform price, and then taking out the highest demand individual, it is straightforward to show that the optimal uniform price in the residual distribution will, in general, fall. By considering successive adjustments of this kind we are drawn to the unsurprising view, for the case of strict 'high-low' segmentation, that it will be optimal to reduce the price level to the low demand segment. This is suggestive from a social welfare point of view, since the lower price will lead to greater consumption efficiency for any given output level. The question is, what happens in the high-demand sector? A general presumption, and one followed by Varian, is that a higher (than OUP) uniform price should be charged in the 'high-demand' sector. If this is so, bearing in mind that many high-demand individuals will usually be rationed in the (unsegmented) OUP case, an increase in price to these individuals *may* reduce consumption in the high-demand segment. However this very rationing characteristic of OUP makes it unlikely that the consumption-efficiency loss in the 'high-demand' sector would outweigh the gain in the 'low-demand' segment. In fact, our own view is that an overall consumption-efficiency gain is even more likely than suggested here, because *the profit-maximising strategy will normally involve all-or-nothing charging (OAN) rather than uniform pricing (OUP).*

This insight, adopted in our earlier work, draws on two results. The first, given in our 1981 paper, notes that in general and in consideration of complete (unsegmented) distributions, there is no reason to expect OUP to have any revenue advantage over OAN (Optimal All-or-Nothing Charging) or *vice versa*. The second result is the expectation that, for any given output level, OAN will involve less consumers than OUP, the difference in the number of consumers becoming more pronounced as output increases. This latter result also draws on our 1981 paper which demonstrated that OAN and OUP tend to be identical as output tends to zero, but that under very general conditions as output increases the optimal uniform price (and hence the number of consumers) would be expected to fall. The symmetry between OAN and OUP leads to the expectation that as output increases the optimal number of consumers under OAN should decrease. Taking these results together, consider a 'high-demand' segment of a market which would be represented geometrically by a truncated distribution. Now it may be that the degree of truncation interferes with neither the OAN nor OUP solutions for the unsegmented case. In this case, the expectation would be that it does not matter (in a revenue sense) whether we use OAN or OUP. However, from our discussion above, if truncation does interfere with the unsegmented OAN and OUP solutions our expectation would be that it *either* affects OUP and not OAN or it affects OUP more than it affects OAN. In an uncertain world clearly OAN is to be preferred to OUP as the 'high-demand' segment marketing strategy.

3. A Linear Demand Distribution Approach

Against the background of the general observations concerning the profitability and efficiency of strategies of market segmentation presented in the previous section, in this and the next section we turn to examine some specific examples of such pricing strategies within the more analytically tractable framework of a linear demand distribution. Specifically, we assume a system of parallel, linear, uniformly distributed demand curves:

$$q_i = a_i - bp \qquad (i = 1, ..., N) \tag{5}$$

where the price intercept, a_i/b varies continuously from $a_i/b = P$ for $i = 1$ (the highest demand individual) to $a_i/b = 0$ for $i = N$ (the lowest demand individual).

The demand *distribution* for this case can be straightforwardly illustrated, as in Figures 3 through 10, which may be interpreted as being constructed, in effect, by placing the demand curves (of unit width) of the N individuals side-by-side, ranked from the highest to the lowest. P is the maximum price anyone is willing to pay for a single unit of the excludable public good, and Q is the greatest quantity anyone would consume if price were zero. In this linear case, the bounding values P, Q and N completely define the distribution and may be taken as constant parameters throughout the analysis.

For any per-unit price, p, and output *unit*, q, the value of n defined by the distributional function (2) is located by finding the relevant point on the surface of the distribution. And for any given output level, q_0, and price, p_0, total revenue is found by identifying the value of n for each separate unit in the bundle q_0, and can be represented by the volume of the appropriately drawn solid in the Figures below.

Since we are considering complex pricing strategies for which, in general, income effects may be expected to affect the demand curves, to enable the demand distribution itself to be validly employed we adopt the simplifying assumption that such income effects are negligible. While we cannot rule out the possibility that *some* results might be significantly affected by this assumption (and conceivably even reversed), it is likely in general that substitution effects will dominate and hence our results at least will be qualitatively applicable.

We begin, in this section, by defining the characteristic features of the pricing strategies and revenue functions relevant to our interest in market segmentation:

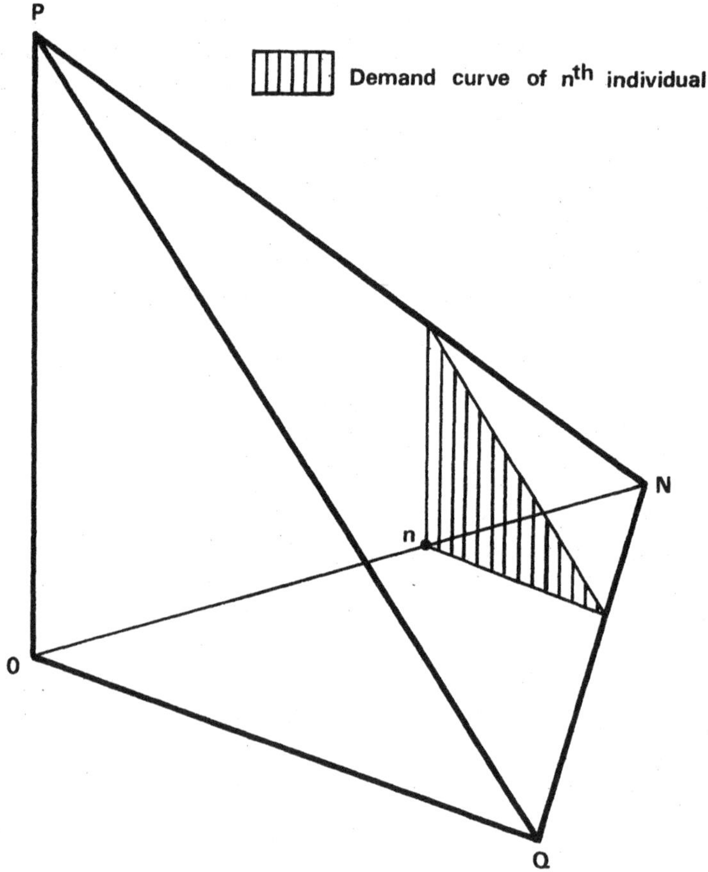

Figure 3: The linear distribution

the choice of output levels and the relative efficiency of the strategies are considered in Section 4. The linear demand distribution enables us to make use of properties of similar triangles and associated proportionality rules. In particular, it is useful to define:

$$\hat{p} = \frac{p}{P};\ \hat{q} = \frac{q}{Q};\ \hat{n} = \frac{n}{N}$$

In Burns and Walsh (1981) we examined a number of uniformly applied pricing strategies, including briefly defining their revenue characteristics in this linear case.[7] Two of those strategies remain of interest to our present endeavour since it can be shown that in various combinations they constitute the fundamental building-blocks of more complex strategies in which interpersonal price discrimination is practised: these are the strategies we defined as Optimal Uniform Pricing (OUP) and Optimal All-or-Nothing Charging (OAN).

Optimal Uniform Pricing (OUP): for a given output level, q, charging the uniform per-unit price which maximises revenue.

As we have already indicated, for price-excludable public goods, it will in general be revenue-maximising (for given output) for the producer to ration high demand individuals by output rather than by price (see Figure 4). If we denote the proportion of all N individuals who are rationed in this sense by $\hat{r}$, inspection of Figure 4 reveals that if $\hat{r}N$ individuals are rationed by output when $\hat{q}Q$ is output, by equal triangles the uniform price must be $(1 - \hat{q} - \hat{r})P$ and a total of $(\hat{q} + \hat{r})N$ individuals will have non-zero consumption. Hence, total revenue is $R(q) = (1-\hat{q}-\hat{r})(\hat{q} + 2\hat{r})\hat{q}\ PQN/2$. However, since $\hat{r}$ must be chosen to maximise revenue for given $\hat{q}$ and $\hat{p}$, we may differentiate R(q) with respect to $\hat{r}$, obtaining the optimality requirement $4\hat{r} = 2 - 3\hat{q}$. Substituting into R(q) enables us to define the following revenue and price functions:

$$R(q)/OUP = \hat{q}(2-\hat{q})^2 PQN/16$$
$$MR(q)/OUP = (2-\hat{q})(2-3\hat{q})PN/16$$
$$p(q)/OUP = (2-\hat{q})P/4.$$

The marginal revenue function for this OUP strategy has a particularly straightforward interpretation. Noting the optimality requirement above, and the expression for p(q)/OUP, we can rewrite

$$MR(q)/OUP = r.\ p(q)/OUP.$$

7) Burns and Walsh (1981), pp. 185-188.

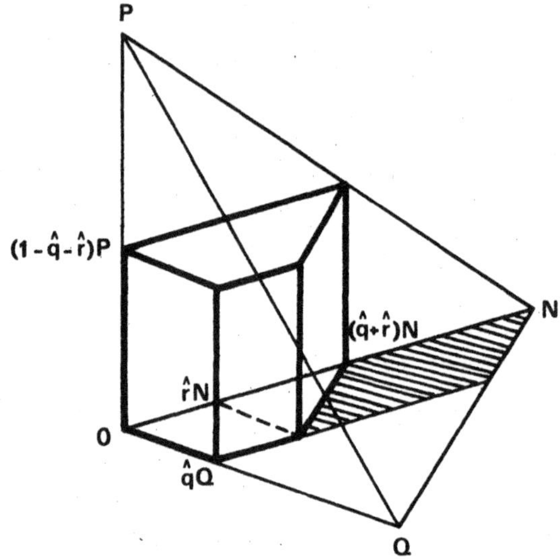

Figure 4: Uniform pricing with linear distribution

That is, marginal revenue is equal to the revenue obtained solely in respect of the final (least consumed) unit of output.

Optimal All-or-Nothing Charging (OAN): for given output level, q, selecting the all-or-nothing charge which maximises revenue.

This OAN strategy is, in fact, symmetrical with OUP, with the roles of p and r reversed. As illustrated in Figure 5, the revenue obtained for output $\hat{q}Q$ is $R(q) = (1 - \hat{q} - \hat{p})(\hat{q} + 2\hat{p})\hat{q}\, PQN/2$. Differentiation with respect to $\hat{p}$ yields the optimality condition $4\hat{p} = 2 - 3\hat{q}$ and it follows that the revenue functions are identical to those for OUP. Moreover, the per-unit price equivalent of the lump-sum OAN charge, $\bar{p}(q)$/OAN, is equivalent to p(q)/OUP. However, OAN is a more complex strategy than OUP: the marginal revenue function cannot be reduced to a simple form like that for OUP and hence testing for whether output has been appropriately selected is more difficult.

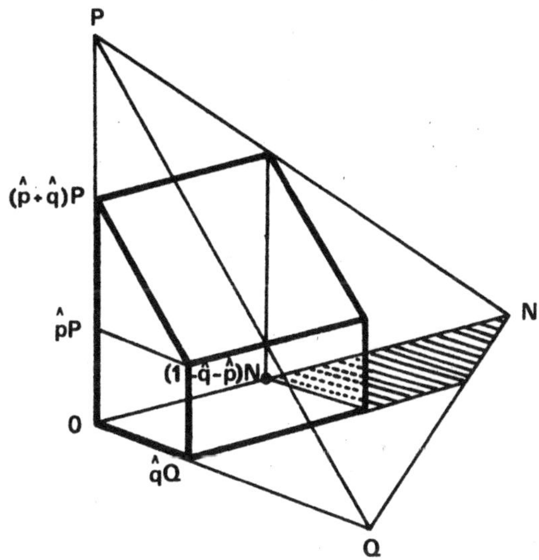

Figure 5: All or nothing charging

These two strategies correspond to simple per-unit pricing and pricing on a season-ticket only basis, as commonly understood: in both cases, the prices (charges) are applied uniformly to all consumers irrespective of the intensity of their demands. As noted earlier, our interest in them here stems from the fact that they constitute important building blocks in analysing the more interesting cases where producers, explicitly or implicitly, attempt to segregate consumers into groups which are charged different prices.

As we have shown in Section 2, from the viewpoint of profitability, it is desirable that segmentation is on a high-low demand basis; and it is trivially obvious that a random allocation of consumers to the different segments would lead to no greater expected revenue, for given q, than if uniform pricing had been applied.

In reality, producers are unlikely to be able to obtain a strict high-low demand segmentation of consumers: segmentation is likely to be based, rather, on identifiable characteristics of groups (segmentation into groups of children, adults, and pensioners, for example), or by "time" of consumption (e.g. peak vs off-peak), which can be expected to reflect intensities of demand only in relatively crude fashion. Moreover, in many cases, producers may not be able to find any objective characteristics of consumer groups that enable them to confidently expect to partition groups of consumers on a basis that is non-random with respect to demand intensities. In these cases, however, it is possible to design "self-selection" strategies in which groups of consumers are given incentives to segment themselves along high-low demand lines.

It is useful, and convenient, to begin, however, by considering the maximum benefits that would flow to producers if they *could* select (and enforce) a high-low demand segmentation of consumers. To simplify, we limit consideration to a case in which consumers are segmented into just two groups: extension to more general cases would be relatively easily achieved.

Even if firms could choose the level of demand at which segmentation occurs and could choose different but uniform prices for each group, the procedure for doing so (for any given q) and selecting the appropriate prices is quite complex even in the linear distribution framework. However, the outcome can be imagined to be something like that illustrated in Figure 6.What is clear, however, is that the segmentation of the distribution eliminates the symmetry between per-unit pricing and all-or-nothing pricing illustrated earlier for the uniform pricing case: the capacity of all-or-nothing pricing to extract additional surplus gives it a substantial comparative advantage in terms of profitability.

To illustrate the power of all-or-nothing pricing in this context, as well as to more formally demonstrate the advantages of segmentation we consider the following strategy, in which both groups ("high" and "low" demand) are offered a similar-sized bundle, q:

Strong Discrimination among Consumers (SDC): assuming that consumers can be segmented into groups, and each group presented with a separate all-or-nothing charge, jointly choosing that segmentation and those charges which maximise revenue for a given output, q.

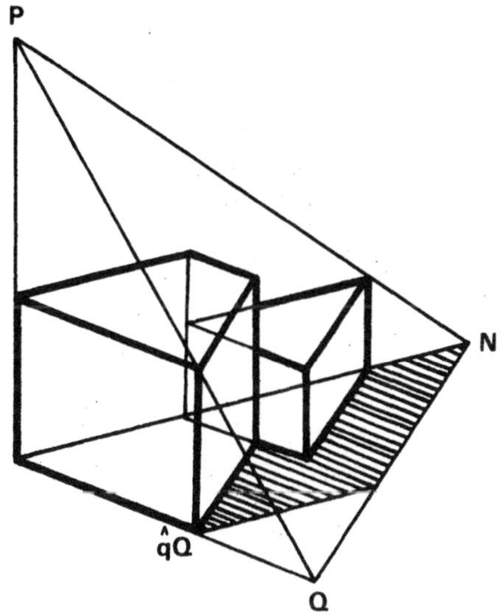

Figure 6: Maximum revenue with segmentation under uniform pricing

We assume here that the (two) groups are offered the same size consumption bundle, though it should be noted that for some higher output levels, selling a slightly smaller output bundle to the lower demand group would increase revenue.[8] To illustrate this strategy, in Figure 7, we examine the case in which there are $(1 - \hat{p} - \hat{q} - \hat{t})N$ individuals in the high demand group and $\hat{t}N$ in the low demand group. Setting optimal all-or-nothing charges separately to each group would yield revenue of:

$$R(q) = \hat{q}(2\hat{p} + \hat{q})(1 - \hat{p} - \hat{q})PQN/2 + \hat{q}(1 - \hat{p} - \hat{q} - \hat{t})\hat{t}\,PQN$$

8) The reasons are fairly obvious. Although the solution requires simultaneous determination of all variables, in effect once output is set for the high demand group, it is a matter of selecting price and output share for the lower demand group. Equal-sized bundles are optimal for $0 < \hat{q} \leq 0.5$.

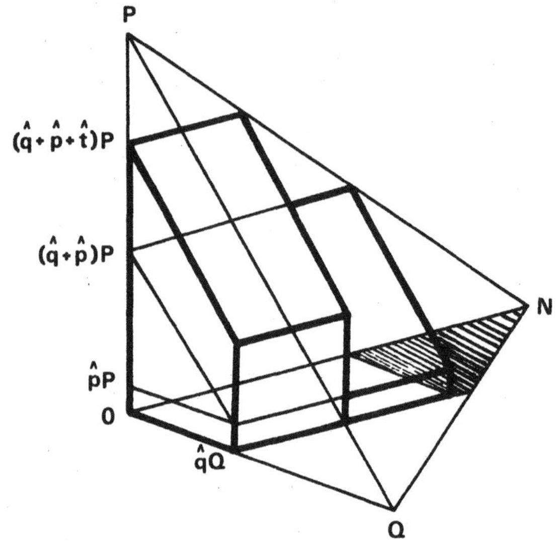

Figure 7: Strong discrimination among consumers

Differentiation with respect to t and p (i.e. to determine optimal segregation and price) yields the conditions

$$\hat{t} = (1 - \hat{p} - \hat{q})/2 \text{ and } \hat{p} = (1 - 2\hat{q})/3$$

Substituting into R(q) yields the revenue and price functions:

$$R(q)/SDC = \hat{q}(2 - \hat{q})^2\, PQN/12 = 4/3\ R(q)/OAN$$

$$MR(q)/SDC = (2 - \hat{q})(2 - 3\hat{q})PN/12 = 4/3\ MR(q)/OAN$$

$$\bar{p}(q)/SDC \begin{cases} = (2 - \hat{q})P/6 \text{ for low demand} \\ = (2 - \hat{q})P/3 \text{ for high demand} \end{cases}$$

The revenue gain for this strategy over uniformly applied all-or-nothing charging (and hence over OUP) is clear, and it can be shown in fact that this strategy dominates all uniformly applied strategies including more sophisticated (but uniform) multi-part pricing (quantity discounting). It is easy to see that (at least where groups are offered equal or very similar-sized consumption bundles) optimal group segregation requires equal sized groups - a result which generalises to the many group case. However, as the number of separate groups increases, it is more likely that revenue can be increased by offering smaller consumption bundles to lower-demand groups. While derivation of revenue functions valid for all q is complex, some idea of the gains possible from varying the size of bundles can be obtained by considering the case of choosing the $\hat{q}$ and $\hat{q}_l$ (consumption for high and low demand groups respectively) which maximise total revenue. As illustrated in Figure 8, the maximum occurs where $\hat{q} = 18/23$ and $\hat{q}_l = 12/23$ (i.e. the lower demand group is offered a bundles 2/3 the size of that of the higher demand group). Clearly, also, the larger the number of groups, the more nearly this SDC strategy gets to being *equivalent* to perfect price discrimination as anaysed in private goods markets.

While this SDC strategy provides a useful strong benchmark case for the analysis of segmentation strategies, its requirements are unquestionably extreme, even for limited numbers of groups. Entrepreneurs may be able to control the size of bundles offered to different groups, but even if they can control group composition, it is unlikely that they can vary group size according to their desired output. However, this is precisely what SDC necessitates: for any given output, equal sized groups should be chosen, with group size dimishing as output increases.

Recognising the difficulties this would create, we now relax the assumption that producers can choose group sizes and assume, instead, that groups are of fixed size. We retain, however, the assumption that segmentation, while fixed, is strictly on a high-low demand basis.

<u>Weak Discrimination among Consumers (WDC)</u>: given fixed groups of consumers within a demand distribution, choosing the all-or-nothing charges to each group which maximise revenue for a given output.

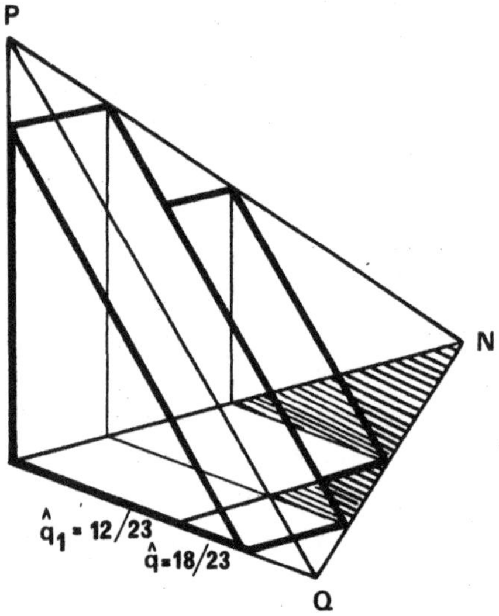

Figure 8: Revenue maximising segmentation

This strategy is closely analogous to so-called "third-degree price discrimination" in private goods analysis and, like that strategy, may be sometimes operationally feasible. Clearly, however, revenue functions and pricing rules for WDC will vary according to the relative magnitudes of the (two) groups considered. In the next Section we consider results for three different relative group magnitudes, denoted WDC (a:b), where the (a:b) ratio compares the magnitude of the high demand group to the low demand group.[9] Although the relevant functions for these and other cases are straightforwardly derived, for our purposes it is sufficient to provide an illustration for just one case. We supposes that (a:b) = (1:2), and note that the total revenue function would then be given by:

9) What is regarded as "fixed" in this context is the total population in each group, not the number of individuals in each who will actually consume the good (which varies according to the charges and output). However, the smaller the "high-demand" group, the more likely that each member will consume the entire output.

$$R(q)/WDC\,(1{:}2) = R_a + R_b, \text{ where}$$

$$R_a = \hat{q}\,(4 - 3\hat{q})PQN/18$$

$$R_b \begin{cases} = \hat{q}(4 - 3\hat{q})^2 PQN/64 \text{ when } 0 \leq \hat{q} \leq 4/9 \\ = 16/127 \text{ when } 4/9 \leq \hat{q} \leq 1 \end{cases}$$

It will be made clear in the next section that even this "weak" discrimination strategy has substantial revenue and profit advantages over uniform pricing strategies. However, while this WDC may be sometimes operationally feasible, in its pure form it still supposes that the (fixed) identifiable groups strictly fall into high-low demand categories. We now turn to consider, as an alternative, strategies where the desired high-low segmentation is actually achieved by setting prices (charges) which induce consumers to segment themselves by self-selection. In fact we consider two such strategies.

Individual or Bulk Purchasing (IBP): for given output, q, charging a per-unit price (p) for units purchased individually or a (discounted) all-or-nothing charge (c) for purchase of the entire output.

Although it occurs, in practice, in many variants and in many contexts, this can be thought of as the "theatre ticket case" where a season of plays (operas or whatever) are offered at single performance prices or entire season charges. The characteristic feature of the strategy (and of the one that follows) is that the higher demand "group" will choose the all-or-nothing charge, and take the entire output, while the lower demand "group" will purchase less than the entire output at single unit prices. The essential analytical feature of the strategy is that the marginal entrant to the higher demand group will be indifferent between (obtain the same surplus from) the two pricing offers, even though his consumption would generally be different in the two groups. Although it is tempting to treat this as a case of "discrimination", in fact the same offer is available to all and the strategy is effectively a uniform pricing strategy similar in complexity (in this "two price" case) to uniform two part pricing.

As Figure 9 illustrates, this IBP strategy can be considered, geometrically and hence analytically, as a combination of OUP at the back of the distribution and

OAN in the remainder of the distribution. Analysis of the optimal choice of p and c is based on the fact that the OUP and OAN components must be chosen to maximise revenue with respect to the particular component of output for which they effectively apply.[10]

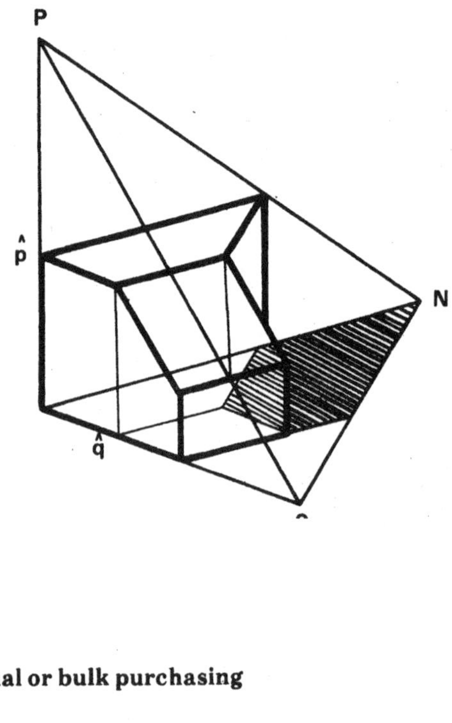

Figure 9: Individual or bulk purchasing

Optimal choice of p and c over all q, in fact can be shown to yield the total revenue function

10) The results which follow for this and the next considered strategy (USP) are based on this fact, and on the fact that for any strategy more complex than second-order, any two adjacent components must reflect the optimal two-part pricing arrangement for the combined output of those components. Hence for the linear distribution, for n-part pricing each component will involve equal amounts (q/n) of output.

$$R(q)/IBP = \hat{q}(2-\hat{q})^2 PQN/16 + \hat{q}^3 PQN/64$$
$$= R(q)/OUP + \hat{q}^3 PQN/64$$
$$MR(q)/IBP = (5\hat{q}-4)(3\hat{q}-4) PN/64$$

Since, as we have seen, OUP and OAN generate identical revenues in the linear case considered here, IBP clearly dominates them both in a revenue sense, but by nowhere near the extent that imposed (high-low) segmentation is able to achieve.

A slightly more sophisticated self-selection strategy can finally be considered - one which partially restores the revenue gains from imposed segmentation:

Uniform Separate Pricing (USP): charging a uniform per-unit price, p_1, up to some consumption level, q_1, and a uniform per-unit price, $p_2 < p_1$, for all additional units above q_1.

As illustrated in Figure 10, this strategy involves the choice of three parameters:

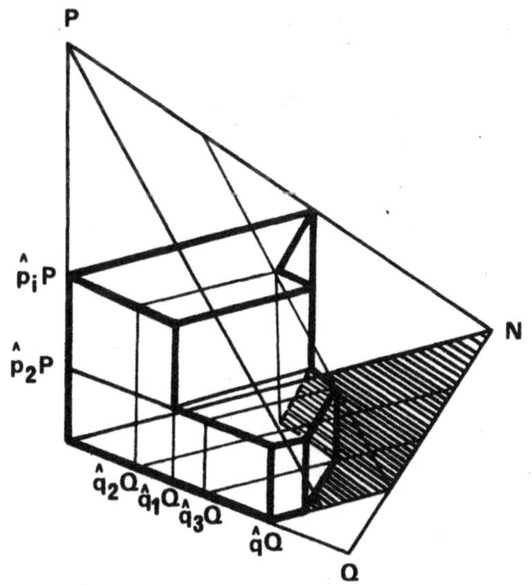

Figure 10: Uniform separate pricing

p_1, q_1 and p_2. Again, the marginal entrant to the higher consumption "group" is indifferent between the groups, although he consumes q_3 units when he would have only purchased q_2 units faced by a simple uniform price p_1. In fact, this strategy is equivalent to a number of other strategies, such as:

(a) a three-part pricing strategy involving an optimal uniform price p_1 for quantities up to q_2, an optimal all-or-nothing charge for the next $q_3 - q_2$ units, and a lower price p_3 for all further units (optimal for segment $q - q_3$);

(b) an optimal uniform price p_1 for consumption up to q_1 and an optimal two-part system for outputs q_1 up to q.

Not surprisingly, the quantity divisions, q_2, $q_3 - q_2$ and $q - q_3$, are equal for optimal pricing arrangements, the revenue functions being given by:

$$R(q)/USP = \hat{q}(2 - \hat{q})^2 PQN/16 + \hat{q}^3 PQN/54$$
$$MR(q)/USP = (6 - 7\hat{q})(6 - 5\hat{q})PN/144$$

Maximum revenue of 0.8163 PQN is obtained at $\hat{q} = 6/7$, once again falling well below that theoretically obtained with imposed segmentation. An intuitive explanation is straightforward - imposed segmentation enables intensive surplus extraction from high demand individuals, whereas self-selective segmentation actually requires that lower average prices be paid by those who consume more. With self-selection, we no longer have genuine interpersonal discrimination, but rather discrimination across units.

4. Profitability and Efficiency

Two matters can now be dealt with more-or-less in combination. First, we provide comparisons of the profitability of the strategies discussed above and of the outputs that are likely to emerge; and, second, we offer a comparison of the welfare effects - the inefficiencies - associated with their use. As indicated earlier, for this latter purpose, information on relative outputs alone is not adequate: the relative welfare effects of alternative marketing strategies involve the combined effects of output *and* consumption inefficiencies, which may be to some extent offsetting. Output and consumption effects initially are considered separately but are brought together in the final sub-section.

4.1. Profitability, output levels and output efficiency

Consider, first, the relative profitability and output levels associated with the various strategies. We follow the usual convention, comparing pricing procedures under the assumption that the equality of marginal revenues and marginal costs will be secured. However, to retain generality, we do not specify any particular cost structure at the present stage since most of our conclusions may be obtained from consideration of properties of the revenue functions alone.

Using the results derived in the previous Section, Figure 11 and 12 can be generated. The total revenue functions in Figure 11 yield profitability rankings and indicate which strategies should, or are likely to be, chosen by entrepreneurs. The marginal revenue functions in Figure 12 can be used to indicate relative outputs for any cost structure we care to impose. On these figures, and those that follow, we show as a benchmark the graphs relevant to the extreme case of multipart pricing (MPP), a strategy reflecting the theoretical possibility of pricing each unit of output separately. [See Burns and Walsh (1981, 1984)]. We also include there a function showing the sum of individual marginal valuations as output varies: optimally efficient output would be where this function intersects the marginal cost function.

Exposition is aided by first dealing separately with those strategies that do not involve discrimination across consumers. Here, the first (quite unsurprising) conclusion indicated by Figure 11 is that profitability depends upon the complexity of the optimisation procedures associated with particular strategies. Three levels of complexity are involved, and might be termed: *first-order, second-order and third-order optimisation processes*. OUP and OAN involve a *first-order process* because for any given output level a choice of price level (or total charge) exists; IBP involves a *second-order process* because two (simultaneously determined) choices have to be made concerning pricing; and *third-order complexity* occurs with USP where two different prices and a quantity have to be chosen simultaneously. This categorising paradigm - based on consideration of the complexity of the optimising process involved - appears to be both novel and

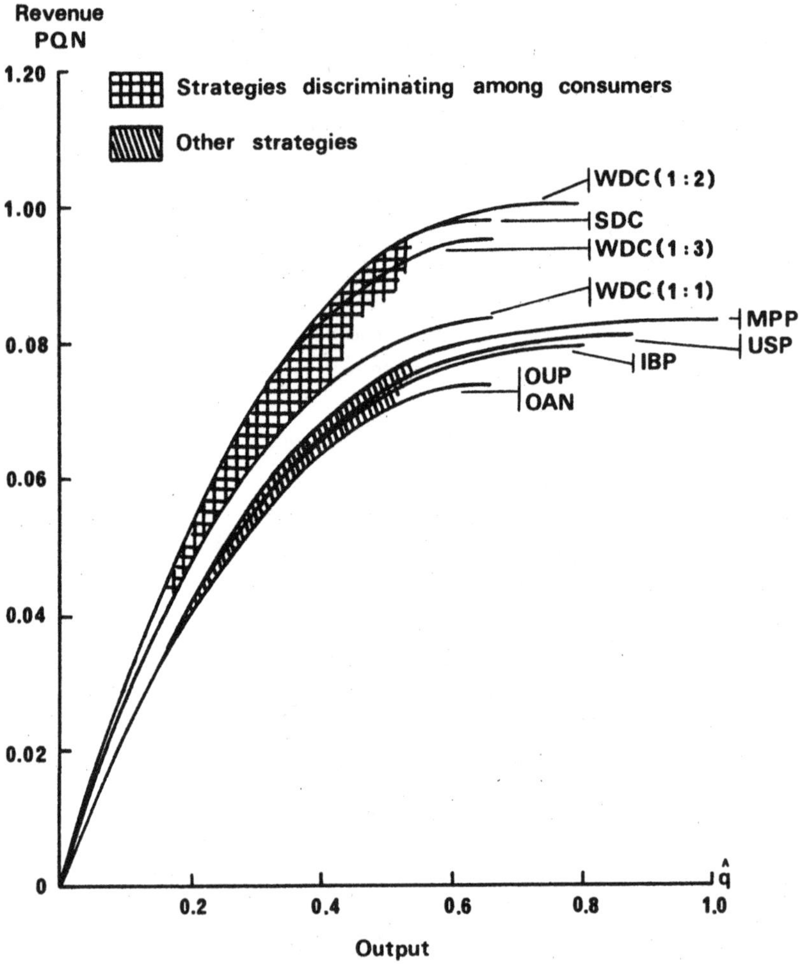

Figure 11: Total revenue functions

more general than the conventional attempts to force procedures into the Pigovian (degrees of discrimination) categories.

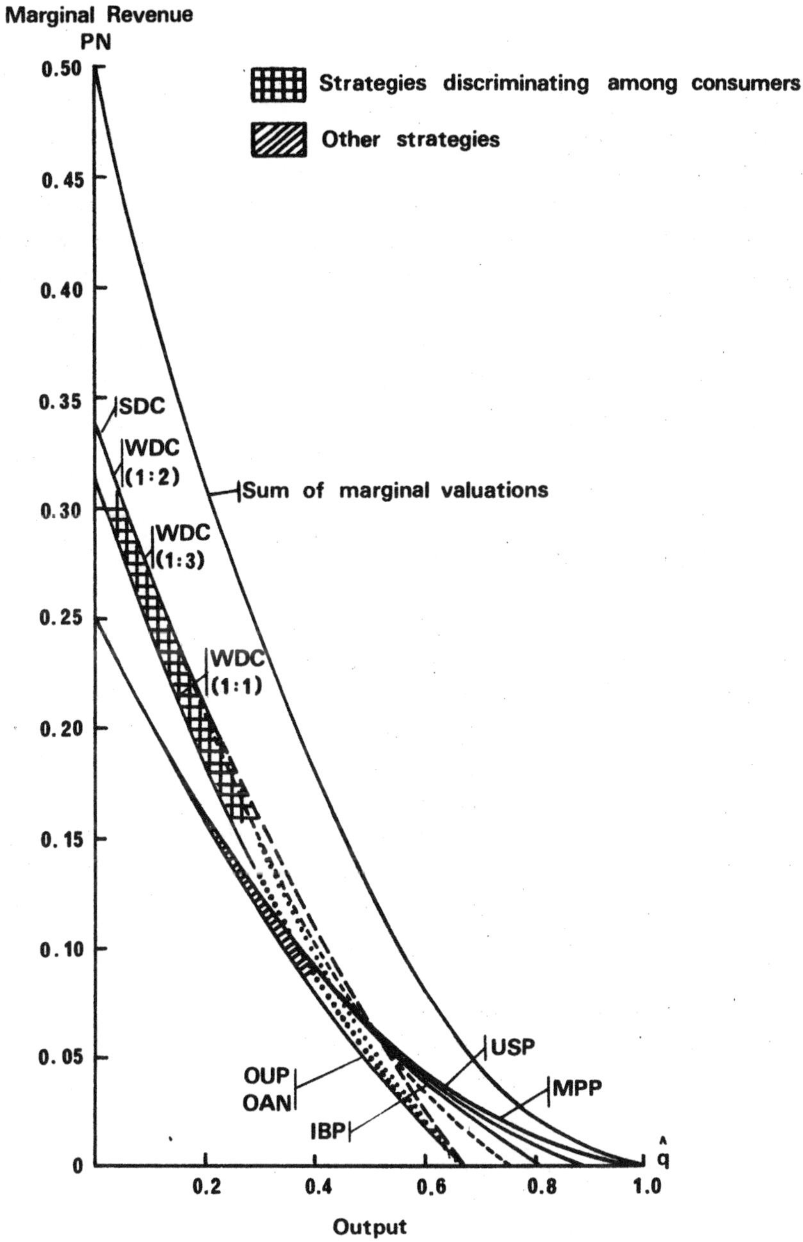

Figure 12: Marginal revenue functions

While, for the linear distribution, strategies of similar complexity have similar revenue functions, these symmetries will not carry through *exactly* to non-linear cases. However, whether, for example, OAN is more or less profitable than OUP in the non-linear case depends upon whether the distribution's surface is concave or convex (or both). Since the exact form of a demand distribution cannot be predicted *a priori*, nor determined empirically beyond a simple (and probably local) approximation, the entrepreneur might reasonably work on the basis that *similarly complex strategies will indeed generate similar revenues.* Figure 11 points to a further important observation. The gains from using more complex strategies appear negligible in the lower output ranges - at least up to $\hat{q} = 0.3$. Beyond that level there are potential gains: a *second-order* process (such as IBP) could increase revenues by up to six per cent. But there are greatly decreasing returns to increased sophistication, even assuming accurate and costless determination of the additional choice parameters.

With regard to the *output* levels for these strategies, the marginal revenue functions in Figure 12 display characteristics broadly in line with expectations generated in the preceding paragraph. Thus, output would vary little between strategies for high levels of marginal cost, unless marginal costs were strongly decreasing in the relevant range of output. For lower levels of marginal cost, however, with constant or decreasing marginal costs the *second-order process* IBP could easily generate output levels twenty per cent higher than under OUP or OAN. All of the strategies entail significant underproduction (relative to efficient output), particularly for high levels of marginal cost, but less severely so where marginal cost is an increasing function of output.

Turning to the cases where discrimination between consumers is practiced, the revenue functions in Figure 11 indicate substantial revenue gains from applying procedures such as SDC and WDC. If the entrepreneur could vary group composition, SDC would dominate all other procedures of comparable complexity (and far more complex strategies that do not discriminate among consumers). But, interestingly, even with fixed group composition, WDC performs nearly as well as SDC, the critical factor, in the two-group case, being that the higher-demand group should contain fewer individuals - probably between 25 and 35 per cent of the demand population. Were the lower-demand group to be the smaller there could be very little additional revenue from WDC relative to non-discriminatory strategies.

Figure 12 confirms the relevance of the magnitudes of the different groups of consumers: output will tend to be greater the smaller the high demand group. However, almost independently of group sizes, *interpersonal discrimination leads to greater output for most, and particularly higher, levels of marginal cost.* Clearly, there is greater 'output inefficiency' (measured relative to optimally efficient output) at higher marginal cost levels; decreasing marginal costs make 'underproduction' greater than otherwise; and increasing marginal costs generate a smaller divergence between actual and efficient output levels.

A final observation can be made which suggests that the output rankings here will apply for a wide range of distributional forms. In all cases the value of marginal revenue for a given output level q will be given, explicitly or implicitly, by the revenue associated only with the qth unit of output. This will be so because incremental changes in output will be associated with marginal changes in prices and all-or-nothing charges that will not alter the revenues associated with the previous output. In the limit, as Δq tends to zero, marginal revenue must therefore approach the revenue associated solely with respect to the additional unit of output. This result can be used to show that the rankings for a linear distribution are quite general.

4.2. Consumption efficiency

We can now compare the consumption efficiency of different strategies at common output levels. Since the different strategies yield different output levels for almost any cost structure, that comparison cannot yield a measure of *overall* efficiency; nonetheless, it provides information useful later. We simply derive, for each strategy, the function (of output) describing the sum of individual valuations of all consumption units. These are presented in Table 1 in an order, and with rearranged expressions (explained below), which heightens interesting symmetries between pricing procedures: graphs of the functions are in Figure 13.

The most important observation is that the procedures involving interpersonal discrimination dominate all others. Indeed, providing the higher-demand group is

Table 1: Consumption Efficiency Functions
(Linear Distribution)

Optimal Strategies Uniform across Individuals:[1]

E(q)/OAN	$= 1.5[\hat{q}(2-\hat{q})^2PQN/16]$
E(q)/OUP	$= 1.5[\hat{q}(2-\hat{q})^2PQN/16] + \hat{q}^3PQN/24$
E(q)/SPB	$= 1.5[\hat{q}(2-\hat{q})^2PQN/16 + \hat{q}^3PQN/64]$
E(q)/TPP	$= 1.5[\hat{q}(2-\hat{q})^2PQN/16 + \hat{q}^3PQN/64] + \hat{q}^3PQN/192$
E(q)/IBP	$= 1.5[\hat{q}(2-\hat{q})^2PQN/16 + \hat{q}^3PQN/64] + \hat{q}^3PQN/192$
E(q)/3PB	$= 1.5[\hat{q}(2-\hat{q})^2PQN/16 + \hat{q}^3PQN/54]$
E(q)/USP	$= 1.5[\hat{q}(2-\hat{q})^2PQN/16 + \hat{q}^3PQN/54] + \hat{q}^3PQN/324$
E(q)/MPP	$= 1.5[\hat{q}(2-\hat{q})^2PQN/16 + \hat{q}^3PQN/48]$

Optimal Efficiency:

E*(q)	$= 2[\hat{q}(2-\hat{q})^2PQN/16 + \hat{q}^3PQN/48]$

Optimal Strategies discriminating across Individuals:

E(q)/SDC	$= 1.33R(q)/SDC = 1.185\,E(q)/OAN = 1.78[\hat{q}(2-\hat{q})^2PQN/16]$
E(q)/WDC(1:1)	$= E(q)/OAN + [E(2q)/OAN]/8 \quad : 0 \le \hat{q} \le 1/3$
	$= E(q)/OAN + [E(2Q/3)/OAN]/8 : 1/3 \le \hat{q} \le 2/3$
E(q)/WDC(1:2)	$= \hat{q}(4-3\hat{q})PQN/18 + 8[E(3q/2)/OAN]/27 : 0 \le \hat{q} \le 4/9$
	$= \hat{q}(4-3\hat{q})PQN/18 + 8[E(2Q/3)/OAN]/27 : 4/9 \le \hat{q} \le 2/3$
E(q)/WDC(1:3)	$= \hat{q}(3-2\hat{q})PQN/8 + 27[E(4q/3)/OAN/64 : 0 \le \hat{q} \le 1/2$
	$= \hat{q}(3-2\hat{q})PQN/8 + 27[E(2Q/3)/OAN]64 : 1/2 \le \hat{q} \le 2/3$

1) For completeness, we have included in this table four strategies not discussed in detail in the text. These are SPB (Separate Pricing of Bundles), TPP (Two Part Pricing), 3PB (a three part version of SPB) and MPP (Multi Part Pricing). Discussion of their characteristic features may be found in Burns and Walsh (1984). Note, also that for those strategies uniform across individuals, consumption efficiency has been presented in the form discussed in the text: (1.5) x Revenue *plus* a component associated with the efficiency gains from any use of uniform pricing.

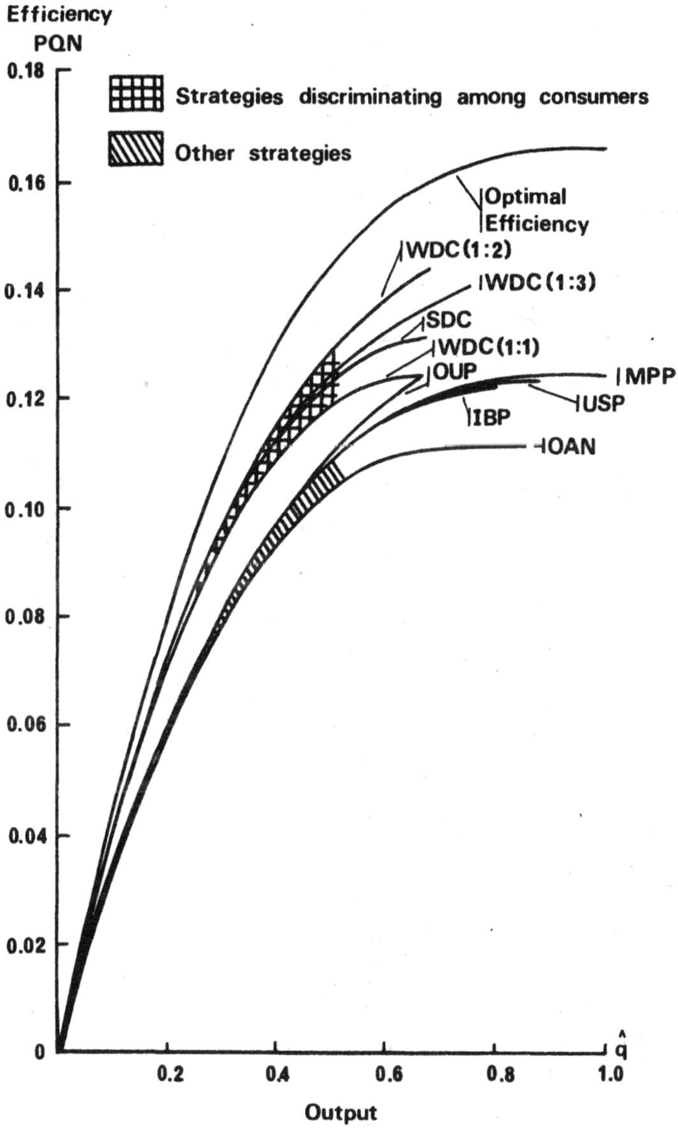

Figure 13: Consumption efficiency functions

smaller than the lower-demand group, discrimination between only two groups will approximately halve the welfare loss associated with the most efficient alternative.

The fact that this next-most efficient alternative is a simple (first-order) uniform pricing regime, OUP, and that the ranking in Figure 13 is likely to apply to a wide distributional range of forms, deserves particular emphasis. The geometric symmetry of the revenue volumes of OAN and OUP suggest certain welfare implications, OUP becoming increasingly more efficient than OAN as the (common) output level increases: although total consumption will remain similar (identical for the linear distribution) for OUP and OAN, *OAN encourages greater consumption of higher-level (but lower-valued) units of output at the expense of some consumption of low-level (but higher -valued) output units.*

Notwithstanding these remarks, as with revenues, *consumption efficiencies* are practically indistinguishable in the lower output ranges ($0 < \hat{q} < 0.3$) except for the dominance of those strategies involving discrimination among consumers. Indeed, there is a straightforward reason for this similarity between the (total) revenue and consumption efficiency graphs. For any bundle of output sold under an all-or-nothing arrangement, the surplus accruing to the consumers will be exactly half the associated revenue (with a linear distribution). Thus for OAN and MPP, consumption efficiency is one and a half times revenue. However, any bundle of output sold under an OUP arrangement has greater consumption efficiency: for bundle size $\tilde{q}$ an efficiency gain of $\tilde{q}^3/4$ relative to OAN always applies.[11] Clearly the magnitude of the efficiency gain diminishes considerably as $\tilde{q}$ becomes smaller, which may reflect either low output or increased sophistication of pricing strategy. These observations explain the changes in ranking between the revenue and consumption efficiency diagrams, and also why the self-selection strategy IBP should yield both identical revenue and efficiency functions to TPP. In each case the strategies are equivalent to marketing half the output under OAN and the remainder under OUP.

11) Thus in Table 1, for strategies uniform across consumers, consumption efficiency is shown as a sum of two components: a revenue-related component, reflecting only the complexity (order) of the strategy; and that other component which depends upon the degree to which uniform pricing is embodied in the strategy.

This latter insight draws attention to the fact that the overall revenue solid for *any* pricing strategy may be regarded as a combination of the two fundamental revenue shapes: OAN and OUP. Not surprisingly, the number of such fundamental shapes making up a particular revenue solid is directly related to the number of choice parameters involved in the optimisation process. These observations lend support to the notion that the *natural* categorising paradigm for price discriminating strategies, as adopted by us above, should be one based upon these well-defined levels of algebraic and geometric complexity.

4.3. Overall efficiency

Meaningful indicators of overall efficiency must account for *both* production and consumption effects. Because output levels will generally differ between strategies, account must also be taken of the different costs of production associated with different output levels. To simplify matters, we follow a common convention of limiting attention to the case of constant marginal cost. For a given level of marginal cost, the marginal revenue functions in Figure 12 identify output and therefore total variable costs for each strategy, while 'gross' efficiency for a given output level is obtained from Figure 13. The overall efficiency measure is obtained by subtracting variable costs from 'gross' efficiency (any fixed cost element does not affect the *relative* performance of different strategies).

In Figure 14 we characterise the performance of the various pricing strategies in relation to the level of marginal cost, including a function relating to the optimally efficient provision of the good. It is confirmed that discrimination among consumers (on a high-low demand basis) is a significant source of increased efficiency and that at higher levels of marginal cost there is no significant difference between any of the procedures not involving such discrimination. As lower values of marginal cost are considered, the greater output efficiency of the more complex strategies such as IBP, just offsets the consumption efficiency of OUP which, however, retains an (almost indiscernible) advantage over USP. The fact that OAN, whose output efficiency equals that of OUP, does so much worse than OUP in terms of overall efficiency provides a striking demonstration of the error in making welfare judgements solely on the basis of output efficiencies.

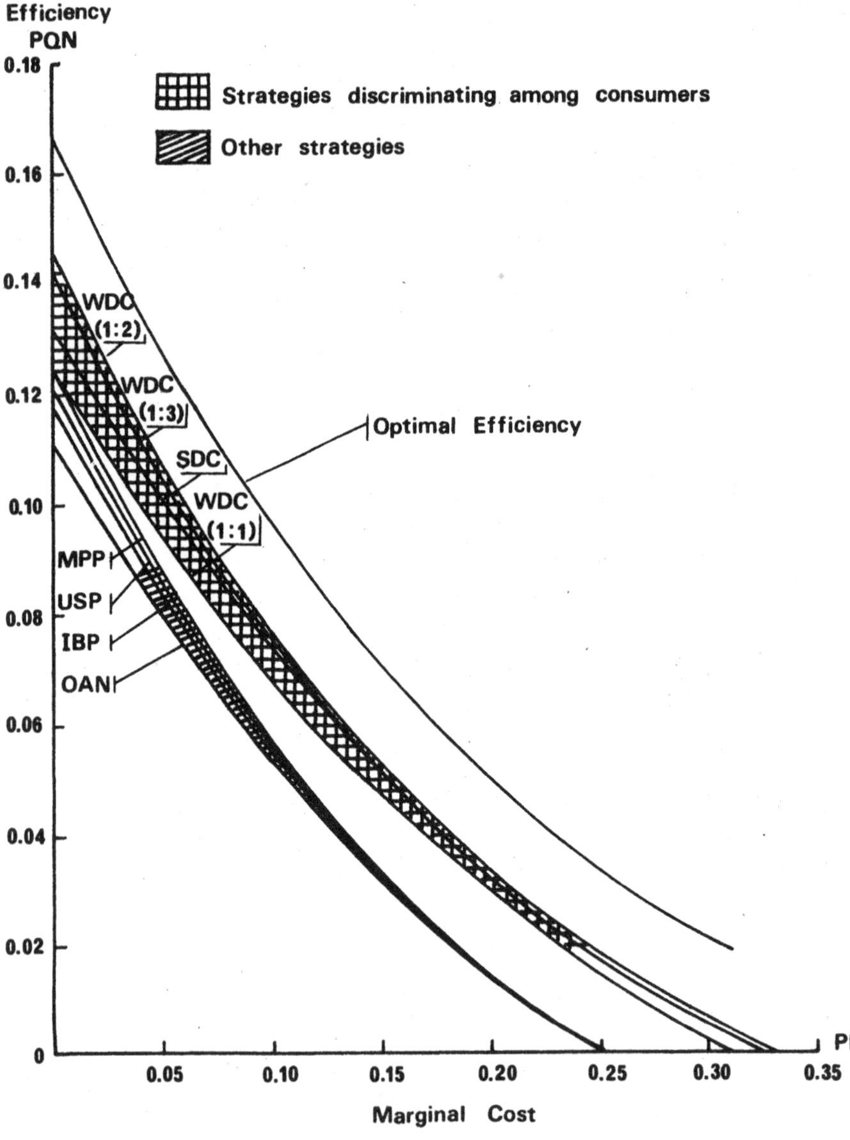

Figure 14: Overall efficiency

5. Conclusions

This paper has been concerned to investigate and clarify important issues that arise in the provision of public goods when price exclusion is both possible and profitable. In the process we have sought to generate further insights into new frameworks of analysis which embody distributional information indispensible to analysis of private provision of public goods under all pricing strategies and to analysis of private goods provision when discriminatory pricing is practiced. In particular, we make use of a linear demand distribution, for both pedagogic and practical reasons.

We have illustrated the use of this framework, and generated new results, in the context of pricing strategies involving segmentation of consumers into groups which are charged different prices. As expected, where producers can impose such segmentation on a strict high-low demand basis the gains in profitability and efficiency over other pricing strategies are very substantial - even when producers cannot choose the size of the different groups.

It has to be conceded, however, that while producers may find some bases on which to segment consumers into identifiable groups, it is unlikely that they will be able to do so on anything like a strict high-low demand basis. Accordingly we consider strategies in which consumers are induced to segment themselves into high-low demand groups by self selection, as in the case of a season of operas and plays offered on both a season-ticket and single performance access basis. Again, as expected, there are revenue and profit gains from these strategies compared to less complex pricing arrangements. However, in terms of efficiency, there is little to commend such strategies over such a basic strategy as uniform per-unit pricing.

Admittedly the results generated here rely to some extent on a number of assumptions that might be considered somewhat special. In particular, we have assumed that jointness remains pure - facilities do not become crowded - and that different output units can be considered to be essentially homogeneous.While it would be useful to consider relaxing these assumptions, there is good reason for believing our results to be reasonably indicative of the more general results that would emerge. Moreover, to a significant extent our analysis has been expository rather than definitive - to illustrate the use of, and importance of, analysis employing the demand distribution. We believe this construct to be an important tool that will find increasing use and application in microeconomic analysis, even where private goods provision is the core of attention.

References

Brennan, Geoffrey, and Walsh, Cliff (1981), "A monopoly model of public goods provision: The uniform pricing case", *American Economic Review* 71, March, 196-206

Brito, Dagobert L., and Oakland, William H. (1980), "On the monopolistic provision of excludable public goods", *American Economic Review* 70, September, 691-704

Burns, Michael E. (1978), The Market Provision of Public Goods: A General Analysis, Department of Economics, Monash University, *Working Paper No. 76*

Burns, Michael E., and Walsh, Cliff (1981), "Market provision of excludable public goods: A general analysis", *Journal of Political Economy* 89, February, 166-191

Burns, Michael E., and Walsh, Cliff (1982), A Linear Demand Distribution Approach to Analysis of Excludable Public Goods Provision, *mimeo*, University of Adelaide and University of Western Ontario

Burns, Michael E., and Walsh, Cliff (1984), Pricing, Profitability and Efficiency in the Provision of Excludable Public Goods: A Demand Distribution Approach, University of Adelaide, Dept of Economics, *Working Paper No. 84-4*,

Musgrave, R.A. (1959), *The Theory of Public Finance*, McGraw-Hill, New York

Musgrave, R.A. and Peacock, A.T. (1958), *Classics in the Theory of Public Finance*, Macmillan, London

Oakland, William H. (1974), "Public goods, perfect competition and under-production", *Journal of Political Economy* 82, September-October, 927-939

Samuelson, Paul A. (1954), "The pure theory of public expenditure", *Review of Economics and Statistics* 36, November, 387-389

Samuelson, Paul A. (1955), " A diagrammatic exposition of a theory of public expenditure", *Review of Economics and Statistics* 37, November, 350-356

Spence, Michael (1978), "Nonlinear prices and welfare", *Journal of Public Economics* 9, 1-18

Thompson, Earl A. (1968), "The perfectly competitive production of collective goods", *Review of Economics and Statistics* 50, February, 1-12

Varian, Hal R. (1984), Price Discrimination and Social Welfare, *Research Paper C-57*, Centre for Research in Economics and Social Theory, University of Michigan

Free Riders and Band Wagons: On the Optimal Supply of Public Goods

by

Bengt-Arne Wickström*

1. Introduction

It is commonly assumed that the supply of public goods in a decentralized environment will be suboptimal. Each agent has a strong incentive to be a "free rider" (see for instance Olson, 1965).[1] The validity of this hypothesis has been empirically tested in a number of experiments. The results have been contradictory (see Marwell and Ames, 1981, Kim and Walker, 1984, and Isaac, Walker, and Thomas, 1984, as well as other work referred to by these authors). It has also been suggested that the behavioral assumptions behind the free-riding hypothesis might not be realistic. Social pressure or genuine desire to contribute to the common good might provide strong incentives against free riding (compare Olson, 1965, and Johansen, 1977).

This essay studies the optimality properties of an economy where such "external" effects play a role. We will assume that the agents have a desire to partake in the financing of a public good. This desire is motivated by the status the agent obtains by such giving. Each agent evaluates his contribution in relation to what everyone else contributes. The one who gives most towards financing a public good, gains the highest social status. We will refer to this as the band-wagon effect (compare Leibenstein, 1950).

*) The author has benefitted from discussions with, and comments from, R. Pethig, Å. Risan, B. Sandvik, and L. Thorlund-Petersen, all of which is gratefully acknowledged. This work was begun when the author, as a research fellow of the Alexander von Humboldt Foundation, was visiting the Fakultät für Volkswirtschaftslehre und Statistik, Universität Mannheim. The author thanks the Alexander von Humbold Foundation, the Fakultät, and Sonderforschungsbereich 5, Universität Mannheim, for their support.

1) With "free riding" one generally refers to a situation where an individual promoting his self-interest has incentives to misrepresent his true preferences. If such a situation leads to an equilibrium, the equilibrium outcome will as a rule not be Pareto optimal. In this essay we use the term "free riding" also to characterize this suboptimal equilibrium.

Such behavior does not appear to be in conflict with observations during voluntary collections for idealistic organisations. It also seems to catch some of the motives behind private support for the Arts; generally, donors get their names published, as well as the size of their donations.

In Section 2 a formal model is developed, a Nash equilibrium, a natural concept for a decentralized solution, is defined, and two alternative definitions of a Pareto optimum are given. Section 3 studies the relationship between the Nash equilibrium and the different Pareto optima. It is shown that if the Nash equilibrium possesses some optimality property, then it also is a first-best Pareto optimum. It is further demonstrated that the band-wagon effect is necessary for a Nash equilibrium to be optimal. Finally, the existence of an income distribution that guarantees the Pareto optimality of the Nash equilibrium, is proved. An example demonstrating some of the results, is found in Section 4.

2. The Model

We study an economy with n individuals, one private good, x, and one public good, y.[2)] Each individual, i, is characterized by a utility function, U^i, and an initial endowment, w^i. The utility of the individual is increasing in his consumption of the private good, x^i, in the supply of the public good, y, and in his contribution, t^i, to finance the production of the public good, and it is decreasing in the averge contribution of everyone else, $\bar{t}^i$:[3)]

(1) $$U^i = U^i(x^i,y,t^i,\bar{t}^i),$$

2) The analysis could easily be extended to cover several private and several public goods. However, this would unnecessarily complicate the exposition without providing any additional insight. The existence theorem of Section 3 would then only hold if rather strong separability assumptions on the public goods in the utility functions were made.

3) The dependence of U^i on t^i is not necessary for all of the results. It is used below in (5b) as a convenience to obtain interior solutions. Not only is the presence of t^i in the utility function not necessary for most of our results, it is also never sufficient for any of them. The intuitive reason for including t^i as a variable in the utility function is the idea that the individual evaluates his own contribution in relation to the contribution of everyone else. One effect of having t^i in the utility function is that the demand for the public good is strengthened in some sense that could be made precise

such that

(2) $$\bar{t}^i := \frac{1}{n-1}\sum_{j\neq i} t^j.$$

Each individual faces two constraints:

(3) $$x^i + t^i = w^i,$$

and

(4) $$y - t^i = (n-1)\bar{t}^i.$$

The first constraint is the normal budget constraint; the second one says that the total supply of the public good equals the total revenues payed for it. We are here implicitly assuming that the production technology for the public good is linear in the private good and that, by a suitable choice of units, the rate of transformation is set equal to one.[4)]

In order to avoid corner solutions we make some technical assumptions on U^i:

(5b) $$U^i_x \rightarrow \infty \quad \text{as} \quad x^i \rightarrow 0,$$

(5b) $$U^i_t \rightarrow \infty \quad \text{as} \quad t^i \rightarrow 0,$$

and

(5c) $$U^i_y \rightarrow \infty \quad \text{as} \quad y \rightarrow 0.$$

4) Alternatively, one can define the size of the public good by equation (4), that is by the total expenditure. The concavity assumptions on U are then the crucial assumptions which can result from quasi-concavity of the utilty function in the physical quantities of the public good, from diminishing returns to scale in its production, or from a combination of both.

The subscripts here indicate partial derivatives. Further, in order to guarantee unique solutions, we assume that U^i is strictly quasi-concave in its arguments.[5)]

Various solution concepts can be defined. We will study two: a Nash equilibrium and Pareto-optimal solutions. In the Nash equilibrium each individual takes the contribution to the public good from the other individuals as a given datum and determines his own contribution such that his utility is maximized.[6)] The Pareto-optimal solutions are found by maximizing a welfare function that is monotone in the utility of each agent. The Nash equilibrium constitutes a decentralized solution, whereas the realization of a Pareto optimum as a rule requires cooperation, coordination, and centralization.

2.1 The Nash equilibrium

The problem facing each individual, is that he wants to maximize his own utility, taking the actions of others, $\bar{t}^i$, as given data. We write:

(6)
$$\begin{aligned} &\underset{x^i,t^i,y}{\text{maximize}} && U^i(x^i,y,t^i,\bar{t}^i), \\ &\text{such that} && x^i + t^i = w^i \\ &\text{and} && y - t^i = (n-1)\bar{t}^i. \end{aligned}$$

The solution to (6) gives us the demand and supply functions

(7a)
$$x^{Di} = x^{Di}(w^i,\bar{t}^i)$$

and

(7b)
$$t^{Di} = t^{Di}(w^i,\bar{t}^i).$$

5) Strict quasi-concavity in t^i is not necessary.

6) In the literature this is also referred to as a voluntary-contributions equilibrium (see for instance Atkinson and Stiglitz, 1980).

Strict quasi-concavity of U^i and convexity of the constraint set imply that x^{Di} and t^{Di} are continuous.

For each individual we thus have a continuous function t^{Di}. Denoting by t the n-vector $(t^1,...,t^n)$ and by w the n-vector $(w^1,...,w^n)$, we have

(8) $$t^D = t^D(w,t).$$

Continuity of t^{Di} implies continuity of t^D. Further, t^i is in the interval $[0,w^i]$. Thus, t^D is a continuous mapping from a convex compact set into itself for a given w. By Brouwer's fixed-point theorem, there exists a fixed point $t^N(w)$ such that $t^N(w) = t^D(w,t^N(w))$. This function is the Nash equilibrium. We thus have:

Proposition 1: There exists a Nash equilibrium in the contributions to the public good.

For the further analysis, the first-order conditions for a solution of (6) will prove useful. We have that t^{Di}, x^{Di}, and $y^{Di} = t^{Di} + (n-1)\,\bar{t}^i$ will satisfy the following equation:

(9) $$\frac{U^i_t}{U^i_x} + \frac{U^i_y}{U^i_x} = 1.$$

Strict quasi-concavity implies that (9), together with the constraints (3) and (4), uniquely determines t^{Di} as a function of w^i and $\bar{t}^i$.

2.2 The Pareto-optimal solutions

Defining the welfare, W, by

(10) $$W = W(x,y,t,a) := \sum_i a^i U^i(x^i,y,t^i,\bar{t}^i),$$

such that

(11) $$\sum_i \alpha^i = 1,$$

$\alpha^i > 0$ for all i, we can find all Pareto optima by maximizing W for different α, subject to constraints.

Two polar assumptions on the constraints are of interest. Either one can respect the initial income distribution w and write the resource constraint as

(12) $$w = x + t,$$

or one allows income transfers, in which case the resource constraint becomes

(13) $$n\bar{w} := \sum_i w^i = \sum_i x^i + \sum_i t^i,$$

where the mean endowment, $\bar{w}$, is defined by (13). In addition we have that

(14) $$\sum_i t^i = y.$$

If t did not explicitly enter the welfare function, (12) and (13) would be equivalent. However, since W depends on t and (12) defines a smaller set of alternatives, a Pareto optimum constrained by (12) will be dominated by, or identical to, some Pareto optimum constrained by (13).

Strict quasi-concavity of each U^i implies that also W is strictly quasi-concave. This, together with the convexity of the constraint sets, implies that, for a given α, the maximum of W is unique and occurs for unique values of t, y, and x. We call the maximum of W, subject to (12) and (14), the second-best optimum and write the optimal values of t and x as

(15a) $$\tilde{t} = \tilde{t}(\alpha, w)$$

and

(15b) $\tilde{x} = \tilde{x}(a,w)$.

Maximizing W subject to (13) and (14) gives us the first-best optimum:

(16a) $t^P = t^P(a,\bar{w})$

and

(16b) $x^P = x^P(a,\bar{w})$.

We note that, for any value of a, there exists an income distribution $\tilde{w}(a)$, with mean endowment $\bar{w}$, such that the second-best optimum is first best:

(17a) $\tilde{t}(a,\tilde{w}(a)) = t^P(a,\bar{w})$

and

(17b) $\tilde{x}(a,\tilde{w}(a)) = x^P(a,\bar{w})$.

Just choose $\tilde{w}(a)$ such that

(18) $\tilde{w}(a) = x^P(a,\bar{w}). + t^P(a,\bar{w})$.

The optimal values $\tilde{t}$ and $\tilde{x}$ are uniquely determined by the constraints (12) and (14) and by the first-order conditions

(19) $$a^iU^i_x[1 - \frac{U^i_t}{U^i_x} + \frac{1}{n-1}\frac{U^i_{\tilde{t}}}{U^i_x}] = a^jU^j_x[1 - \frac{U^j_t}{U^j_x} + \frac{1}{n-1}\frac{U^j_{\tilde{t}}}{U^j_x}],$$

for all i and j, and

(20) $$\sum_i \beta^i \left[\frac{U^i_y}{U^i_x} + \frac{1}{n} \left\{ \frac{U^i_t}{U^i_x} + \frac{U^{\underline{i}}_t}{U^i_x} \right\} \right] = 1,$$

such that

(21) $$\beta^i := n \frac{\alpha^i U^i_x}{\sum_j \alpha^j U^j_x}.$$

Similarly, t^P and x^P are uniquely determined by (13), (14), and the first-order conditions

(22) $$\frac{U^i_t}{U^i_x} - \frac{1}{n-1} \frac{U^{\underline{i}}_t}{U^i_x} = \frac{U^j_t}{U^j_x} - \frac{1}{n-1} \frac{U^{\underline{j}}_t}{U^j_x},$$

for all i and j,

(23) $$\sum_j \frac{U^j_y}{U^j_x} + \frac{1}{n} \sum_j \left(\frac{U^j_t}{U^j_x} + \frac{U^{\underline{j}}_t}{U^j_x} \right) = 1,$$

and

(24) $$\alpha^i U^i_x = \alpha^j U^j_x,$$

for all i and j.

3. Comparing the Nash Equilibrium with the Pareto-optimal Solutions

It is obvious that as a rule the Nash equilibrium will not be Pareto optimal. The interesting question is if there ever will be a coincidence of the Nash equilibrium with a Pareto optimum. This question will be addressed in this section.

We start out by proving a proposition.

Proposition 2: If a Nash equilibrium is a second-best Pareto optimum, then this second-best Pareto optimum is unique, given the income distribution, and it is also a first-best Pareto optimum.

Proof: Assume that (9), (19), and (20) hold. Substituting (9) into (20), we obtain

$$(25) \qquad \sum_i \alpha^i U^i_x [1 - \frac{U^i_t}{U^i_x} + \frac{1}{n-1} \frac{U^i_{\tilde{t}}}{U^i_x}] = 0.$$

From (19) it follows that (25), independently of the value of α, can hold only if each term of the sum is zero, that is, if

$$(26) \qquad 1 - \frac{U^i_t}{U^i_x} + \frac{1}{n-1} \frac{U^i_{\tilde{t}}}{U^i_x} = 0$$

for all i. But (9) and (26) imply that (22) and (23) are satisfied. Now, choose α such that (24) is satisfied. The Nash equilibrium is a first-best optimum, q.e.d.

Corollary: If there is no band-wagon effect, that is, if $U_{\tilde{t}} = 0$, then the Nash equilibrium will never be Pareto optimal.

The pure desire to contribute to the common good is thus not enough for an allocation to become Pareto optimal.

Another way of formulating Proposition 2 is as follows: If there exists an income distribution w such that $t^N(w) = \tilde{t}(\alpha,w)$ for some α, then it holds for all α, and there exists some $\tilde{\alpha}$, $\tilde{\alpha}^i > 0$ for all i, such that $w = \tilde{w}(\tilde{\alpha})$. The question now to be addressed, is whether such an income distribution exists. An affirmative reply presupposes certain assumptions.

Equations (26) and (9) imply that a Pareto-optimal Nash equilibrium satisfies the expression

(27)
$$-\frac{U^i_{\bar{t}}}{U^i_y} = n-1.$$

The existence of an optimal equilibrium requires that the value of the function

(28)
$$g^i(w^i,t) := -\frac{1}{n-1}\,\frac{U^i_{\bar{t}}(w^i-t^i,\sum t^j,t^i,\bar{t}^i)}{U^i_y(w^i-t^i,\sum t^j,t^i,\bar{t}^i)}$$

can be made to "vary enough" for different values of w, when $t=t^N(w)$.

The function g^i is the marginal rate of substitution between $\bar{t}^i$ and y on the manifold defined by the constraints (3) and (4). This marginal rate of substitution measures the subjective cost to the individual, in units of the public good, of an increase in the contribution t from everyone else. That is, it is the cost to him of others gaining status.

We basically want g^i to increase in value from below one to above one as w increases. We thus need assumptions like the following:

(29)
$$g^i(w^i,t^N(w)) < 1,$$

if some w's are small enough, and

(30)
$$g^i(w^i,t^N(w)) > 1,$$

if some w's are big enough.

The properties (29) and (30) can be derived from assumptions on the form of the utility functions. Several different assumptions would be sufficient. In general, a normality assumption, making t^D strictly increasing in w, is needed. In addition, some assumptions on the concavity properties of the utility functions are necessary.

We define the function $t^{Mi}(w)$ by

(31) $$t^{Mi}(w) := \min_{\bar{t}^i \leq w} \{t^{Di}(w,\bar{t}^i)\}.$$

The property needed, is that $t^{Mi}(w)$ can be made large enough by choosing w suitable large. Clearly, it is the dependence of t^{Di} on $\bar{t}^i$ that is critical, and, hence, it is the properties of $t^{Di}(w,w)$ that are of interest. In general, an increase in $\bar{t}^i$ will have two direct effects and one indirect effect on the individual's maximization problem. It will increase the supply of y which implies an increase in the individual's "income" and, through the constraint (4), act as a direct substitute for t^i. The indirect effect is that it influences the form of the utility function.

Returning to $t^{Di}(w,w)$, we will need that both the direct effect on t^{Di} of an increase in w and the indirect effect through the utility function be positive. The indirect effect will be positive if we assume that t^i in a certain way is a complement[7] to $\bar{t}^i$. That is, we assume that an increase in everyone else's status, *ceteris paribus*, will cause an individual to want to increase his own status, or at least not to want to decrease it.

Assumption 1: The utility function of each individual, i, satisfies the following conditions:

(32a) $$\frac{\partial(U^i_t/U^i_x)}{\partial\bar{t}^i} \geq 0,$$

(32b) $$\frac{\partial(U^i_y/U^i_x)}{\partial\bar{t}^i} \geq 0,$$

(33a) $$\frac{\partial(U^i_t/U^i_x)}{\partial y} \leq 0,$$

7) Complementarity and substitutability are of course properties of the utility function, and do not imply any structure on the constraint set.

and

(33b) $$\frac{\partial(U^i_y/U^i_x)}{\partial t^i} \leq 0.$$ [8]

<u>Remark</u>: If x^i, t^i, and y are normal goods, [9] then conditions (33a) and (33b) imply that $x^{Di}{}_w(w^i,\bar{t}^i)$, $t^{Di}{}_w(w^i,\bar{t}^i)$, and $y^{Di}{}_w(w^i,\bar{t}^i)$ all are greater than zero.

Conditions (32a) and (32b) are the complementarity assumptions. An increase in the values of $\bar{t}^i$, *ceteris paribus*, causes an increase in the individual's demand for t, both directly and, possibly, indirectly. The indirect effect is caused by an alteration of the individual's preferences for the collective good. Conditions (33a) and (33b) are substitutability assumptions on y and t.

In order to get a positive direct effect on $t^{Di}(w,w)$ we need a homogeneity assumption. The budget constraint corresponding to $t^{Di}(w,w)$, is

(34) $$x^i + y = nw$$

and

(35) $$x^i + t^i = w.$$

We note that the budget constraint is homothetic in x^i, y, and t^i. A general assumption that leads to the desired result is the following:

<u>Assumption 2</u>: The utility function, U^i, is homothetic in x^i, y, and t^i.

8) Alternatively, one could assume full separability, that is, assume that the above expressions, (33a) and (33b), are zero. That, together with homotheticity, would imply a CES utility function. See Samuelson (1965).

9) Normal and inferior are here defined in terms of the shape of the indifference surfaces. The projection into the x-y plane, say, of any curve, defined by a constant gradient of the utility function, is increasing.

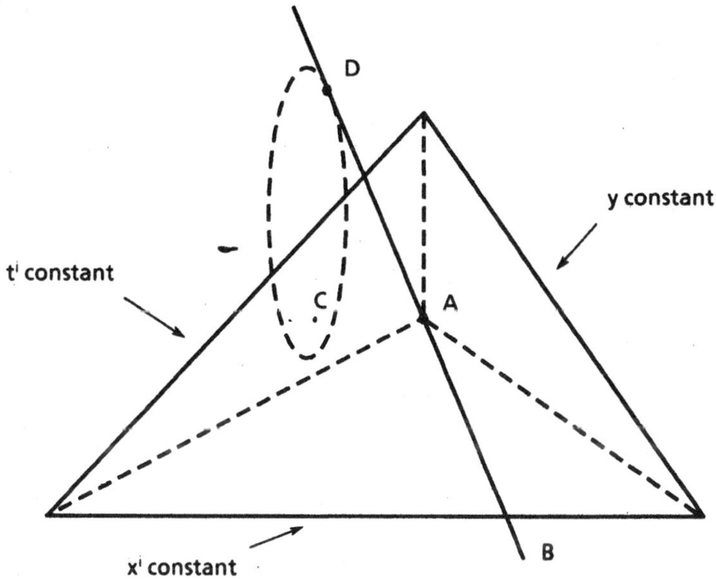

Figure 1: Individually optimal adjustments

That normality is not sufficient, is demonstrated in Figure 1. The point A is the optimum corresponding to the endowment w. The figure is projected perpendicularly to the plane of the paper from the origo. The line B is the budget line. The triangle is parallell to the tangent at A of the indifference surface through A. It gives us the loci of greater values of x^i, y, and t^i, than in point A, that intersect the budget line for a larger value of w. Normality of all goods implies that the optimum, constrained only by the plane in which the triangle lies, will lie in the triangle. C is such a point. As the indifference curve shows, the optimum constrained by the budget constraint, D, does not have to occur for a larger value of t^i than in point A.

Remark: Assumption 1 and 2 imply that $t^{Mi}(w)$ is increasing in w for all individuals.

We also need some assumptions on the marginal rate of substitution between $\bar{t}^i$ and y:

Assumption 3: The partial derivatives of the marginal rate of substitution between $\bar{t}^i$ and y, $U^i_{\bar{t}}/U^i_y$, satisfy the following conditions:

(36a) $$-\frac{\partial(U^i_{\bar{t}}/U^i_y)}{\partial y} \geq 0,$$

(36b) $$-\frac{\partial(U^i_{\bar{t}}/U^i_y)}{\partial \bar{t}^i} \geq 0,$$

(36c) $$-\frac{\partial(U^i_{\bar{t}}/U^i_y)}{\partial t^i} \geq 0,$$

and

(36d) $$-\frac{\partial(U^i_{\bar{t}}/U^i_y)}{\partial x^i} = 0.$$

Furthermore, for any $\Omega > 0$ there exists a positive number, L, such that

(37a) $$-\frac{U^i_{\bar{t}}}{U^i_y} < n-1,$$

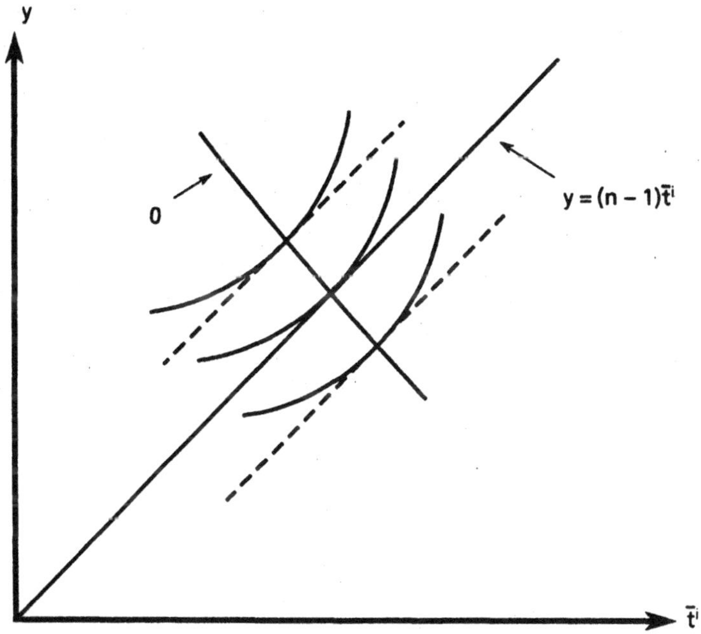

Figure 2: Indifference diagram in the $y-\bar{t}^i$ plane

if $t^i \leq L$ and $\bar{t}^i \leq y/(n-1) \leq \Omega + L/(n-1)$. Finally, there exists a positive number, K, such that

(37b) $$-\frac{U^i_{\bar{t}}}{U^i_y} > n-1.$$

if $y \geq t^i \geq K$ and $\bar{t}^i \geq 0$.

Conditions (36a) and (36b) are normality assumptions and imply that the indifference curves in the y-$\bar{t}$ plane have the form of Figure 2. Only the part of the figure that is above the line $y = (n-1)\bar{t}^i$ is of interest. The optimality condition (27) implies that an optimum must lie on the curve marked 0 in the figure. At the optimum, the vertical distance between the curve 0 and the line $y = (n-1)\bar{t}^i$ should be $t^i = t^{Di}(w^i,\bar{t}^i)$. The two conditions imply that 0 has a non-positive slope.

If we regard the band-wagon effect, reflected in the dependence of U^i on $\bar{t}^i$, as the cost to an individual of other individuals obtaining higher social status, then condition (36c) says that the more status has an individual, the costlier to him is an increase in someone else's status. That is, an increase in status makes an indivudal more status conscious. Equation (36d) is a separability assumption.

Given Assumptions 1, 2, and 3, we can prove that there exists an income distribution such that the Nash equilibrium is Pareto optimal.

Theorem: There exists an income distribution, w^P, with $w^{Pi} > 0$ for all agents i, such that $t^N(w^P) = \tilde{t}(\alpha,w^P) = t^P(\alpha,\bar{w}^P)$, for some α, $\alpha^i > 0$ for all i.

Proof: Choose Ω, and consequently a suitable L, such that

(38) $$t^{Mi}(w^i) \geq K,$$

for all i if $w^i > \Omega$-1. We thus find that the condition $w^i > \Omega$-1 implies that

(39) $$g^i(w^i,t^D(w,t)) > 1.$$

Further, we see that, for each given i, if $w^i = L$ and $w^j \leq \Omega$, for all $j \neq i$, then

(40) $$g^i(w^i,t^D(w,t)) < 1.$$

We construct a function, $(f^i) = (f^i_1, f^i_2)$, on the set A defined by

(41) $$A = \{(w^i,t^i) | L \leq w^i \leq \Omega, 0 \leq t^i \leq w^i\}.$$

Let

(42a) $$f^i_1(w,t) := \max\{w^i + 1 - g^i(w^i,t^D(w,t)), L\}$$

and

(42b) $$f^i_2(w,t) := t^{Di}(w^i,\bar{t}^i).$$

It is readily seen that f is a continuous function from A into A, and that A is a convex, compact set. Thus, the conditions of Brouwer's fixed-point theorem are satisfied, and there exists a fixed point (w^P,t^P) such that $f(w^P,t^P) = (w^P,t^P)$. The contribution t^P is the Nash equilibrium evaluated at w^P, $t^P = t^N(w^P)$. The endowments w^{Pi} satisfy

(43) $$w^{Pi} = \max\{w^{Pi} + 1 - g^i(w^{Pi},t^P), L\}.$$

Since $g^i(w^i,t^P) < 1$ if $t^i \leq L$, and since $t^i \leq w^i$, we have that $w^{Pi} > L$. Hence, w^{Pi} satisfies

(44) $$g^i(w^{Pi},t^P) = 1,$$

for all i. But (44), together with (9), implies (26). Hence, the income distribution w^P, with $w^{Pi} \geq L > 0$ for all i, gives us a Nash equilibrium which is a first-best Pareto optimum, q.e.d.

The theorem states that we can always find an income distribution such that the resulting Nash equilibrium is a first-best Pareto optimum.[10] However, we can not

10) We note that if we had several public goods, we could in general in this manner only guarantee the Pareto-optimal supply of one, since we would have a condition like equation (44) that needed to be satisfied for each of them. This would, of course, not be the case unless some rather strong assumptions were made on the form of the utility functions. Compare footnote 2).

generate any Pareto optimum. That is, the choice of income distribution solves the efficiency problem, but can at the same time create an equity problem. The Pareto optimum is determined by the form of the utility functions and it is achieved when

$$\frac{1}{n-1}\,\frac{U^i_{\bar{t}}}{U^i_y} = -1 \tag{45}$$

for all individuals. That implies that the Pareto-optimal income distribution is such that the endowment of the individuals least status conscious should be the highest. Those who are the first to jump on the band-wagon should be the last when it comes to the distribution of the resources. Alternatively, one can say that those most prone to be free riders, ought to have the largest endowments.

To conclude this section, we sum up the results. First, the band-wagon effect is necessary for a Nash equilibrium to be optimal. Second, the income distribution has to be chosen very carefully, and even then, rather strict assumptions on the form of the utility functions seem to be required. The incentive-incompatibility problems associated with the optimal supply of public goods, can thus in general *not* be solved by the processes studied in this essay. The success is limited to rather special cases.

4. An Example

We will illustrate some of the results with a simple example. We assume that all individuals have identical utility functions of the form

$$U(x,y,t,\bar{t}) = x^{\alpha}\, y^{\beta}\, t^{\gamma}\, e^{-\delta\bar{t}}. \tag{46}$$

The relevant marginal rates of substitution are

(47a) $$\frac{U_y}{U_x} = \frac{\beta}{\alpha}\frac{x}{y},$$

(47b) $$\frac{U_t}{U_x} = \frac{\gamma}{\alpha}\frac{x}{t},$$

and

(47c) $$\frac{U_{\bar{t}}}{U_y} = -\frac{\delta}{\beta}\,y.$$

Since all individuals have the same preferences, the Pareto optimum will be achieved with an equal income distribution. It thus suffices to find the Nash equilibrium for equal endowments. By symmetry the t's will then be identical and we can substitute t for $\bar{t}$ in equation (9):

(48) $$\frac{\gamma}{\alpha}\frac{w-t}{t} + \frac{\beta}{\alpha}\frac{w-t}{nt} = 1.$$

We solve (48) to find the Nash equilibrium $t^N(w)$:

(49) $$t^N(w) = w\,\frac{\frac{\beta}{n} + \gamma}{\alpha + \frac{\beta}{n} + \gamma}.$$

In order for $t^N(w)$ to be Pareto optimal it needs to satisfy equation (45):

(50) $$\frac{1}{n-1}\frac{\delta}{\beta}\,nt = 1$$

or

(51) $$t = [1 - \frac{1}{n}]\,\frac{\beta}{\delta}.$$

That is, the optimal endowment w^P should be

(52) $$w^P = [1 - \frac{1}{n}]\ [1 + \frac{\alpha}{\frac{\beta}{n} + \gamma}]\ \frac{\beta}{\delta}.$$

The important parameters here are β and δ. The desire for the public good is measured by β and the band-wagon effect by δ. The larger is β, the greater is the optimal supply of the public good, and the greater has w to be in order to insure a sufficiently high value of t^D. The larger is δ, the stronger is the band-wagon effect, and the smaller is the optimal w. As δ vanishes, the size of the endowments has to increase to infinity.

We also note that the optimal income distribution is largely independent of the size of the population, n. This has to do with the fact that the marginal rate of substitution betwen the collective good and the private good, equation (47a), is inversely proportional to y, and that the optimality condition (20), for large n, implies that the marginal rate of substitution be inversely proportional to n. We thus have a near scale invariance with respect to the size of the population.

The size of the endowment of each individual, which leads to a Pareto-optimal state, thus can be almost the same for a small group of individuals as for a large group. However, as the group becomes large, the preferences might change. Since the individuals then become more anonymous, they might not relate to the average donation of the entire population but to some subgroup of individuals to which they belong. Such behavior would, of course, complicate the model.

References

Atkinson, A.B., and Stiglitz, J.E.(1980), *Lectures on Public Economics*, McGraw-Hill, Maidenhead

Isaac, R.M., Walker, J.M., and Thomas, S.H.(1984), "Divergent evidence on free riding: An experimental examination of possible explanation", *Public Choice 43*, 113-149

Johansen, L. (1977), "The theory of public goods: Misplaced emphasis?" *Journal of Public Economics* 7, 147-152

Kim, O., and Walker, M. (1984), "The free rider problem: Experimental evidence", *Public Choice* 43, 3-24

Leibenstein, H. (1950), "Bandwagon, snob, and Veblen effects in the theory of consumers' demand", *Quarterly Journal of Economics* 64, 183-207

Marwell, G., and Ames, R.E. (1981), "Economists free ride, does anyone else? Experiments on the provision of public goods, IV". *Journal of Public Economics* 15, 295-310

Olson, M. (1965), *The Logic of Collective Actions: Public Goods and the Theory of Groups*, Harvard University Press, Cambridge, (Mass.)

Samuelson, P.A. (1965), "Using full duality to show that simultaneous additive direct and indirect utilities implies unitary price elasticity of demand," *Econometrica* 33, 781-796

Competitive Lobbying for Group-Specific Public Goods *

by

Rüdiger Pethig

1. The Problem

In this paper we define public goods as jointly consumable goods (Blümel, Pethig, von dem Hagen 1984) and assume, in addition, that they are non-excludable and group specific[1]. The latter qualification means that only a proper subset of all agents in the economy has preferences on a particular public good while all other agents are indifferent toward that good. We envisage an economy with two of these excludable public goods and with two disjoint groups of agents, each of which is constituted by its members' "common interest" for one and only one of these goods.

If consumers' preferences were known the goods could be provided and financed in a Pareto-optimal way according to the benefit principle (Lindahl equilibrium)[2]. In contrast, we assume that information on preferences is strictly private. Since, in addition, the public goods to be considered are non-excludable, the only way to finance them is by voluntary contributions or by coercive taxation. In this paper we focus our attention entirely on tax-financed provision. Then the relevant

* This paper is part of the author's research program of the "Sonderforschungsbereich 5 der DFG: Staatliche Allokationspolitk im marktwirtschaftlichen System" at the University of Mannheim. Helpful comments from W. Blümel and O. von dem Hagen are gratefully acknowledged. Remaining errors are the author's sole responsibility, however.

1) The seminal work on group-specific public goods is, of course, Olson (1965), who claimed (p. 14) "... that most collective goods can only be defined with respect to some specific group." For Olson (1965, p. 14) a group-specific public good is such that if any person in a group "... consumes it, it cannot feasibly be withheld from others in that group." But he also suggests that joint consumability (or jointness) is not a necessary attribute of a public good. Here we disagree, but we also conjecture that Olson's view does not differ substantively from ours. Suppose, for example, the issue is on passing money transfers to all families with children. The respective piece of legislation is clearly a group-specific public good whereas the individual transfer payments are private (and excludable) goods.

2) Observe that under these assumptions the fact that public goods are group specific does not pose any particular problems in general equilibrium analysis.

issues are (i) the size of the overall budget for all public goods, (ii) the distribution of the tax burden depending on the type of taxes being levied and, finally, (iii) the public-goods distribution, that is, the allocation of funds to each public good. All of these problems involve conflicting group interests and all of them are clearly interdependent. Nevertheless, these issues can be separated on a conceptual level and so the ceteris-paribus clause is used here assuming the tax revenue and the budget size as given. Hence we are confronted with a distributional "tug of war" between different groups. We are left with a non-positive sum game in the sense that each group cannot gain except at the expense of all other groups.

Which are the rules of this game? Let us assume that the ultimate decision on the distribution of public goods is made by the incumbent administration (executive) that has limited information on voters' preferences and whose aim is to maximize the probability of reelection.[3)] The administration is assumed to be responsive to redistributive lobbies on the basis of its conjecture that the intensity of a group's lobbying indicates its preference intensity for the pertaining public good. Therefore, the administration follows the motto: 'he who cries loudest gets most' in an attempt to maximize its expected probability to be reelected.

In order to study competitive lobbying as viewed above, the issue of lobby formation must be addressed and this issue will, in fact, account for the major part of the paper. A lobby is defined here as a special-interest organization or association consisting of all those members of some given group who contribute to finance the promotion of group interest by lobbying.[4)] Suppose for a moment that such an organization exists and lobbies successfully for an improved provision of the group-specific public good. Then the benefits accrue to all group members whether or not they are members of the lobby.[5)] If the revenue from voluntary

3) Alternatively, the decision may be thought to result from majority voting of some legislative body whose majority party (fraction or coalition) elects the administration.

4) It is not necessary to specify here the particular activities that constitute lobbying. They may consist in campaign contributions, threats to withdraw some given support of the administration or the intensity of campaigning against the incumbent administration etc.

5) The principle difference between a lobby and a public-good club is that the club good is exclusively used by club members while group members who do not join the lobby cannot be excluded from consumption of the group-specific public good.

contributions is too small for effective lobbying, it follows - as Olson (1965) argued forcefully - that group members will not join the lobby unless the organization is engaged in two separate activities, namely in lobbying and in creating selective incentives by which non-members are somehow punished and/or members are rewarded. The important point about these selective incentives is that "... those who do not join the organization ... can be treated differently from those who do" (Olson 1965, p. 51).

It is easy to see that positive and negative selective incentives (coercion versus inducement to become a lobby member) are equivalent for analytical purposes since it is the relative discrimination of non-members that counts. Therefore, we may restrict our subsequent model to negative selective incentives without loss of generality. Olson (1965, p. 51) was very clear about the working of coercion as an incentive to join the organization: "Coercion ... leaves an individual on a lower indifference curve than he would have been on had he borne his allocated share of the cost of the collective good and not been coerced."

Section 2 of the present paper serves to elaborate in a formal model the micro-economic foundations of lobby formation, simultaneously taking into account both the political decision process and competitive lobbying. The solution concept being employed for noncooperative lobbying is the Nash equilibrium. In Section 3, more specific assumptions on preferences are introduced in order to gain further insights into competitive lobbying. The conditions for successful lobby formation are studied and the lobbying outcome is characterized. Due to the rather restrictive assumptions on preferences it turns out that lobby membership is independent of the amount of public good provided and that, under some qualifications, each lobby has a dominant strategy. These somewhat implausible results are "generalized" in Section 4, where alternative assumptions on preferences and incentive generation are applied.

2. The Conceptual Framework

In much of what follows competitive lobbying is studied from the point of view of one group. Variables referring to this group are not marked by a special symbol.

Without loss of generality, all other groups are "aggregated" to one other group.[6] The variables referring to this second group are characterized by a plus sign as a superscript. Capital letters are reserved for functions (and sets). Subscripts that are attached to functions indicate partial derivatives (e.g. $F_x := \partial F/\partial x$). If F is a monotone function, its inverse is denoted by $\bar{F}$.

2.1 The group and its lobby

The group under consideration consists of m members, where group members are indexed by $i = 1,...,m$. The lobby has n members with $o \leq n \leq m$, and, if it exists, it is involved in three distinct activities: membership recruiting, lobbying (or rent seeking), and dues collection. We denote by f (for fund raising) and r (for lobbying or rent seeking) the respective resource investments and by g the uniform membership dues[7] being fixed by the lobby. Consequently, an action of the lobby is a triple (f,r,g). The lobby's revenue is ng while its expenditure is f+r. Its net revenue is

(1) $$b := ng - f$$

2.2 The political decision of allocating public goods

There is a fixed amount of tax revenue that is to be spent for the two group-specific public goods. The production functions are linear and the units of the public goods are so defined, that tax money can be transformed into either public good on a one-to-one basis. The assignment of public goods to each group depends on each lobby's rent-seeking effort (r and r^+, respectively). More specifically, we assume that there are two functions Z and Z^+ such that

(2) $$z = \hat{Z}(r,r^+)$$ $$z^+ = \hat{Z}^+(r,r^+)$$

6) It is true, of course, that two-person games are in various aspects special as compared to n-person games ($n > 2$). But here we do not focus on these differences.

7) One could introduce more sophisticated dues policies analogue to price differentiation or multipart pricing as discussed by Burns and Walsh (1981) in a different context. However, this is beyond the scope of the present paper.

is the respective amount of public good allocated to each group if rent-seeking investments are given by (r,r^+). The functions $\hat{Z}$ and $\hat{Z}^+$ have the following properties:

(i) $\hat{Z}$ ($\hat{Z}^+$, respectively) is non-decreasing and concave in r (r^+) but non-increasing and convex in r^+ (r);

(ii) For all $(r,r^+) \geq 0$:
$\hat{Z}(r,r^+) + \hat{Z}^+(r,r^+) = \hat{z}$ (with $\hat{z}$ exhausting the overall budget for public goods) and $\hat{Z}(r,r^+) \in [0,\hat{z}]$;

(iii) For given $(r,r^+) \geq 0$, the incumbent administration determines the public-goods distribution $[\hat{Z}(r,r^+), \hat{Z}^+(r,r^+)]$, and, by assumption, this distribution maximizes its expected probability for reelection.

2.3 The individual's decision problem

For $i = 1,\ldots,m$ agent i's utility is given by

(3) $$u^i = U(i,x^i,a^i,z),$$

where $x^i \geq 0$ is his or her consumption of the (only) private good [8] and where $z \geq 0$ is the amount of the group-specific public good provided. For convenience, the private good is taken as numéraire. In (3) we assume $U_a < 0$ and

(4) $$a^i \begin{cases} = \dfrac{(g-g^i)a}{g} & \text{if } g > 0 \\ = 0 & \text{if } g = 0 \end{cases}$$

where $g^i \geq 0$ is agent i's contribution for the lobby (in terms of the numéraire) and where $g \geq 0$ is the membership dues as fixed by the lobby. The parameter a is also controlled by the lobby through its recruiting effort. More formally,

8) For the purpose of this paper it is sufficient to consider only one private good, even though the commodity space could be easily expanded.

(5) $a = A(f)$,

where $A(0) = 0$ and A is assumed to be concave and nondecreasing. Some remarks on the economic interpretation of equations (3) to (5) seem to be in order.

Suppose first that there is no lobby, or equivalently, that the lobby's action is ($f = 0$, $g = 0$, $r = 0$). Then $a^i = a = 0$ by (4) and (5). It follows that, through $a^i > 0$, the lobby's (non-zero) activity creates an externality for group members. A necessary, though not sufficient condition for this externality is $f > 0$. The fund-raising activity ($f > 0$) may take the form of moral suasion, or advertising for joining the lobby or appealing to the group member's solidarity to contribute to the furthering of the common interest; it may also consist of coercive pressure or threats against non-members of the lobby or other negative sanctions, e.g. concerning social status. The intensity of this kind of activity is measured by $A(f)$. Exposure to this activity is perceived by the individual as an uncomfortable feeling or even as punishment. This hypothesis is expressed in $U_a < 0$, where the magnitude of $|U_a|$ indicates the individual's degree of sensitivity towards the lobby's coercive pressure. $U_a < 0$ implies, of course, that the individual is left on a lower indifference curve - as Olson (1965, p. 51) suggested.[9]

However, the individual is not inevitably and helplessly exposed to this externality. By choosing to join the lobby ($g^i = g$) he or she can entirely escape from the coercive pressure of the lobby. An impressive example of wide-ranging symbolic relevance is the institution of indulgence in the Catholic Church during the Reformation era: At that time, priests devoted much effort to making their faithfuls believe that every human being's fate was misery and hell unless he or she bought a letter of indulgence which in our context corresponds to the

9) Observe that negative selective incentives, as conceived in this paper, take the form of a group-specific public good (or rather "bad") that is rejectable by group members under certain qualifications (specified in (4) and interpreted below). Olson (1965) suggested, instead, that selective incentives often consist of a private good, so that the group-specific public good which is lobbied for becomes a by-product of that private good. Stigler (1974) is correct in criticising this view on the ground that other firms could try to provide the private good cheaper and thus destroy the lobby's financial basis for lobbying.

individual's decision to become a member of the lobby. It is important to emphasize that it is the agent's decision variable g^i which turns the lobby-created externality A(f) into a selective incentive.[10)]

What is, then, the individual's decision problem in such an environment? The agent's choice of (g^i, x^i) is assumed to be constrained by

(6) $(g^i,x^i) \in \{(g^i,x^i) | g^i \in \{0,g\} \text{ and } x^i + g^i \leq w^i\}$

where w^i is the agent's given income or wealth net of taxes being measured in terms of numéraire. Constraining the variable g^i to $g^i = 0$ or $g^i = g$ is a somewhat crude assumption serving to simplify the analysis.[11)] It means that membership is an all-or-none option: If the agent wants to contribute more or less than g he or she cannot become a lobby member.

For alternatively predetermined values of a, g and z (and for exogeneous w^i) agent i solves

Problem 1: Maximize u^i with respect to g^i and x^i subject to (3), (4) and (6).

Clearly, a solution (g^{i*},x^{i*}) of Problem 1 implies either $g^{i*} = 0$ or $g^{i*} = g$ or both, in which case we assume that the agent joins the organization.

Figure 1 illustrates the solution to Problem 1 for some individual i when $\bar{a} > 0$ and $\bar{g} > 0$ are given and when z is changed parametrically. Observe first, that the curve WP^i_1 represents agent i's absolute (rather than marginal) willingness-to-pay for alternative levels of public-good provision if no lobby exists. The other two

10) In public-goods terminology, the public bad A(f) is rejectable, but rejection is costly and the individual's decision whether or not to reject the public bad depends on the comparison of the cost (g) and the benefit ($a^i = 0$) of rejection.

11) The analytical framework given by (4) is wide enough to take as the range of g^i the entire set of nonnegative real numbers. In this case g should be interpreted as the amount of dues recommended by the lobby. For $A(f) > 0$ then a positive incentive is created for each agent to contribute $g^i > g$. Investigation of this much more general approach would appear to be interesting and promising. It is, however, beyond the scope of the present paper.

curves depict the willingness-to-pay, if the individual chooses to be (WP^i_2) or not to be (WP^i_3) a member of the lobby. For small levels of public good ($0 \leq z < z_b$) the agent is better off if he or she does not join the lobby, because the opportunity costs of dues payment (private-good consumption foregone) are greater than the loss of utility resulting from the lobby's coercive pressure. At $z > z_b$ the reverse result holds. Hence at z_b the individual is indifferent with respect to the available options.

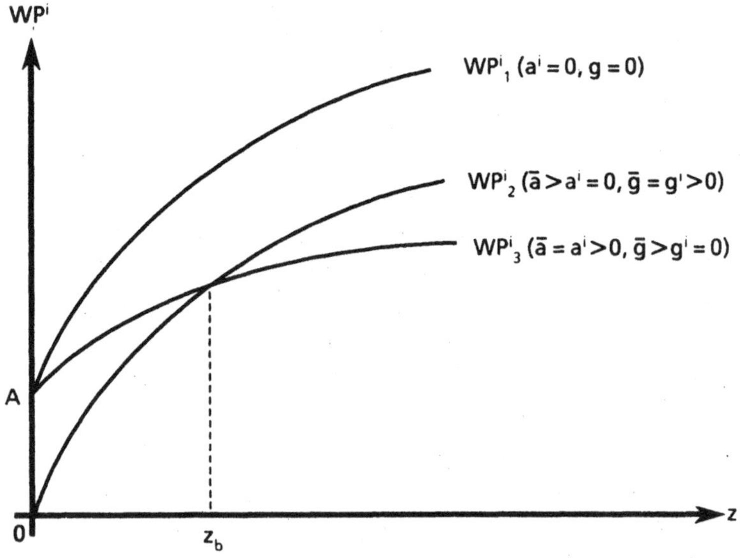

Figure 1: The individual 's decision problem

Figure 1 also clarifies that an agent's decision to join the lobby does not depend on his or her expectations as to the effectiveness of the lobby. A fortiori, the agent does not consider the impact of his or her membership on the outcome. Aside from the analytical difficulties to model these interdependencies and reactions, they appear to be relevant only for small groups.[12]

2.4 The lobby's decision problem

Suppose that all individuals maximize utility for some given (a,g,z). Then

(7) $n = \hat{N}(a,g,z)$

is defined as the number of elements in the set $\{i \mid g^i = g \text{ solves Problem 1}\}$. With the help of (2) and (5) we rewrite

(7') $\hat{N}(a,g,z) = \hat{N}[A(f), g, \hat{Z}(r,r^+)] =: N(f,g,r;r^+)$.

It follows that the lobby's net revenue is

(1') $b = B(f,g,r;r^+) := gN(f,g,r;r^+) - f$

It is obvious that, for given r^+, an action (f,g,r) of the lobby is not feasible unless

(8) $B(f,g,r;r^+) \geq r.$

Due to (8) the lobby cannot spend more money on lobbying than it raised (net of fund-raising costs). An inequality sign in (8) (budget surplus) clearly implies feasibility even though it is plausible that the lobby members will strongly urge their officials not to use funds for other purposes than furthering the common interest. A thorough analysis of this issue would require to focus on the organizational structure of the lobby, on its decision-making procedures and on the discretion of lobby officials.[13] One would also have to answer the question in

12) This argument is analogous to the observation that Nash equilibria of voluntary contributions cannot be expected in large groups (Olson (1965)).

13) It may not be possible for self-interested lobby officials to use a budget surplus for raising their remuneration directly. But they may be able to increase their utility by rendering the organization X-inefficient (overstaffing etc.).

which way and to which extent member preferences translate into the lobby's actions. However, it is beyond the scope of the present paper to study these important issues adequately. We assume, instead, that the lobby

- takes efficient actions and
- secures the maximum possible amount of the group-specific public good for (alternatively) given lobbying effort of the other group.[14])

In order to specify the efficiency requirement, consider first the set
$S(z,r^+) := \{ (f,g,r) \mid z = \hat{Z}(r,r^+) \text{ and (8) holds} \}$
of feasible actions for given z and r^+. An action (f,g,r) is said to be efficient, if for every (z, r^+)

(9) $(f,g,r) \in S(z,r^+)$ and $f+r \leq f' + r'$ for all $(f',g',r') \in S(z,r^+)$.

Hence the lobby's objective requires to solve

Problem 2: For every given r^+: Maximize z with respect to (f,g,r) subject to (9)

It is tempting to argue that maximizing z with respect to f, g and r implies efficiency. However, it is easy to see and made explicit in Section 3 below that this conjecture may be incorrect, if $\hat{Z}$ is bounded from above.

2.5 Lobbying equilibrium

It has become obvious by now that our model is constructed in such a way that it forms a noncooperative game in which two lobbies are the players whose strategies are rent-seeking investments. For this type of game, the Nash equilibrium appears to be an adequate solution concept. The strategy tuple $(\hat{r},\hat{r}^+)$ constitutes a Nash equilibrium - called *lobbying equilibrium* -, if $\hat{r}$ solves Problem 2 for given $\hat{r}^+$ and if $\hat{r}^+$ solves the other group's analogue problem for given $\hat{r}$.

14) Other variables such as revenue or membership may be considered either as alternative objectives or (minimum-level) side constraints. As argued above, it is conceivable, however, that the lobby's actions are "collectively irrational" in the sense of being "non-optimizing" altogether.

If the solutions are unique the lobbying equilibrium can also be described with the help of Cournot-type reaction functions. Suppose, that for predetermined r^+ the unique solution of Problem 2 is (f,g,r). Since r is uniquely assigned to r^+ in this way, there is a function R satisfying

(10) $$r = R(r^+),$$

where R denotes the lobby's reaction function. $(\hat{r},\hat{r}^+)$ constitutes a lobbying equililbrium, if $\hat{r} = R(\hat{r}^+)$ and $\hat{r}^+ = R^+(\hat{r})$.

It is well known from various fields of economic theory that there is a severe trade-off between the generality of a model and the possibility to derive meaningful and economically interesting implications. The model as outlined above clarifies the conceptual framework and the relevant interdependencies. But due to its generality it does not yield specific information on questions such as the condition for non-zero lobby activity, or the lobby membership and how it depends on the lobby's action, or the conditions for the existence of an interior lobbying equilibrium. In the next section, we introduce more restrictive assumptions in order to gain further insight into the driving forces of competitive lobbying.

3. A Simplified Version of the Model

The simplifications to be introduced in this section are related to individual preferences (3) and to the rent-seeking technology (2). We assume now that all group members have quasi-linear preferences being represented by

(11) $$U(i,x^i,a^i,z) = V(i,z) - (e_0 - e_1(m-i))a^i + x^i$$

In (11) the function V may remain unspecified. $e_0 > 0$ and $e_1 \geq 0$ are two parameters by which all group members are ordered according to their sensitivity for the lobby's coercive pressure. Observe that $i = m$ $(i = 0)$ is the most (least) sensitive agent, if $e_1 > 0$ and that all group members' sensitivity is the same if $e_1 = 0$. It is also assumed that $e_0 \geq me_1$, which ensures that the lobby's coercive pressure is a 'bad' rather than a good for everybody in the group who is not a member of the lobby.

The second simplification of Section 3 as compared to Section 2 is to require that $\hat{Z}$ and $\hat{Z}^+$ from (2) are separable[15] in r and r^+.

More specifically, we introduce

(12) $\tilde{Z}(r,r^+) := Z(r) + z_0 - Z^+(r^+)$ and $\tilde{Z}^+(r,r^+) := Z^+(r^+) + z_0^+ - Z(r)$

with $z_0 + z^+_0 = \hat{z}$ and assume that the functions Z and Z^+ are concave, non-negative, non-decreasing and satisfy $Z(0) = Z^+(0) = 0$. Then we set

$$(13)\qquad \hat{Z}(r,r^+) = \begin{cases} \tilde{Z}(r,r^+) \\ \hat{z} \\ 0 \end{cases} \quad \text{if } \tilde{Z}(r,r^+) \begin{cases} \in [0,\hat{z}] \\ > \hat{z} \\ < 0 \end{cases}$$

In view of (12) it is straightforward that the analogue of (13) for $\hat{Z}^+$ (substituting in (13) $\hat{Z}$ by $\hat{Z}^+$ and $\tilde{Z}$ by $\tilde{Z}^+$) is satisfied, if and only if (13) holds. It follows from this observation that the present specification of (2) by (12) and (13) satisfies the properties (i) and (ii) as required for $\hat{Z}$ and $\hat{Z}^+$ in Section 2.

For given $(a,g > 0,z)$ the individual's decision problem is now specified by using (5) and the budget constraint $x^i = w^i - g^i$ in order to turn (11) into

$$\hat{U}(i,g^i;a,g,z) = V(i,z) - (e_0 - e_1(m-i))\,\frac{g-g^i}{g}\,a + w^i - g^i$$

There is a solution to Problem 1, if $x^i \geq 0$ or

(14) $g \leq w^i$.

15) As to empirical plausibility, we consider separability a severe restriction. The efforts of one lobby seem to be the more effective, ceteris paribus, the weaker the other lobby's counter-attacks are. For an elaborate parametric, but non-separable rent-seeking technology see Pethig (1984).

Recall that if $g^i = g$ solves Problem 1 then agent i chooses to be a member of the lobby. Obviously he does so, if and only if[16] $\hat{U}(i, g^i=g; a,g,z) \geq \hat{U}(i,g^i=0; a,g,z)$, or equivalently, if and only if $g \leq (e_0 - e_1(m-i))a$.

Note first that unlike in the illustration in Figure 1, here agent i's decision to join the lobby is independent of z. This is due to the specification of preferences in (11). It is also important to observe that if there is i_1 such that $g \leq (e_0 - e_1(m-i_1))$ a then $g \leq (e_0 - e_1(m-i))a$ for all $i = i_1, i_1+1,...,m$. Define i_0 to be that particular agent who satisfies (for given g and a) $g \leq (e_0 - e_1(m-i_0))a$ and $g > (e_0 - e_1(m-i))a$ for all $i < i_0$. Clearly, then $n = m-i_0$ is the lobby membership and n is a discontinuous function of g and a.

Since it is more convenient to work with smooth functions we apply the real-number approximation for group members by substituting the set of integers $\{1,...,m\}$ by the closed interval $[0,m]$. When we use the notation $i \in [0,m]$ in the following, it is not implied that there is a continuum of agents. It rather means that if $i \in [0,m]$ is not an integer, it "approximates" that agent who is indexed by the next lower integer. Using this convention, for given g and $a>0$, $g = (e_0 - e_1(m-i_0))a$ uniquely defines that "approximated" agent i_0 who is indifferent between joining and not joining the lobby (and hence is a member). It follows from the argument of the preceding paragraph that $n = m-i_0$ is the lobby membership - the only difference being that n is now a real number and the true membership is the next lower integer to n. Due to the real-number approximation we can write

(15) $$g = (e_0 - e_1 n)a.$$

For $a > 0$, (7) now takes the form

(7") $$n = m - i_0 = \frac{1}{e_1}(e_0 - \frac{g}{a}) = \hat{N}(a,g,z) \text{ for all z.}$$

16) Recall the convention that in case of indifference an agent is assumed to be a lobby member.

Since i_0 is restricted to the interval [0,m], we also require $0 \leq n \leq m$ and therefore, from (7")

$$(16) \qquad \frac{g}{a} \in [e_0 - me_1, e_0] \quad \text{for } a > 0.$$

We emphasized that (7") presupposes $a > 0$ and hence $f > 0$ due to (5). If (7") were used in (1) to specify the net revenue, it would no longer be possible to determine, under which conditions the zero action would be the lobby's best response. It is therefore preferable to use (15) for substituting g by n as a decision variable of the lobby. In other words, we consider (f,n,r) as the lobby's action rather than (f,g,r) so that the budget constraint (8) becomes[17)]

$$(8') \qquad b = B(f,n) := n(e_0 - e_1 n)A(f) - f \geq r.$$

We are now in the position to address Problem 2. Hence we have to maximize the variable z with respect to f, n and r subject to (8'), (9) and (12) - (16). Due to (8') the lobby's net revenue B(f,n) does not depend on r. This suggests to determine the maximum possible net revenue and to ask, in particular,under which conditions the lobby is able to raise a positive net revenue. From $B_n = A(f)(e_0 - 2e_1 n) = 0$ it follows that - for every given f - b attains its maximum if

$$(17) \qquad n = e_0/2e_1.$$

For the time being we postulate $(e_0/2e_1) \in [0,m]$ postponing to check the implications of (16). Substituting n from (17) in B(f,n) yields

$$(18) \qquad B(f) = \frac{e_0^2}{4e_1} A(f) - f.$$

17) The function B from (1') and (8) is clearly different from that in (8'), which should be indicated by choosing a different functional sign in (8'). For the ease of exposition we will accept this lack of differentiation in (8') and in what follows. At the same time confusion is avoided by sufficient reference to where the respective function B is defined.

Recall from (5) that A is a concave function satisfying $A(f) \geq 0$ and $A(0) = 0$. Hence the lobby is able to raise positive net revenue if and only if

$$(19) \qquad A_f(f) > \frac{4e_1}{e_0^2} \quad \text{for } f = 0.$$

In Olson's (1965) terminology, a latent special-interest group can be mobilized by a lobbying organization (under the assumptions of the present model), if and only if (19) holds[18]. From here our analysis proceeds in several steps. The first is to determine the upper bound for the membership dues. According to (5), (15) and (17) the maximum net revenue requires to set $g = (e_0/2)A(f)$. The dues are clearly bounded from above by (15) that is by the individual budget constraint. In order to keep the analysis simple we restrict our further investigation to the case $w^i = w$ for all i.

If the domain of A is not bounded from above, then $a_1 = 2w/e_0$ is the maximum possible value of the externality satisfying $g = w = (e_0/2)a_1$. In this case, the dues exhaust the entire individual budget, i.e. (15) holds as an equality[19]. Suppose now that there is a finite limiting value, say a_2, for A if f tends to infinity. Define $a_3 = a_2$, if A is bounded from above and $a_3 = a_1$ otherwise. Clearly, then

$$\bar{g} := (e_0/2)\bar{a} \qquad \text{with } \bar{a} := \min\,[a_1, a_3]$$

is the upper bound for g. If a_2 is finite the inverse of function A is set-valued at a_2. It is then a necessary condition for efficient lobbying to choose the smallest recruiting effort for the maximum possible outcome. For convenience, we denote this efficient input by $\bar{A}(a_2)$.

18) An additional condition is $Z_r(r) > 0$ for $r = 0$, which is, of course the raison d'être of the entire issue.

19) Empirically, this case does not seem to be relevant, since individuals will leave the lobby long before $g = w^i$. But due to the quasi-linear utility function (11), the individuals' marginal utility for the private consumption good is constant in our model rather than increasing with decreasing amounts of the private good available for consumption. Hence $g = w^i$ is not ruled out as a possible solution to our model.

The next step is to define three levels of fund-raising investment, namely f^w, f^z and f^m, that will turn out to be relevant for a solution to Problem 2:

- $f^w := \bar{A}(\bar{a})$ with $\bar{a} := \min [a_1,a_3]$ as specified above; in this case either the lobby members spend all their income on membership dues or additional fund-raising effort is ineffective.
- $f^m := \bar{A}_f(4e_1/e^2_0)$ if $(4e_1/e^2_0)$ belongs to the range of A_f, and $f^m = f^w$ otherwise. f^m is the unique maximizer of B from (18) if there exists a positive-valued maximum for B.
- f^z is determined with the help of r^z which in turn is a maximizer of Z (for given r^+) satisfying $Z(r) < Z(r^z)$ for all $r \in [0,r^z)$. We assign $f^z = f^w$, if r^z does not exist <u>or</u> if $r^z \geq B(f^m)$. Otherwise f^z is specified by the two conditions (i) $r^z = B(f^z)$ and (ii) there is no $f \in (0,f^z)$ such that $r^z = B(f)$. If $f^z < f^w$ and $0 < f^m < f^w$, then clearly $f^z < f^m$. Under these conditions the lobby is able to raise more lobbying funds than can be spent for effective lobbying. Hence under $f^z < f^m$, $(f^z, g = (e_0/2)A(f^z), r = B(f^z))$ is the solution to Problem 2.

The rationale for defining f^w, f^m and f^z is to determine the maximum possible public-goods increment to be secured by the lobby for predetermined lobbying effort of the other group. Observe that under condition (16) $f = \min [f^w,f^m]$ yields the maximum net revenue. In Figure 2 one has $f^m < f^w$ and it is straightforward that for $Z = Z^1$ the lobby's maximizing action is $(f^m, (e_0/2)\ A(f^m), B(f^m))$. The same action yields the maximum attainable public-good provision under $Z = Z^2$, too, but it would be inefficient, because the same result can be achieved with $(f^z, (e_0/2)A(f^z), r^z)$.

Unfortunately, two more complications must be "removed" on our way to determine the lobby's reaction function as defined in (9): We still have to consider (a) the constraint (16) and (b) the constraints involved in (13).

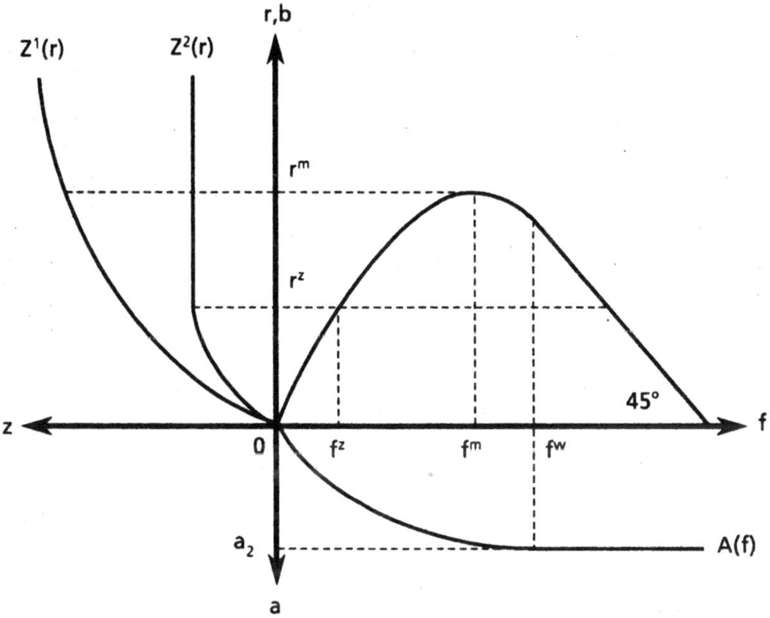

Figure 2: The lobby 's decision problem

(a) With the help of (15) and (17) the constraint (16) becomes $(e_0/2) \in [e_0 - me_1, e_0]$. Obviously, the upper bound is never violated, but if e_0, e_1, m are such that $e_0 > 2e_1m$, then (16) is violated under (15) and (17). So the implicit assumption up to now, namely that (15), (16) and (17) are generally compatible, cannot be maintained. If $(e_0/2e_1) > m$, it is easy to see that we have to set n = m in (15) and (9'). Hence

(18') $$B'(f) := m(e_0 - e_1m)\, A(f) - f$$

and in this case

(19') $$A_f(f) > \frac{1}{m(e_0 - e_1 m)} \quad \text{for } f = 0$$

is the necessary and sufficient condition for the lobby's ability to raise positive net revenue. Since under $e_0 > 2e_1m$ (18) is substituted by (18') it is also necessary to adjust the values f^w, f^z and f^m. This is easily done by defining three values $f^{w'}$, $f^{z'}$ and $f^{m'}$ in complete analogy to f^w, f^z and f^m, respectively. The only differences are, that B' is substituted for B, $1/m(e_0 - e_1m)$ for $4e_1/e^2_0$, and a_1 by $a'_1 := w/(e_0 - e_1m)$.

(b) The second (and last) complication in solving Problem 2 are the constraints involved in (13). For that purpose it is convenient to introduce the following notation:

$$r^* \begin{cases} = B(f^*) \text{ with } f^* = \min\,[f^z, f^w, f^m], \text{ if } e_0 \le 2e_1 m \\ = B'(f^{*'}) \text{ with } f^{*'} = \min\,[f^{z'}, f^{w'}, f^{m'}] \text{ otherwise} \end{cases}$$

(20) $$r = \bar{Z}[z^+_0 + Z^+(r^+)] =: F^1(r^+)$$

(21) $$r = \bar{Z}[Z^+(r^+) - z_0] =: F^2(r^+)$$

$r^+_1 := \bar{F}^1(r^*)$, if $F^1(0) < r^*$, and $r^+_1 = 0$ otherwise

$r^+_2 := \bar{F}^2(r^*)$

With the help of these definitions we now substantiate two claims:

<u>Claim 1</u>: $R(r^+) = F^1(r^+)$ on $[0, r^+_1]$.

Suppose that (for sufficiently small r^+) r is chosen so that $\hat{z}$, the maximum possible value is secured. Substituting $z = z_0 + z^+_0$ in (12) yields (20). F^1 is positively sloped (in the relevant domain[20]) and $F^1(0) > 0$. If $r^+ = 0$ and $F^1(0) < r^*$, then $r = F^1(0)$ solves Problem 2. Correspondingly, $R(r^+) = F^1(r^+)$ as long as $F^1(r^+) \le r$. If $F^1(0) > r^*$, then $[0, r^+_1] = \{0\}$ and $R(r^+) = r^*$.

20) F^1 is positively sloped if $Z_r > 0$ and $Z^+_{r+} > 0$ which is here assumed to hold in the relevant domain. Situations where $Z_r = 0$ or $Z^+_{r+} = 0$ can be handled by the model, but the pertinent analytical complications are left to the reader.

Claim 2: $R(r^+) = 0$ on $[r^+_2,\infty)$.
Suppose that (for sufficiently large r^+) r is chosen such as to maintain $z = 0$. Using (12) gives us (21). Again, F^2 is positively sloped and $r^+ = \bar{F}^2(r=0) > 0$. At r^+_2 the organization's maximizing action implies $r = r^*$ and $z = 0$. But since the other group cannot gain more than to take everything from the group under consideration, $z = 0$ is obviously secured at $r = 0$ for every "excessive" lobbying effort r^+ satisfying $F^2(r^+) \geq r^*$.

The preceding results are summarized as follows:

Proposition
Under the assumptions of Section 3, the reaction function R from (10) is given by $R(r^+) = 0$ on $[0,\infty)$, if and only if

either: $e_0 \leq 2e_1m$ and condition (19) does not hold,

or: $e_0 > 2e_1m$ and conditon (19') does not hold.

Otherwise, the reaction function satisfies

$$(22) \qquad R(r^+) \begin{cases} = F^2(r^+) \text{ on } [0, r^+_1], \\ = r^* \text{ on } [r^+_1, r^+_2], \\ = 0 \text{ on } [r^+_2,\infty). \end{cases}$$

Figure 3 illustrates (22) for positive r^+_1. The reaction curve R is given by the line segment $F^1(0)ABr^+_2$ and by the positive abscissa from r^+_2 to the right.

According to (22) the domain of R is partitioned into three intervals. In the first interval $[0,r^+_1]$ (that may be empty), the group under consideration dominates the other group so that the other group does not get any public good at all. The third interval $[r^+_2,\infty)$ is associated with the opposite all-or-none situation, but values r^+ in the interval $[r^+_1,r^+_2]$ lead to intermediate public-goods distributions. Observe that for this part of the domain the lobby's best response is a dominant strategy being completely determined by the group size (m), by the preferences of group members as well as the preference distribution and by the lobby's capacity of creating negative selective incentives. The dominant-strategy property does not depend on the lobby's "productivity" of lobbying as reflected in the function Z. This function has an impact, however, on the functions F^1 and F^2, on the reaction function over the interval $[0,r^+_1]$ and on the boundary points r^+_1 and r^+_2,

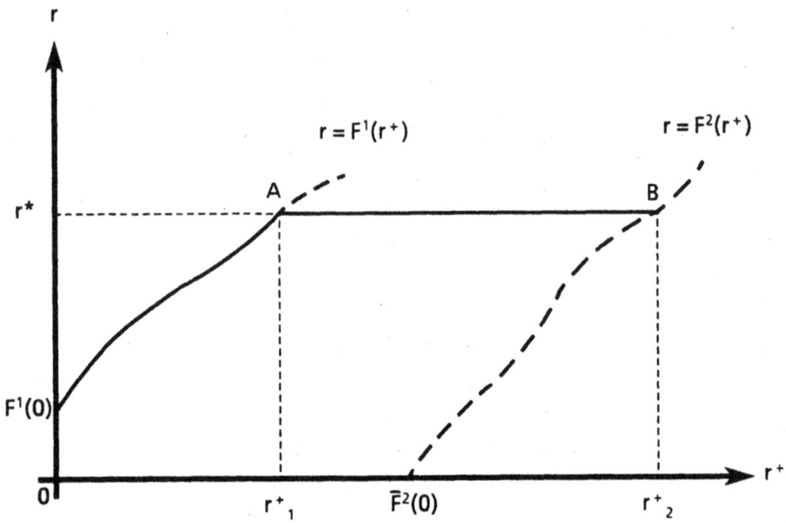

Figure 3: The lobby 's reaction curve

themselves. Moreover, for every given $r^+ \in [r^+_1, r^+_2]$ the amount of public good secured for the group by the lobby's best response is the greater, the more efficient its "lobbying technology" (Z) is.

From the above investigation of the reaction function(s) the properties of a lobbying equilibrium are straightforward. We leave aside the discussion of equilibria associated with all-or-none public-goods distributions and focus our attention, instead, on lobbying equilibria $(r^*, r^{+*}) \in [r_1, r_2] \times [r^+_1, r^+_2]$.

The solid straight lines in quadrant 1 of Figure 4 represent the (relevant parts of the) reaction functions. The quadrants 2 and 4 indicate the amount of public good being assigned to one group if this group varies its lobbying effort while the other group plays its dominant strategy. It turns out that at the lobbying equilibrium E_1 (in Figure 4) the associated public-goods distribution is D_1. Assume that the distribution (z_0,z^+_0) being legislated in the absence of lobbying is given by D_0 in quadrant 3. Then Figure 4 shows that the tug of war favoured the group marked with superscript 'plus' while the other group gets less than it would have got in the absence of lobbying. What happens if preference parameters or the capacity to generate selective incentives change? To fix our ideas suppose that r^{+*} remains

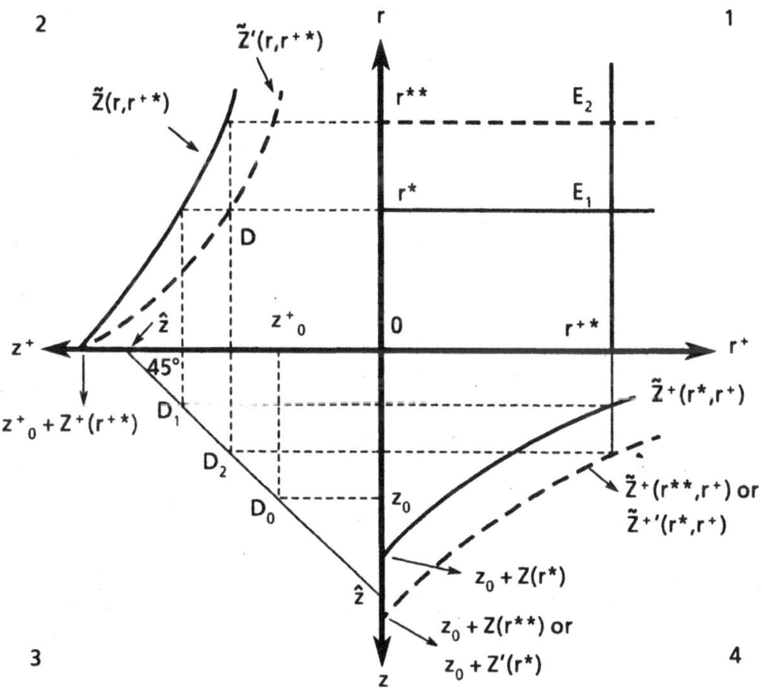

Figure 4: Lobbying equilibrium and comparative statics

unchanged and that $r^* = B(f^m)$. If, in addition, we specify A from (5) by

(23) $A(f) = f^v$ with constant $v \in (0,1)$

then we obtain, after some rearrangement of terms,

$$r^* = R^*(e_0,e_1,v) := \frac{e_0^2(1-v)}{4e_1}\left(\frac{e_0^2 v}{4e_1}\right)^{\frac{v}{1-v}}.$$

Inspection of this equation shows immediately that $r^* > 0$ for all $v \in (0,1)$. Moreover, differentiation yields

$R^*_v = (1/(1-v)^2)R^*(e_0,e_1,v) \ln (e^2_0 v/4e_1)$
implying that $R^*_v \gtreqless 0$ for $v \gtreqless 4e_1/e^2_0$. We obtain, in addition, $R^*_{e0} > 0$ and $R^*_{e1} < 0$.

Consider now a change of e_0, e_1 or v resulting in a new best response $r^{**} > r^*$. This change is reflected by the dotted lines in the quadrants 1 and 4 of Figure 4. In quadrant 2 the solid line is still the relevant one. The new lobbying equilibrium is E_2 with D_2 being the associated distribution.

Suppose, finally, that the lobbying equilibrium is E_1 in Figure 4, but now the political weight of one group rises. More specifically, we substitute Z by Z' satisfying $Z'(r) > Z(r)$ for all positive r. This change shifts the solid lines in the quadrants 2 and 4 to the right and downward, respectively. For convenience of illustration, we constructed the shifts in Z and Z^+ in such a way, that the function $Z^+(r^{**}, \cdot)$ and $Z^{+\prime}(r^*, \cdot)$ coincide and that the function $Z'(\cdot, r^{+*})$ passes through point D. Consequently, the public-goods distribution D_2 is now associated to the lobbying equilibrium E_1.

4. A Different Specification of Preferences

It is obvious that the results of Section 3 depend heavily on the utility functions as specified in (11). In particular, the dominant-strategy property and hence the fact that membership does not depend on the quantity of public good provided may be considered quite implausible. We therefore want to complement our analysis of Section 3 by employing the following specification of utility functions:

(24) $U(i,x^i,a^i,z) = (1-a^i)\,[(e_0-(m-i)e_1)z-e_2z^2] + x^i.$

This completely parametrized, quadratic utility function is clearly not very general. Its advantage is, however, that U is no longer separable in a^i and z (while still remaining manageable), that is, the disutility as derived from increased coercive pressure or moral suasion consists of a diminution of satisfaction derived from public-good consumption. Again (24), (4) and the budget equation $x^i = w^i - g^i$ yield (for $g > 0$)

$$\hat{U}(i,g^i;a,g,z) = (1-\frac{g-g^i}{g}a)\,[(e_0-(m-i)e_1)z-e_2z^2] + w^i-g^i$$

By the same line of argument used in the previous section [21] one obtains

(25) $g = az(e_0-e_1n-e_2z)$

or for $a > 0$

(8''') $$n = \frac{1}{e_1}(e_0-e_2z-\frac{g}{az}).$$

Hence

(26) $B(f,n,z) := A(f)(e_0-e_1n-e_2z)nz-f.$

For simplicity, we specify A from (5) as in (23). The next step of our analysis is to maximize B with respect to n and f. For that purpose we first derive

(27) $$n = \frac{1}{2e_1}(e_0-e_2z)$$

21) Figure 1 illustrates an individual's decision problem for this utility function. The line 0A corresponds to w^i, and we have $g = w^i$.

from $B_n = 0$ and substitute (27) in (26) to obtain

$$(28) \qquad B(f,z;v) := \frac{z(e_0 - e_2 z)^2}{2e_1} f^v - f.$$

Maximizing B from (28) with respect to f requires $B_f = [vz(e_0\text{-}e_2z)^2/2e_1]f^{v-1}\text{-}1 = 0$ and yields, after some rearrangements,

$$(29) \qquad B(z;v) := E(v)z^h(e_0 - e_2 z)^{2h} \text{ with } h := \frac{1}{1-v} \text{ and with } E(v) := (1-v)[v^v/2e_1]^h$$

Which are the properties of B with respect to z? Observe first, that it is sufficient to restrict the domain of B to $[0,z_1]$ with $z_1 := e_0/e_2$, since by (27) $n < 0$ if $z > z_1$. Obviously, for all $v \in (0,1)$ it is true that $B(0;v) = B(z_1;v) = 0$ and $B(z;v) > 0$ for all $z \in (0,z_1)$. The derivatives of B from (29) are

$$(30) \qquad B_z = hE(v)\, z^{h-1}(e_0\text{-}e_2z)^{2h-1}(e_0\text{-}3e_2z)$$

$$(31) \qquad B_{zz} = hE(v)\, z^{h-2}(e_0\text{-}e_2z)^{2h-2}D(z) \text{ with } D(z) := (h\text{-}1)e_0^2\text{-}(6h\text{-}2)e_0e_2z + (5h\text{-}1)e_2^2z^2.$$

Inspection of (30) and (31) shows that the function B attains its unique maximum over $[0,z_1]$ at $z_2 := z_1/3$. Moreover, B is strictly convex on $[0,z_3]$ and strictly concave on $[z_3,z_1]$, where

$$z_3 := \frac{(h-1)e_0}{(5h-1)e_2} \text{ (with } z_3 < z_2 \text{ since } h > 1 \text{ by (23)).}$$

With this information we proceed to derive the reaction function diagrammatically[22]. Part 1 of Figure 5 depicts the lobbying budget curve by the line

22) In this section we leave aside all difficulties stemming from boundary solutions either with respect to lobby membership or with respect to upper and lower bounds for public-good provision.

$Ob_ab_4b_5b_6b_7b_8z_1$. For alternatively given $\bar{z}_4,...,\bar{z}_8$ the points $b_4,...,b_8$ satisfy the balanced-budget condition for the maximum attainable z[23]. Part 2 of Figure 5 serves to transform $\bar{z}$ into r^+ via the definition $\bar{z} = z_0\text{-}Z^+(r^+)$, and Part 3 takes r^+ to the upper left quadrant. This section of Figure 5 contains the lobby's reaction curve, since to each given r^+_j $(j = 4,...,8)$ it associates the best response r_j taken from Part 1 and satisfying the condition $r_j = b_j$ $(j = 4,...,8)$. The lower panel of Figure 5 complements these results by elaborating on the relationships between z and $\bar{z}$ (Part 5) and z and r^+ (Part 6), respectively.

In summary, the following properties characterize a lobby's reaction function if the group members' preferences are given by (11):

(i) There is no dominant strategy for the lobbying organization.

(ii) If $z \geq e_0/3e_2$ can be secured without lobbying (that is, if $\bar{z} \geq e_0/3e_2$) then the best response to increasing $\bar{z}$ is a less than proportional increase in z.

(iii) If the technology for creating negative selective incentives changes, the pertinent shifts of the reaction curve are not clear-cut. Its direction of change does not only depend on the initial value of v - as in Section 3 - but also on the value of z.[24]

23) For $\bar{z}_5 = 0$ budget balance is attained at three different budgets: $b = 0$, $b = b_a$ and $b = b_5$. The unique solution of Problem 2 is reached for $b = b_5$ as is straightforward from Figure 5.

24) More specifically, equation (29) can be rearranged to read

$B(z;v) = (1\text{-}v)\,(e_0\text{-}e_2z)^2[(z(e_0\text{-}e_2z)/2e_1)v^v]^h$. Hence

$B_v = (1/1\text{-}v)B(z;v)[(1+v)\ln(z(e_0\text{-}e_2z)/2e_1)v - 1]$

and $B_v \gtreqless 0$, iff $\ln v \gtreqless \frac{1}{1+v} - \ln z\,(e_0 - e_2z)/2e_1$.

But we want to know, how the lobby adjusts its best-response rent-seeking investment $R(r^+;v)$ if v changes. From Figure 5 it is straigthforward that for given r^+ one obtains sign B_v = sign R_v.

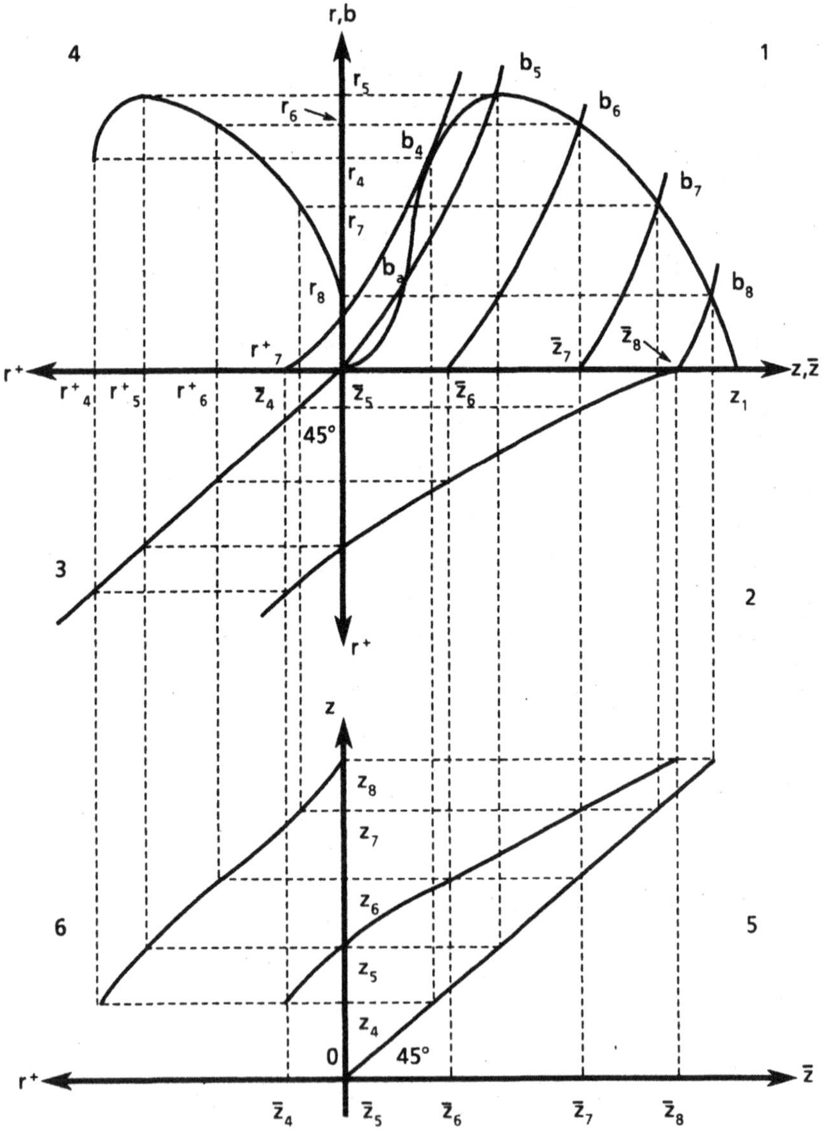

Figure 5: Derivation of the lobby's reaction function in the case of quadratic individual preferences

(iv) If the group's political weight improves, then the maximum z secured for given r^+ increases unambiguously, whereas the best-response rent-seeking investment diminishes for low r^+ and rises for large r^+.

(v) The optimum lobby membership decreases uniformly with increasing provision of the public good. In contrast, the optimum dues are positively correlated to growing public good provision as long as $z < e_0/2e_2$ and the correlation is negative for $z > e_0/2e_2$.

5. Concluding Remarks

So far our analysis has been strictly positive (descriptive), but it has, of course, far-reaching normative implications. The most obvious conclusion seems to be that any recruiting and lobbying effort is socially wasteful, since, by the assumption of a given overall budget for public goods, lobbying cannot affect anything but redistribution. Since society already paid for the public goods irrespective of each group's share by taxation the aggregate recruiting and lobbying expenditures $(r+r^+ +f+f^+)$ may be considered an adequate measure for social waste.

The problem with such an argument is, however, that it applies to groups and to society rather than to the constituent individuals. If we restrict welfare judgements to the Pareto criterion one relevant question is whether the allocation associated to the lobbying equilibrium is Pareto-superior to that emerging in the absence of lobbying. For convenience we refer to the group, marked by a plus sign, as the second group and to the other group as the first group. Suppose now that (r,r^+) is the unique lobbying equilibrium and that $z := \hat{Z}(r,r^+) > \hat{Z}(0,0) =: z_0$. Then all members of the second group are clearly worse off as compared to the non-lobbying situation. But for the members of the first group the utility comparison is not so clear-cut. Those individuals who are not lobby members enjoy the increment of public good provided but they also suffer from the disutility of the negative selective incentive. They are better off, if the former effect overcompensates the latter. For lobby members there is a similar trade-off. Their additional utility from public-good consumption may or may not be overcompensated by the disutility from private-good consumption forgone that is the opportunity cost of dues payment.[25] If marginal utility for the public good is positive in the relevant domain, members of the first group are the more likely to be better off in the lobbying equilibrium, the larger the difference $\hat{Z}(r,r^+)-z_0$. It follows that, in general, the lobbying equilibrium is not Pareto-dominated by the non-lobbying situation. On the other hand, it is also obvious, that the former allocation cannot, in any case, be Pareto-superior to the latter.

Choosing the non-lobbying allocation as a normative point of reference raises two critical issues:

(i) Recall that the (non-lobbying) public-goods distribution (z_0,z^+_0) was assumed to maximize the administration's probability to be reelected. We did not inquire into the relationship between this distribution and individual preferences. Simple median-voter considerations cannot be applied in the framework of the present paper, since voting models implicitly assume that administrations implement the winning election platform without any discretion. Rather than investigating this important issue in detail, let us now suppose that all preferences are separable in the public-good (as assumed in Sections 3 and 4), that there is a unique Pareto-efficient public-goods distribution (z_p,z^+_p)[26]), that $\hat{z} = z_p+z^+_p$ and that, finally, $(z_p,z^+_p) \neq (z_0,z^+_0)$ which is equivalent to $z_p \neq z_0$ (because $z^+_p = \hat{z}-z_p$). Without loss of generality, let us consider $z_0 < z_p$. If the distribution (z_0,z^+_0) is turned into the lobbying equilibrium, (z,z^+), then one of three situations occurs:
(a) $z < z_0 < z_p$, (b) $z_0 < z \leq z_p$ or (c) $z_0 < z_p < z$.
Under (a) and possibly under (c) lobbying increases the deviation from Pareto efficiency which is (or may be) reduced under the conditions (b) and (c). Even though we put forward this argument here in a very restrictive and sketchy way, it should have become clear that it further complicates the normative assessment of lobbying.

25) One may argue that this condition is a 'conditio sine qua non' for a 'rational' individual's decision to join the lobby. Such a behavioral hypothesis would result in an entirely different lobbying game, since $z^+ < \hat{Z}^+(0,0)$ would imply that no member of the second group would ever join its lobby. Compare also the remarks made in the context of Figure 1.

26) If preferences are separable one obtains Pareto-efficient public-goods distributions independent of the tax structure and the distribution of the tax burden. The uniqueness of (z_p,z^+_p) is secured, for example, if preferences are given by (11) in Section 4. As shown in Pethig (1983), assumption (11) yields $z_p = e_0/2e_2$ and $z^+_p = e^+_0/2e^+_2$.

(ii) Another issue relating to the nonlobbying allocation as a reference point is its lack of group-incentive compatibility. When the "lobbying technology" of (2) is specified by (12) and (13) and when footnote 18 is recalled, it is apparent that, by assumption, the administration is not able to find any public-goods proposal (z_0, z^+_0) which does not trigger contradiction, that is, lobbying by at least one group.[27] In our view this assumption makes sense since we deal with a situation of pure redistribution. The alternative assumption, that there is a distribution $(\hat{Z}(0,0), \hat{Z}^+(0,0))$ such that $\hat{Z}_r(0,0) = \hat{Z}^+_{r+}(0,0) = 0$, would simply deny the basic conflict of interests. If this view is accepted the administration's proposal (z_0, z^+_0) becomes dubious as a normative point of reference, since, in general, it cannot be an outcome of the political process.[28]

A final remark refers to the necessity of giving more explicit analytical structure to both lobby formation and to the processes of political response to lobbying. The "lobbying technology" depends on political institutions and rules suggesting that a comparative institutional analysis is needed both for further positive and normative research. Tullock (1980, p. 104) argued in a different context that in order to discourage rent seeking, political institutions should be chosen so that lobbying costs are high relative to the outcome. Observe, however, that in the present paper lobbying is almost insensitive to its productivity (the steepness of the functions Z and Z^+). Lobby formation is a complex organizational process, and it is an empirical question whether the lobby taken as a unit behaves like a rational rent seeker. Our hypothesis was, that "collective rationality" cannot be expected.

27) The qualifications for zero lobbying are, of course, given in Section 3. They relate to insufficient capacity to generate coercion or to the dominance of the adversary.

28) The rather common view to characterize lobbying as policy failure is then subject to an inverse Nirwana reproach, since the reference situation is not implementable.

References

Blümel, Wolfgang, Pethig, Rüdiger, and von dem Hagen, Oskar (1984), The Theory of Public Goods: A Survey of Recent Issues, Economics Department of the University of Oldenburg, Discussion Paper No. 80-84

Burns, Michael E., and Walsh, Cliff (1981), "Market provision of price-excludable public goods: A general analysis", *Journal of Political Economy* 89, 166-191

Olson, Mancur (1965), *The Logic of Collective Action*, Harvard University Press, Cambridge (Mass.)

Pethig, Rüdiger (1983), "On the production and distribution of information, *Zeitschrift für Nationalökonomie* 43, 383 - 403

Pethig, Rüdiger (1984), A Basic Model of Rent Seeking, Economics Department of the University of Oldenburg, Discussion Paper No. 74-84

Stigler, George J. (1974), "Free riders and collective action", *Bell Journal of Economics* 5, 359-365

Tullock, Gordon (1980), "Efficient rent seeking", in: Buchanan, James M., Tollison, Robert D., and Tullock, Gordon (eds.), *Toward a Theory of the Rent-Seeking Society*, Texas A&M University Press, College Station, 97-112

The MDP-Procedure in a Regional Economy

by

Oskar von dem Hagen*)

1. Introduction

Although it may be obvious to many people that one can express one's feelings on something with words or by actions, this is not generally true for political scientists or economists. Economic agents either buy something or they do not. Expressing one's feelings in any other way one has to put up with "cumbrous political channels" as Friedman (1962, 91) calls them. Political scientists on the other hand are more used to verbal communication and have labelled other behaviour desertion and treason. When Hirschman (1970) examined the interaction between these modes of expressing oneself, he not only provided the profession with an extremely stimulating analysis, but he also introduced a neutral terminology that does not discriminate against either mode: "exit" and "voice".

In many cases either the exit or voice behaviour dominates. However, Hirschman points out that they do not necessarily complement each other in cases where both coexist. The performance of a polito-economic system based on voice behaviour may improve or deteriorate if exit behaviour becomes possible. This is the problem we want to examine in the framework of a regional economy with local public goods.

When Samuelson (1954) formulated the efficiency conditions for public goods, he examined the case of a pure public good[1] where exit from its consumption is

---

*) This paper is part of the author's research at the Sonderforschungsbereich 5 of the Deutsche Forschungsgemeinschaft. It benefitted from several discussions with Richard Arnott, Russell Davidson, and Rüdiger Pethig as well as helpful comments by Wolfgang Ströbele. Their help is gratefully acknowledged.

1) Because the term "pure" public good may be ambiguous, this type of public good is said to be non-excludable, non-rejectable, and non-congestible (cf. Blümel, Pethig, and von dem Hagen, 1985).

impossible. The necessary information to provide a public good efficiently is private information about individual preferences. Voice is then necessary for efficiency. Unfortunately, as Samuelson was quick to point out, it is "in the selfish interest of each person to give false signals, to pretend to have less interest in a given collective consumption acitivity" (p.388).

The relevance of this so-called free-rider behaviour is still controversial. One of the earliest partial counter-arguments is due to Tiebout (1956). He argues that most of the public goods are of local nature in the sense that only residents of a given area can consume them. By choosing a residence, each individual implicitly reveals his preferences over bundles of public goods. More specifically, he suggests that individuals would form homogeneous communities[2)] to achieve efficient provision of local public goods. While in Samuelson's model exit is impossible and only voice behaviour can lead to efficiency, Tiebout allows for exit and claims that exit behaviour is sufficient for efficiency even in the presence of (local) public goods. He considers the case of an impure local public good where the average cost of production is a U-shaped function of the number of residents and assumes that community governments are only concerned with attracting the optimal number of residents to provide a fixed level of the public good at minimum average cost. In other words, the government only cares about the number of citizens and is completely irresponsive to their preferences.[3)]

One of the most controversial issues in this context is the requirement of homogeneous communities in order to achieve efficiency. Two recent comments on the subject indicate the wide range of different opinions. Bewley (1981) wishes to make the point that "one cannot extend Tiebout's analysis to heterogeneous

2) The term "homogeneous" applies to identical residents as well as "similar" residents. If individuals form a continuum with respect to one characteristic, then homogeneity should mean that a community population corresponds to a single interval of individuals (cf. Westhoff, 1977). Tiebout himself is not very specific about the interpretation of his statement "the consumer-voters will move to that community which *exactly* satisfies their preferences" (p.421). If the local public good is financed through a poll-tax, then Tiebout's statement seems to imply that all individuals within a community have to be identical with respect to income and preferences.

3) We therefore disagree with Pestieau's (1983) view that Tiebout built a bridge between exit and voice. While this is true for some later "Tiebout-type" models, it is not true for Tiebout's own contribution.

communities" (p.725), while Stiglitz (1983) opposes that "the focus on homogeneity in so much of the literature is simply a red herring" (p.27). Recent contributions to the discussion include Berglas (1984a, 1984b), Berglas, Helpman and Pines (1982), Berglas and Pines (1984), Sandler (1984), and Sandler and Tschirhart (1980, 1984).

In simple two-good models where, furthermore, preferences and production do not distinguish between types, there will generally be a homogeneous community structure that is Pareto non-inferior to a heterogeneous structure (cf. Berglas, 1984a, and Berglas, Helpman, and Pines 1982). The model of section 3 belongs to this class as will be demonstrated in section 3.4. However, since the question of heterogeneity in not of primary concern in the present paper we have no qualms about using such a simple model.

In the following section some results of exit-only and voice-exit models of economies with local public goods will be surveyed. In section 3 a model will be presented where voice influences public provision through regional MDP-procedures. The steady states, Tiebout equilibria, and social optima of the model will be examined. Section 4 contains concluding remarks.

2. Some Results of the Theory of Local Public Goods

2.1. Exit-only models

A central concept of the theory of local public goods is the so-called Tiebout equilibrium. In such an equilibrium no individual has an incentive to leave his community of residence. Intuitively this notion seems clear. A formal definition, however, has to specify the information or expectations an individual has about other communities. While it is generally assumed that he has perfect information about the status quo, it is not clear which of the changes due to his moving to a different community he anticipates. In the case of a continuum of consumers there is no ambiguity because the movement of a single consumer does not cause any changes. However, models where a single individual does not have or does not perceive any effect on the performance of the system are exactly the economist's way of making voice behaviour redundant.[4)]

When does a Tiebout equilibrium exist and under which circumstances will it be efficient? Tiebout suggests that in his model an equilibrium with homogeneous communities exists and is efficient. Later analyses demonstrate this rigorously but all require rather special assumptions about the form of government, the tax system within a community or the cost function for the public good.[5)] The problem encountered quite often is that a Tiebout equilibrium exists if the government is sufficiently inflexible (or is expected to be inflexible) - but this equilibrium can be inefficient. On the other hand, a flexible government could guarantee efficiency of an equilibrium - but the latter may not exist.

Bewley (1981) distinguishes between democratic and entrepreneurial governments. Democratic governments are assumed to be concerned only with the welfare of the present residents. This can give rise to inefficient equilibria as is often demonstrated with the help of the beach/ski-resort example:

> There are two communities and two types of consumers. Both communities can develop beach and ski resorts, but community 1 has a comparative advantage in developing a beach resort. Type 1 consumers only care for swimming while type 2 individuals enjoy just skiing. If all type 2 individuals happen to reside in community 1 and all type 1 individuals in community 2, then the best a "democratic" government of region 1 can do is to develop skiing-facilities while community 2 would develop swimming facilities.

This type of inefficiency is called "mismatching": no single individual has an incentive to move, but obviously a Pareto improvement can be achieved if all tpe 1 and type 2 individuals are swapped. "Entrepreneurial" governments can detect this deficiency and initiate the necessary policy changes.

---

4) Tiebout (1956) makes the less elegant assumption that a community government simply does not respond to residents' preferences.

5) Cf. Rothenberg (1970), Barr (1973), McGuire (1974), Pestieau (1977), Sonstelie and Portney (1978), Wooders (1978) and Bewley (1981).

Wooders (1978) uses the core concept of cooperative game theory and proves that an efficient equilibrium exists if the nunber of consumers of each type is "sufficiently" large. The core concept requires individuals not only to know the status quo but also to have information about all possible community formations ("quasi-regions"). This information precludes inefficient community formation, but leads to the non-existence of equilibrium if the number of consumers of a given type is too small. This may be illustrated by the following example:

> There are three identical consumers who care about a public good which can be produced with decreasing returns to labour. Symmetrial payoffs for members of a coalition of size n are given by
>
> $$v(n) = \begin{cases} 0 \text{ if } n=0,1 \\ 2 \text{ if } n=2 \\ 1 \text{ if } n=3. \end{cases}$$
>
> If the individuals only consider moving alone then n=3 is a stable community. But two consumers together would prefer to move to the other community.

Bewley (1981) shows that a public good which is consumed in equal amounts by all residents and whose cost is proportional to the number of consumers (what he calls a "pure public service") will lead to an efficient Tiebout equilibrium if there is free trade and if governments are entrepreneurial and competitive. By means of examples he shows that if any of the assumptions are violated either efficiency or existence of an equilibrium cannot be guaranteed.[6]

2.2 Voice-and-exit models

The no-exit model of Samuelson and the no-voice model of Tiebout are, of course, just "polar cases". It is therefore desirable to develop an integrated model with voice and exit behaviour. In many models voice behaviour is treated implicitly. This is true for the assumption of cooperative behaviour where only the *outcomes* of voice behaviour within a coalition are analyzed (e.g. in Wooders, 1978, and, in a similar spirit, Richter, 1982). This is also true for models which employ the assumption that residents of a homogeneous community will truthfully reveal their preferences. For example, Zodrow (1983, 4) states that homogeneity "with

6) More positive results have been derived by Schweizer (1982) who relaxes the zero-profit condition, and by Berglas (1984b) who shows that one of Bewley's non-existence results only holds in an economy without private goods.

respect to tastes for public services ... eliminates the local public choice problem". This may be true for some special cases like majority voting in communities with identical individuals. But in general the incentives for truthful revelation in a homogeneous community are not different from those in a heterogeneous one. In her survey on the subject Rose-Ackerman (1983, 56) therefore concludes that "the economist's dream of doing away with politics cannot be realized even in the local government context".

However, the prospects of developing an empirically interesting voice-and-exit model where Tiebout equilibria are efficient appeas to be dim. The restrictions on exit-only models to achieve such a result are so severe that the pursuit of similar conditions for models that allow voice behaviour as well seems to be rather pointless. Other authors on the subject share this view and restrict themselves to the questions of existence of a Tiebout equilibrium and its properties - especially its stability properties (e.g. Westhoff, 1977, 1979, Rose-Ackerman, 1979, Brueckner, 1979, Beliveau, 1981, Epple, Filimon, and Romer, 1984).

Westhoff (1977) presents one of the most satisfying models that incorporates voice and exit. He considers a two-good economy with a fixed number of communities and a continuum of consumers. The level of local public goods is determined by majority voting and is paid for by a proportional income tax. For this economy he is able to prove the existence of a Tiebout equilibrium with every community populated.[7] It may be interesting to note that the proof is valid not only for local public goods but for Samuelsonian pure public goods as well. However, standard assumptions on preferences are not sufficient to establish this result. Westhoff imposes the additional restrictions that individuals can be ranked continuously by their marginal rate of substitution and that this ranking is independent of the level of local public-good provision. A similar model that includes a housing market is presented by Epple, Filimon, and Romer (1984). They also give a numerical example where the Tiebout equilibrium is unique (and stable) for a variety of parameter values.

7) In a later article Westhoff (1979) shows that a uniqueequilibrium in his model is necessarily unstable.

In a model where the level of public-good provision is determined efficiently and not by majority rule, Wheaton (1975) has shown that financing the public good by means of benefit taxation will lead to the instability of Tiebout equilibria. Since the model to be developed in section 3 will lead to efficient provision of a public good within each community and benefit taxation at the margin, Wheaton's argument has to be examined more closely.

Wheaton considers a large number of communities, each inhabited by n individuals. Individuals differ only with respect to their income. There is one pure local public good y and one private good x, both of which have "normal" positive income effects. C(y) is the input requirement for y in terms of x and exhibits constant marginal cost. The level of public-good provision satisfies the Samuelson condition $\Sigma_i MRS^i = C_y$ where superscripts refer to individuals and subscripts denote partial derivatives. Wheaton examines the effect of an increase in person 1's income on individual i's utility ($i \neq 1$) and argues that the effect would be the same as individual i moving to an infinitesimally richer community. This effect is given by

(1) $$\frac{dU^i}{dI^1} = U^i_y \frac{dy}{dI^1} + U^i_x \frac{dx^i}{dI^1}.$$

Using i's budget constraint

(2) $$I^i = MRS^i y + x^i$$

(1) can be rewritten as

$$\frac{dU^i}{dI^1} = U^i_x \frac{dy}{dI^1} \left(MRS^i - \frac{MRS^i + y\, MRS^i_y}{1 + y MRS^i_x} \right)$$

$$= U^i_x \frac{dy}{dI^1} \frac{MRS^i - MRS^i_y / MRS^i_x}{1 + 1/y MRS^i_x}.$$

dy/dI^1 can be obtained by differentiating $\Sigma_i MRS^i = C_y$ with respect to I^1 which yields

$$\frac{dy}{dI^1} = \frac{-m^1}{\Sigma_i MRS^i_y(1 - ym^i) - \Sigma_i MRS^i m^i}$$

where $m^i = MRS^i_x/(1 + y\ MRS^i_x)$. Since y and x are normal goods $dy/dI^1 > 0$, $MRS^i_y < 0$ and $MRS^i_x > 0$. Therefore $dU^i/dI^1 > 0$, i.e. everybody would like to move to a richer community.

This result demonstrates that the exit option may well upset the performance even of the idealized Lindahl mechanism with truthful revelation, which would lead to benefit taxes according to (2). The deteriorating effect of the exit option is by no means new. It was already one of the central issues in Hirschman's book. We will return to this problem in the next section and discuss why the result does not apply to the MDP-mechanism.

3. Voice as MDP-Procedure

We are going to consider a model where government behaviour and individual voicing behaviour are described by the MDP-procedure (Malinvaud 1971, Drèze and de la Vallée Poussin, 1971). This is an incremental procedure where individuals are asked to voice (in continuous time) their marginal willingness to pay (σ^i) for the public good. In an economy with one public good and one private good the MDP-procedure can be defined by the following differential equations:[8]

$$(3)\quad y' = \begin{cases} \Sigma_i \sigma^i - C_y & \text{if } y > 0 \\ \max(0, \Sigma_i \sigma^i - C_y) & \text{if } y = 0 \end{cases}$$

$$(4)\quad x^{i'} = -\sigma^i y' + \delta^i y'^2$$

8) It is important to notice that it is the flow of the public good which enters utility and production functions. However, and this is a central feature of the MDP-procedure, the level of public-good provision is institutionally fixed, i.e. the level of y is given at each instant. It is only the rate of change of y (3) which is affected by individuals' voices.

where a prime denotes the forward derivative with respect to time and $\delta^i > 0$ is a distributional parameter with $\Sigma_i \delta^i = 1$. This procedure guarantees a balanced public budget and a non-decreasing utility level for every individual who reports $\sigma^i = MRS^i$.[9] This property is called individual rationality.

3.1 The model

We are considering a continuum of consumers with utility functions $U(i,y,x^i) = iay - by^2 + x^i$ and identical initial endowment I_0. a und b are positive parameters and i is distributed uniformly between 0 and 1.. There are two communities with population P_j ($j=1,2$). The size of these populations $N_j := \mu(P_j)$ is the Lebesgue measure. The size of the total population is N, i.e. $N = N_1 + N_2$. The cost of local public-good production is allowed to depend on the community size and is given by

$$(5) \qquad C^*(y_j,N_j) = (\alpha^* + \beta N_j)y_j$$

where y_j is the level of public-good provision in community j. β reflects the cost to community size or congestion. (5) can be rewritten as

$$C^*(y_j,N_j) = N(\alpha^*/N + \beta N_j/N)y_j.$$

Introducing $n_j := N_j/N$ as the fraction of individuals residing in community j and $\alpha := \alpha^*/N$, the production costs can be defined as

$$(6) \qquad C(y_j,n_j) = N(\alpha + \beta n_j)y_j.$$

The level of public-good provision in each community is determined by a regional MDP-procedure. Every individual within a community is supposed to receive the same share of the surplus $\delta^i_j = 1/N_j$. At this stage we will ignore any difficulties due to strategic misrepresentation and assume that the marginal rates of

9) The properties of this procedure under truthful revelation and myopically strategic behaviour area surveyed by von dem Hagen (1984a).

substitution are revealed truthfully.[10]

The initial level of public-good provision is zero in each community and its adjustment with truthful revelation becomes

$$(3')\qquad y'_j = aS_j - 2bN_j y_j - N\gamma_j, \text{where } S_j = \int_{P_j} i\, d\mu(i)$$

and $\gamma_j = \alpha + \beta n_j$.

3.2 <u>Dynamic behaviour and steady states</u>

The explicit solution of (3') gives the level of public-good provision:

$$(7)\qquad y_j(t) = [(as_j - \gamma_j) - (as_j - \gamma_j)\exp(-2bN_j t)]/2bn_j,$$

where $s_j = S_j/N$ and t denotes time. The corresponding solution for x^i can be obtained by integrating (4).[11] After changing the variable of integration from t to y this yields (10). The following derivation is less direct but adds more to the understanding of the model. It is a property of the MDP-procedure that under truthful revelation the change in utility is

$$(8)\qquad U^{i'} = U^i_x\, \delta^i (y'_j)^2.$$

Integrating (8) by parts and using $\delta^i = 1/N_j$ and $U^i_x = 1$ we get

$$\begin{aligned} U^i(t) &= I_0 + \textstyle\int_0^{y(t)} y'_j/N_j\, dy \\ (9)\qquad &= I_0 + y_j(t)\,[(as_j - \gamma_j)/n_j - by_j(t)]. \end{aligned}$$

---

10) Truthful revelation is the only strategy that guarantees a monotonically increasing level of utility (Drèze and de la Vallée Poussin, 1971). Furthermore, if the share of the surplus is the same for everybody, as assumed above, the procedure has the same time-path under truthful revelation and myopically strategic behaviour - only the rate of convergence is slower under the latter regime (Roberts, 1979). And the property of the MDP-procedure to converge to a Pareto-optimal allocation seems to be robust even with respect to intertemporal strategic behaviour (cf. Champsaur and Laroque, 1981, and von dem Hagen, 1984b). Therefore, as a first approach the assumption of truthful revelation does not seem unreasonable.

11) In the following the subscript of individual variables or parameters indicating the community of residence will often be omitted where this can be done without ambiguity.

The right hand side does not contain any individual variables. In other words the utility level within a given community is always the same for everybody. This is due to the assumptions that preferences are revealed truthfully, the shares in the surplus are identical, utility functions are linear in x, and the initial utililty levels are identical.

From (9) and the utility function it follows that

(10) $x^i = I_o + y_j\,[a(s_j/n_j - i) - \gamma_j/n_j].$

This can be interpreted as everybody paying the same financing tax

$$\tau_j = C(y_j,n_j)/N_j$$
$$= (\gamma_j/n_j)y_j$$
(11) $$= (\alpha/n_j + \beta)y_j.$$

The remaining tax payment can then be interpreted as a transfer tax which is proportional to an individual's deviation from the average willingness to pay

(12) $\rho^i_j = (s_j/n_j - i)y_j.$

An individuals's level of utility at a steady state can be calculated from (9) using (7) as

(13) $U^i(\infty) = by^2_j + I_o.$

Restricting ourselves to homogeneous communities (see fn.2) we can introduce the notation $n_1 = n$ and $n_2 = 1 - n$ and assume that low demanders live in community 1. Then $s_1 = n^2/2$, $s_2 = (1-n^2)/2$ and the final levels of public-good provision can be calculated from (7) as

(14) $y_1 = \max\,\{0,\ (an/2 - \alpha/n - \beta)/2b\}$

and

(15) $y_2 = \max\{0, [a(1+n)/2 - \alpha/(1-n) - \beta]/2b\}$.

where the non-negativity constraint is explicitly taken into account. If $y_1 > 0$, it follows from (14) that

$$\partial y_1/\partial n = a/2 + \alpha/n^2 > 0,$$

i.e. steady-state provision of the public good always increases in community 1 when high demand individuals immigrate. There is a critical community size

$$n^* := \beta/a + SQRT[(\beta/a)^2 + 2\alpha/a].$$

below which no public good will be provided. For community 2

$$\partial y_2/\partial n = a/2 - \alpha/(1-n)^2$$

indicates that public-good provision increases with the population if the latter is small, achieves a maximum when

$$1 - n = SQRT(2\alpha/a),$$

and decreases again when the population continues to grow. The population of community 2 can be too small for the public good to be provided which occurs at

$$n^{***} := \beta/a + SQRT[(\beta/a)^2 + 1 - 2(\alpha + \beta)/a].$$

On the other hand, at

$$n^{**} := \beta/a - SQRT[(\beta/a)^2 + 1 - 2(\alpha + \beta)/a]$$

community 2 has reached a size beyond which no public good will be provided anymore.

3.3 Tiebout equilibria

To discuss efficiency and stability properties of Tiebout equilibria we will restrict ourselves to steady states of the MDP-procedure. In fact, we will not consider simultaneous occurence of voice and exit but only an alternating sequence. A common approach is to let individuals choose a community of residence before any voice mechanism starts. Individuals are assumed to foresee the subsequent allocation adjustments and a Tiebout equilibrium is a situation where the expected utility level is higher nowhere else than in the chosen community of residence. We call this framework (A). It is not really a voice-exit framework because exit is not defined after the voice procedure has started.

In the alternative framework (B) the MDP-procedure is assumed to converge infinitely fast. The exit option then is a movement from a steady state in one community to a steady state in another community. Since we are dealing with a continuum of consumers, there is not going to be any allocative effect of individual exit decisions.

For the analysis of Tiebout equilibria it will be useful to distinguish the following cases:

	$n \leq n^{**}$	$n^{**} < n < n^{***}$	$n \geq n^{***}$
$n \leq n^*$	Case 1: $y_1 = 0$ $y_2 = 0$	Case 2: $y_1 = 0$ $y_2 > 0$	Case 3: $y_1 = 0$ $y_2 = 0$
$n > n^*$	Case 4: $y_1 > 0$ $y_2 = 0$	Case 5: $y_1 > 0$ $y_2 > 0$	Case 6: $y_1 > 0$ $y_2 = 0$

Table 1

Cases 1 and 3 are trivial Tiebout equilibria in both framework (A) and (B). They will obviously be locally stable if n lies inside the respective intervals. For non-trivial equilibria where the public good is provided in at least one community we have to distinguish between framework (A) and(B).

(A) Exit-voice sequence

For any partition into homogeneous communities an individual knows the final level of public-good provision given by (14) and (15).The corresponding utility level is given by (13). For a Tiebout equilibrium the final utility level and thus, according to (13), the final level of public-good provision has to be the same in both communities. In this framework only case 5 of table 1 can contain a non-trivial Tiebout equilibrium. At such an equilibrium every individual will be indifferent between communities 1 and 2. According to (14) and (15) we can define

$$n^{iv} := -2\alpha/a + 1/2 + \mathrm{SQRT}[(2\alpha/a)^2 + 1/4]$$

as the unique partition giving rise to a Tiebout equilibrium in framework (A). However, depending on the parameter values, a Tiebout equilibrium with $y_1 = y_2$ may not exist. If it exists the size of community 1 (n^{iv}) has to be greater than 1/2 and therefore greater than the size of community 2.[12)]

To examine the stability properties of the equilibrium with homogeneous communities, we define a pseudo adjustment mechanism

$$(16) \quad n' = u_1 - u_2,$$

where u_1 and u_2 are the common utility levels in communities 1 and 2 respectively as derived in (13). The equilibrium of this process is stable if $\partial n'/\partial n < 0$ at least at the equilibrium. Differentiating (16) with respect to n yields

12) The fact that everybody is indifferent at such an equilibrium raises the question why people would sort themselves into homogeneous communities. It follows from the above analysis that $y_1 = y_2$ is a sufficient condition for a Tiebout equilibrium and this can be satisfied by heterogeneous communities as well. Nothing can then be said about the relative size of the communities. But see 3.4.

(17) $\partial n'/\partial n = 2b(y_1\, \partial y_1/\partial n - y_2\, \partial y_2/\partial n).$

It follows from (14) and (15) that

$$\partial y_1/\partial n = (a/2 + \alpha/n^2)/2b$$

and

$$\partial y_2/\partial n = [(a/2 - \alpha/(1\text{-}n)^2]/2b.$$

(17) can therefore be rewritten as

$$\begin{aligned}\partial n'/\partial n &= y_1[a/2 + \alpha/n^2] - y_2[a/2 - \alpha/(1\text{-}n)^2] \\ &= y\alpha\,[1/n^2 + 1/(1\text{-}n)^2] > 0,\end{aligned}$$

where $y = y_1 = y_2$. The equilibrium will thus always be unstable In fact, if exit is allowed at this equilibrium as in the following section, the marginal individual in community 2 will not remain indifferent but rather move to community 1. This mechanism will then always lead to one grand community.

(B) Voice-exit sequence

So far, exit was not allowed once the public good was provided anywhere. Allowing exit at this stage leads to the problem of assigning tax shares to new immigrants. These tax shares should only depend on current observable variables, not on the history of the MDP-process. Furthermore, we should not expect individuals to reveal their true marginal rate of substitution if this is the price they are going to pay even for the infra-marginal units of the public good. The good incentive properties of the MDP-procedure derive from the fact that the revealed willingness-to-pay affects only the price of the marginal unit of the public good.

We are going to assume that the current level of public-good provision remains unaffected by somebody's exit and that everybody in a community is paying the same financing tax (11) - even a new immigrant. Accordingly, an emigrant does not contribute towards financing the public good in his old community of residence.

The treatment of the transfer taxes is more complex and, in fact, indicates the limitations of this model with regional MDP-procedures. In the MDP-procedure the level of public-good provision is institutionally fixed. Ceteris paribus, one more unit of public good provided today implies one more unit forever. For regional MDP-procedures to retain some kind of indidividual rationality we are going to assume that transfer taxes are fixed in the same way as the public-good provision.

Assumption 1: When individual i moves from community j to community k, his financing-tax payment changes from τ_j tro τ_k. His transfer-tax payments ρ^i_j, however, remains unaffected.

For the following discussion it may be helpful to interpret an individual's income as coupons that entitle him to a permanent income.Transfer taxes are then paid with these coupons.

An individual considering to move would compare the level of utility at home with the utility he would receive in another community. For person i in community 1 we can define a switching function

$$(18) \quad S12(i) := u(i,y_1,x^i) - u(i,y_2,x^i + \tau_1 - \tau_2),$$

indicating this person's desire to remain in community 1. The equilibrium level of public good provision in community 2 changes only by an infinitesimal amount but affects individuals differently depending on their type (i). A change in private-good consumption occurs only due to a difference in the financing tax rates τ_1 and τ_2.

While the first expression is the same for all residents of community 1, the second one is not due to differences in private-good consumption.The steady-state level can be derived from (10) and (7) as

$$(19) \quad x^i(\infty) = I_o - iay_j + 2by^2_j$$

In contrast to framework (A) the exit decision here differs among residents. In order to define a community switching function in terms of the marginal consumer (n) it is necessary for the infra-marginal individuals to be less inclined to move. For individuals in community 1, for example, it is required that

$$S12(i) \geq S12(n) \ \forall i \leq n.$$

According to (18) this is equivalent to

$$-U(i, y_2, x^i + \tau_i - \tau_2) \geq -U(n, y_2, x^n + \tau_1 - \tau_2).$$

This can be rewritten using the specifiation of the utility functions and (19) as

$$iay_2 - by_2 + I_o + y_2(2by_2 - ia) \geq nay_2 - by_2 + I_o + y_2(2by_2 - na).$$

which reduces to $i(y_1 - y_2) \geq n(y_1 - y_2)$. Since $n \geq i$ this requires

(20) $y_2 \geq y_1$.

In fact, (20) is also a necessary condition for a Tiebout equilibrium with homogeneous communities. If (20) is violated then $y_1 > y_2$. According to (18) S12(0) is negative in this case indicating that Individual 0 would prefer to move to community 2. Therefore, under framework (B) cases 4 and 6 of table 1 cannot contain any Tiebout equilibria.

If (20) holds, we can define the switching function for community 1 in terms of the marginal individual S12 := S12(n) or

(21) $S12 = an(y_1 - y_2) - b(y^2{}_1 - y^2{}_2) - \tau_1 + \tau_2.$

The value of the switching function is independent of the current level of private-good consumption. Only the levels of public-good provision and the difference in the financing-tax rate matter. It is therefore straightforward that the willingness of the marginal individual to stay in community 2 is

$$S21 = an(y_2-y_1) - b(y^2_2-y^2_1) - \tau_2 + \tau_1$$
$$= -S12.$$

If (20) holds, one can easily show that it is the marginal individual in community 2 (the lowest demander) who has the highest desire to move. Therefore it is a necessary and sufficient condition for a Tiebout equilibrium with homogeneous communities that

$$S12 = S21 = 0.$$

We have already mentioned that cases 1 and 3 of table 1 consist only of trivial Tiebout equilibria while cases 4 and 6 do not contain any Tiebout equilibria. Hence the only cases of interest are 2 and 5. Let us examine case 2 first. The switching functions are

$$S12 = -S21 = -any_2 + by^2_2 + t_2.$$

Using (11) and (15) this is equivalent to

$$(1-n)S12 = y_2[n^2 3a/4 - n(a+\beta/2) + a/4 + (\alpha+\beta)/2]$$

A Tiebout equilibrium where the public good is provided in only one community therefore requires

$$0 = n^2 3a/4 - n(a+\beta/2) + a/4 + (\alpha+\beta)/2.$$

Of the two roots of this equation one would imply the equilibrium to be unstable in terms of the adjustment process

$$(16') \quad n' = u^n_1 - u^n_2.$$

The stable root is

$$n^v := (1/3) \{2 + \beta/a + SQRT[(2+\beta/a)^2 - 3 - 6(\alpha+\beta)/a]\}.$$

In this model it is therefore possible for a Tiebout equilibrium to exist even if the public good is provided in one community but not in the other.

Let us now turn to case 5 where the public good is provided in both communities.

Proposition: A Tiebout equilibrium where the public good is provided in both communities can occur in the voice-exit sequence only if $n=.5$.

Proof: It is tedious but straightforward to rewrite the switching function (21) using (11), (14), and (15) as

$$(18) \qquad S12 = (.5-n)[n^4a^2/2 - n^3a(a-4\alpha) - n^2(4\alpha\beta+4\alpha a-a^2/2) + 4\alpha an + 2\alpha^2] / [4bn^2(1-n)^2].$$

The fourth-order polynomial (in square brackets) is positive at $n=0$ and $n=1$. Furthermore, its slope is positive at $n=0$ and negative at $n=1$. Since the leading term is positive, the graph has to be W-shaped. It follows that the polynomial has to be positive on the whole interval [0,1]. The switching function can thus only be zero if $n=.5$. QED

Corollary: A Tiebout equilibrium at $n=.5$ is stable in terms of the adjustment process (16').

This corollary follows immediately from the proof of the preceding proposition.

3.4 Optimality

A social optimum in an economy with the above type of utility functions requires maximization of total utility $nu_1+(1-n)u_2$. Using (13)-(15) and disregarding the restriction of homogeneous communities, the problem becomes

$$(22) \qquad \max_{n,s_1,s_2} n[(as_1-d\gamma_1)/2bn]^2 + (1-n)[(as_2-\gamma_2)/2b(1-n)]^2$$

s.t.

$$s_1 + s_2 = 1/2$$
$$s_1 \geq n^2/2$$

$$s_2 \leq (1-n^2)/2.$$
$$0 \leq n \leq 1$$

Substituting s_2 by the first constraint an interior maximum with respect to s_1 $(0<s_1<1/2)$ requires

$$2n[(as_1-\gamma_1)/2bn]a/2bn +$$
$$2(1-n)[(a/2-as_1-\gamma_2)/2b(1-n)](-a)/2b(1-n) = 0.$$

This is equivalent to $(as_1-\gamma_1)/2bn = (as_2-\gamma_2)/2b(1-n)$ which can be rewritten using (7) as

(23) $y_1 = y_2$.

Maximization with respect to n, taking account of $y_1 = y_2$, yields

$$n\partial y_1/\partial n + (1-n)\,\partial y_2/\partial n = 0$$
$$= \quad a/2 + \alpha/n - \alpha/(1-n).$$

This condition is equivalent to $n = n^{iv}$. A social optimum in this model thus requires two homogeneous communities with equal public-good provision.

While this is the only non-trivial Tiebout equilibrium of framework (A), we already pointed out that it is neither stable under the adjustment process (16) nor with respect to exit as defined in framework (B).

4. Conclusion

There are two types of conclusions we would like to draw from this model. The first refers to the possibility of exit. In contrast to Tiebout's intention the exit option may upset the performance of an otherwise well-functioning system. While this was already a central argument in Hirschman's book, his framework was somewhat different from ours.

The second type of conclusion is about the MDP-procedure. The preceding discussion seems to suggest that there are limitations to the application of the MDP-procedure to regional economies where exit is possible.[13] The interpretation above requires that individuals' transfer taxes remain unaffected by exit. While this was defined in terms of location, it could also be interpreted as exit from the living. Individulas in this model then have either to live infinitely long or pass their income on their heirs. Since the MDP-procedure is almost exclusively used as a model for public planning procedures, this indicates that the application to regional economies may be questionable.

Another result of the voice-exit sequence in the MDP-model, however, has quite a realistic touch. In framework (B) it is quite important into which community one is "born".[14]

References

Barr, James L. (1973), "Tiebout models of community structure", *Papers of the Regional Science Association* 30, 113-139

Beliveau, Barbara C. (1981), Two Aspects of Market Signaling, Yale University, PhD Dissertation

Berglas, Eitan (1984a), "Quantities, qualities and multiple public services in the Tiebout model", *Journal of Public Economics* 25(3), December, 299-321

Berglas, Eitan (1984b), On the Existence of Equilibrium with Heterogeneous Communities, Foerder Institute for Economic Research, Tel-Aviv University, Ramat Aviv, Working Paper #36-84, November

Berglas, Eitan, Helpman, Elhanan, and Pines, David (1982), "The economic theory of clubs - Some clarifications", *Economics Letters* 10(3-4), 343-348

Berglas, Eitan, and Pines, David (1984), "Resource constraint, replicability and mixed clubs", *Journal of Public Economics* 23(3), April, 391-397

13) In this paper we are only dealing with consumption goods. For an application to public inputs see Tulkens and Kioni Kiabantu (1983).

14) Otherwise identical individuals n starting in community 1 or 2 will end up with different utility levels. This happens because individual n is the highest demander in community 1 and the lowest demander in community 2. The low demanders are in an advantageous position in this model because the status quo ($y_0 = 0$) is in their favour.

Bewley, Truman F. (1981), "A critique of Tiebout's theory of local public expenditures", *Econometrica* 49(3), May, 713-740

Blümel, Wolfgang, Pethig, Rüdiger, and von dem Hagen, Oskar (1985), The Theory of Public Goods: A Survey of Recent Issues, Universität Oldenburg, Wirtschaftswissenschaftliche Diskussionsbeiträge #80-84, revised and extended, April

Brueckner, Jan K. (1979), "Equilibrium in a system of communities with local public goods", *Economics Letters* 2(4), 387-393

Champsaur, Paul, and Laroque, Guy (1981), "Le plan face aux comportements stratégiques des unités décentralisée", *Annales de l'INSEE* 42, Avril-Juin, 3-30

Drèze, Jacques, and de la Vallée Poussin, Dominique (1971), "A tâtonnement process for public goods", *Review of Economic Studies* 38(2), April, 133-150

Epple, Dennis, Filimon, Radu, and Romer, Thomas (1984), "Equilibrium among local jurisdictions: Toward an integrated treatment of voting and residential choice", *Journal of Public Economics* 24(3), August, 281-308

Friedman, Milton (1962), *Capitalism and Freedom*, Chicago University Press, Chicago

Hirschman, Albert O. (1970), *Exit, Voice, and Loyalty*, Harvard University Press, Cambridge

Malinvaud, Edmond (1971), "A planning approach to the public good problem", *Swedish Journal of Economics* 73(1), March, 96-112

McGuire, Martin C. (1974), "Group segregation and optimal jurisdictions", *Journal of Political Economy* 82(1), January-February, 112-132

Pestieau, Pierre (1977), "The optimality limits of the Tiebout model", in: Oates, Wallace E. (ed.), *The Political Economy of Fiscal Federalism*, Heath, Lexington, 173-186

Pestieau, Pierre (1983), "Fiscal mobility and local public goods - A survey of the empirical and theoretical studies of the Tiebout model", in: Thisse, Jacques-François, and Zoller, Henry G. (eds.), *Locational Analysis of Public Facilities*, North-Holland, Amsterdam, 11-41

Richter, Donald K. (1982), "Weakly democratic tax equilibria in a local public goods economy with perfect consumer mobility", *Journal of Economic Theory* 27(1), June, 137-162

Roberts, John (1979), "Incentives in planning procedures for the provision of public goods", *Review of Economic Studies* 46(2), April, 283-292

Rose-Ackerman, Susan (1979), "Market models of local government: Exit, voting, and the land market", *Journal of Urban Economics* 6(3), July, 319-337

Rose-Ackerman, Susan (1983), "Beyond Tiebout: Modeling the political eocnomy of local government", in: Zodrow, George R. (ed.), *Local Provision of Public Services: The Tiebout Model after Twenty-Five Years*, Academic Press, New York, 55-83

Rothenberg, Jerome (1970), "Local decentralization and the theory of optimal government", in: Margolis, Julius (ed.), *The Analysis of Public Output*, Columbia University Press, New York, 31-64

Samuelson, Paul A. (1954), "The pure theory of public expenditure", *Review of Economics and Statistics* 36(4), November, 350-356

Sandler, Todd (1984), "Club optimality - Further clarifications", *Economics Letters* 14(1), 61-65

Sandler, Todd, and Tschirhart, John T. (1980), "The economic theory of clubs: An evaluative survey", *Journal of Economic Literature* 18(4), December, 1481-1521

Sandler, Todd, and Tschirhart, John T. (1984), "Mixed clubs - Further observations", *Journal of Public Economics* 23(3), April, 381-389

Schweizer, Urs (1982), Agglomeration and Mobility, Department of Economics, University of Bielefeld, Discussion Paper #106, March

Sonstelie, Jon C., and Portney, Paul R. (1978), "Profit maximizing communities and the theory of local public expenditure", *Journal of Urban Economics* 5(2), April, 263-277

Stiglitz, Joseph E. (1983), "The theory of local public goods twenty-five years after Tiebout: A perspective", in: Zodrow, George R. (ed.), *Local Provision of Public Services: The Tiebout Model after Twenty-Five Years*, Academic Press, New York, 17-53

Tiebout, Charles M. (1956), "A pure theory of local expenditures", *Journal of Political Economy* 64(5), October, 416-424

Tulkens, Henry, and Kioni Kiabantu, Tomasikila (1983), "A planning process for the efficient allocation of resources to transportation infrastructure", in: Thisse, Jacques-François, and Zoller, Henry G. (eds.), *Locational Analysis of Public Facilities*, North-Holland, Amsterdam, 127-152

von dem Hagen, Oskar (1984a), Truthful Revelation and Myopic Behaviour in the MDP-procedure, Universität Oldenburg, Wirtschaftswissenschaftliche Diskussionsbeiträge #68-84, März

von dem Hagen, Oskar (1984b), "Zur Dynamik der Kollektivgüterallokation", in: Siebert, Horst (ed.), *Intertemporale Allokation*, Lang, Frankfurt, 427-451

Westhoff, Frank H. (1977), "Existence of equilibria in economies with a local public good", *Journal of Economic Theory* 14(1), February, 84-112

Westhoff, Frank H. (1979), "Policy inferences from community choice models: A caution", *Journal of Urban Economics* 6(4), October, 535-549

Wheaton, William C. (1975), "Consumer mobility and consumer tax bases", *Journal of Public Economics* 4(4) November, 377-384

Wooders, Myrna H. (1978), "Equilibria, the core, and jurisdiction structures in economies with a local public good", *Journal of Economic Theory* 18(2), August, 328-348

Zodrow, George R. (1983), "The Tiebout model after twenty-five years: An overview", in: Zodrow, George R. (ed.), *Local Provision of Public Services: The Tiebout Model after Twenty-Five Years*, Academic Press, New York, 1-15

Distributive and Allocative Effects of Individual Voting Behaviour*

by

Horst Hanusch

and

Peter Biene

1. Introduction

Each government's budget can be separated into revenues and expenditures. This procedure is common standard in the literature on public finance and it serves as the point of departure for different models that consider both sides separately. The theory of optimum income taxation based upon the pioneering work of Mirrlees [1971] restricts its analysis to public revenues. In the simpler model of Sheshinski [1972], a certain proportion of the individual gross labour income is collected by the government in form of compulsory taxes which are used to finance the given revenue requirements as well as transfer payments that are distributed equally to everyone. The problem analysed in this theory is the conflict between equity and efficiency: making the income distribution more equal induces the aggregate income to decline.

Concerning the expenditures, the optimal size of the public budget can be determined. In his seminal paper, Samuelson [1954] stated necessary conditions for the optimal allocation of public and private goods. By doing so, his analysis focusses on the allocative efficiency leaving aside the distributive effects that stem from different ways of financing the provision of these public goods.

*) An earlier draft of this paper was presented at the meeting of the European Public Choice Society in Munich, May 2 - 5, 1984. We are indebted to all of the participants in this meeting who commented on our paper, especially to our discussant Kurt Reding. Of course, any remaining errors are evidently ours.

Even though both theories in itself derive interesting results, their solutions depend on each other. For example, Feldstein [1973] pointed out that the solution of the tax model depends on the exogeneous revenue requirements. Moreover, Brito and Oakland [1977] derive a modification of Samuelson's result if the public good is financed by an income tax. These findings lead to the conclusion that both problems are to be analysed simultaneously. Otherwise, it must be presumed that the implications of these models bear only little relevance to the real world. First steps into this direction are the works of Moreh [1983] and Moreland [1984] .

All the above mentioned theories use the social welfare approach to derive their results. A different way is taken if the analysis restricts itself to the individuals and their utility-maximizing behaviour. In this case, the economic choice of the individuals are transformed into the political sphere where they determine government activities via majority voting rule. The well-known model of Bowen [1943] shows how public and private goods are allocated in this setting. Romer [1975] gave the solution of the tax problem. Taking both problems together, Gevers and Proost [1978] analyse the case that the individuals have to decide upon two issues simultaneously: first, on the proportion of the private and government sectors, and second, on the use of tax revenues for public goods and transfer payments.

This paper is in line with the arguments of Gevers and Proost. What we want to stress is the close relationship between problems of distribution and that of allocation. In order to derive clear-cut results, some heroic assumptions will be made. First, we restrict our analysis to a two-goods economy. One is a pure private and the other is a pure public good. Second, the tax function is taken to be linear in before-tax income. Third, we assume that the individuals have identical utility functions. Moreover, they are assumed to be of Cobb-Douglas type. Of course, these simplifications restrict the generality of our approach but we hope that this disadvantage is overcompensated by some new and interesting insights.

Section 2 presents the basic model where the individual behaviour is analysed especially in regard to their labour supply. As the financial system is characterized by a constant marginal tax rate and uniform transfer payments, government revenues solely depend upon the individuals' labour incomes. Section 3 contains a comparative static analysis. It is asked how labour supply alters in response to a change both in the tax rate and in the transfer payments. In general, these instruments of the government's allocational and distributive policy lower the individual labour supply. Additionally, the effects of these instruments interact with each other: the higher the transfer payments the greater is the (negative) impact of a change in the tax rate.

Section 4 analyses how the individuals choose their solution of this conflict between equity and efficiency. Of course, this solution depends upon their ability. Concerning the tax rate and the transfer payments, there are clear-cut results: the higher the individual ability, the lower are the most preferred tax rate and transfer payments. In a system of majority voting, the median voter decides upon the parameters that describe government activities. If the distribution of individual abilities and, hence, incomes is skewed to the right, i.e. the median income is smaller than the mean one, the median is in favour of a positive tax rate but he does not necessarily vote for positive transfer payments. Moreover, under the assumption that everyone works, the median's most preferred tax policy defines an equilibrium under the majority voting rule. To end with, section 5 contains a numerical example and section 6 some concluding remarks.

2. The Model

We consider a closed economy consisting of n individuals. Each individual is characterized by a specific ability (or skill) w_i $(i = 1,...,n)$. We assume

$$(1) \qquad 0 < w_1 \leq ... \leq w_i \leq ... \leq w_n < \infty$$

so that the individuals are ordered according to their ability. Furthermore, it is assumed that the individual wage rate corresponds to the skill level.

An arbitrary individual i can use a given period of time which we take to be unity, as working time l_i or leisure f_i,

$$(2) \qquad l_i + f_i = 1.$$

This choice immediately results in the individual before-tax income

(3) $$z_i = w_i l_i .$$

We assume that the government imposes a constant marginal tax rate t on gross income. On its part, the government uses its tax revenues both for the provision of a public good G, which we assume to be strictly positive ($G > 0$), and for monetary transfer payments from which each individual gets an amout of $k = K/n$. In case of $K < 0$, it is a lump-sum tax.
In a static model, the individual net income will be spent completely for private consumption,

(4) $$x_i = (1-t)z_i + k.$$

It will be assumed that the individuals have identical utility functions whose arguments are private consumption, the public good, and leisure. Furthermore, we take the utility functions to be of Cobb-Douglas form,

(5) $$u_i = x^{\alpha}_i f^{\beta}_i G^{\gamma}$$

where $0 < \alpha, \beta, \gamma < 1$ and $\alpha + \beta + \gamma = 1$. This assumption guarantees that the usual properties of utility functions - positive but decreasing marginal utility - is fulfilled for each argument.

In this economic environment, the individuals try to maximize their utility taking both k and G as given. The Lagrange equation of this problem is

$$L_i = x^{\alpha}_i (1-l_i)^{\beta} G^{\gamma} \cdot \lambda[x_i - (1-t)w_i l_i - k]$$

As it is not ensured that the individual i will work ($l_i > 0$), the Kuhn-Tucker conditions have to be employed for the variable l_i. Thus, the first order conditions for a utility maximizing behaviour are

$$\frac{\partial L_i}{\partial x_i} = \alpha x_i^{\alpha-1} f_i^{\beta} G^{\gamma} - \lambda = 0$$

$$\frac{\partial L_i}{\partial l_i} = -\beta x_i^{\alpha} f_i^{\beta-1} G^Y + \lambda(1-t)w_i \leq 0$$

$$l_i \frac{\partial L_i}{\partial l_i} = 0$$

The assumption concerning the utility functions ensure that the second order conditions are satisfied, too. Rearranging these terms results in

(6) $$\alpha(1\text{-}t)\, w_i f_i \leq \beta x_i$$

where the equality sign holds for $l_i > 0$.

From (6) it follows that in case of $l_i > 0$, the individuals substitute leisure for working time as long as the marginal utility of leisure is equal to the marginal utility of private consumption available for their working timc. In case of $l_i = 0$, the marginal utility of private consumption is always smaller than the marginal utility of leisure regardless of the working time the individual i may choose. In addition, it is to be noticed that the tax rate must be smaller than one,

(7) $$t < 1$$

because in case of $t \geq 0$ nobody will work. This fact also becomes clear if one considers the optimum working time of individual i,

(8) $$l_i = \begin{cases} 0 & \text{for } w_i \leq w_0 \\ \hat{\alpha} - \hat{\beta}k/[(1\text{-}t)w_i] & \text{for } w_i > w_0 \end{cases}$$

where $\hat{\alpha} = \alpha/(\alpha+\beta)$ and $\hat{\beta} = \beta/(\alpha+\beta)$. Additionally, $w_0 = \beta k/\alpha(1\text{-}t)$ denotes the skill level below which everyone will choose to be idle.

The equation (8) can be regarded as the labour-supply function of the individual under consideration. From (3) and (8), the corresponding before-tax income follows

(9)
$$z_i = \begin{cases} 0 & \text{for } w_i \leq w_0 \\ \hat{\alpha} w_i - \hat{\beta} k/(1-t) & \text{for } w_i > w_0 \end{cases}$$

The private consumption of individual i is consequently

(10)
$$x_i = \begin{cases} k & \text{for } w_i \leq w_0 \\ \hat{\alpha}[(1-t)w_i + k] & \text{for } w_i > w_0 \end{cases}$$

We now impose two restrictions on government policy. First, we postulate that nobody drops out of the working force completely. This is ensured by the assumption

(11)
$$t < 1 - \frac{\beta k}{\alpha w_1}.$$

Moreover, we assume that the net income is positive for all individuals,

(12)
$$t < 1 + \frac{k}{w_1}.$$

These conditions are formulated as restrictions on the tax rate where (11) and (12) are more restrictive than the constraint (7) if and only if k represents a positive transfer payment and a lump-sum tax, respectively.

Obviously, the individual working time, before-tax income, and after-tax income depend on individual ability,

(13)
$$\frac{\partial l_i}{\partial w_i} = \frac{\hat{\beta} k}{(1-t)w_i^2} \begin{cases} > 0 \text{ for } k > 0 \\ = \quad\quad\; = \\ < \quad\quad\; < \end{cases}$$

(14)
$$\frac{\partial z_i}{\partial w_i} = \hat{\alpha} > 0.$$

(15) $$\frac{\partial x_i}{\partial w_i} = \hat{a}(1-t) > 0\,.$$

Only in case of $k > 0$, the optimum working time is an increasing function of the individual skill level. On the other hand, for $k < 0$ the reduction in working time is so low that it is overcompensated by the higher ability. Therefore, gross income as well as net income increase with ability. Consequently, for an arbitrary k, relatively low ability is equivalent to relatively low gross income. In case of $k > 0$, gross incomes are distributed more unequally than abilities. This is due to the fact that higher before-tax income results both from higher ability and longer working time.

Given the tax rates and transfer payments, tax revenues $T(> 0)$ solely depend upon the individual labour incomes,

$$T = \sum_{i=1}^{n} t w_i l_i\,.$$

Hence,

(16) $$T = n[\hat{a}\, t\, \bar{w} - \frac{\beta t k}{1-t}]$$

where $\bar{w} = \Sigma\, w_i/n$. The government spends its tax revenues for the provision of public goods as well as for transfer payments. Because of the fact that a market price does not exist for the public good, its value will be identified with the resources used for providing it. In this way, public goods are measured in terms of private goods.

We assume that the government does not want to maximize a social welfare function of its own but that its only task is to balance the budget. Therefore, government expenditures have to be equal to tax revenues,

(17) $$T = K + G\,.$$

From (17), it can be seen that there are three different ways to balance the budget:

- positive income taxes used for the provision of public goods and transfer payments ($t > 0, k > 0$);
- positive income taxes and lump-sum taxes used for the provision of public goods ($t > 0, k < 0$);
- lump-sum taxes used for a negative income tax and the provision of public goods ($t < 0, k < 0$).

Inserting (16) and $K = nk$ into (17) yields an expression for the quantity of public goods,

(18) $$G(k,t) = n[\hat{\alpha}t\bar{w} - \frac{1-\hat{\alpha}t}{1-t}k].$$

Equation (18) indicates the connection between the three variables describing government activities. It states that one parameter is a function of the remaining two. In equation (18), G was taken to be the dependent variable. As the partial derivative of G with respect to k is smaller than zero there is for every value of t a one-to-one correspondence between the quantity of public goods that can be supplied and the transfer payments. Therefore, the problem of determining the government activities is only a two-dimensional choice.

3. The Impact of Government Activities on Economic Performance

In this section, we want to analyze the effect of changes in government policy on economic performance. To begin with, let us consider transfer payments. Because of

(19) $$\frac{\partial l_i}{\partial k} = -\frac{\hat{\beta}}{(1-t)w_i} < 0$$

an increase in transfer payments induces a decrease in the individual supply of labour. If the revenues from the income tax are positive ($t > 0$), the tax revenues will diminish

(20)
$$\frac{\partial T}{\partial k} = -n\frac{\hat{\beta}t}{1-t} \begin{cases} < 0 \text{ for } t > 0 \\ = \qquad = \\ > \qquad < \end{cases}$$

In case of t < 0, the individuals receive an addition to their gross income. If the individuals decide to shorten their working time, their gross incomes decline. Given a t < 0, the additions paid by the government decrease, too.

Therefore, increasing transfer payments and decreasing tax revenues must be compensated for by a drastic reduction in the supply of public goods if the budget is to be balanced

(21)
$$\frac{\partial G}{\partial k} = \frac{\partial T}{\partial k} - \frac{\partial K}{\partial k} = -n\frac{1-\hat{\alpha}t}{1-t} < 0.$$

The second variable of the government is the tax rate. The term

(22)
$$\frac{\partial l_i}{\partial t} = -\frac{\hat{\beta}k}{(1-t)^2 w_i} \begin{cases} < 0 \text{ for } k > 0 \\ = \qquad = \\ > \qquad < . \end{cases}$$

shows that the effect of increasing the tax rate depends on the lump-sum element. In case of transfer payments, it induces the individual labour supply to decline. Lump-sum taxes lead to the reverse effect. Correspondingly, the individual gross income alters due to the change in the tax rate as

(23)
$$\frac{\partial z_i}{\partial t} = \frac{\hat{\beta}k}{(1-t)^2} \begin{cases} < 0 \text{ for } k > 0 \\ = \qquad = \\ > \qquad < . \end{cases}$$

This is the basis for the effect on tax revenues

(24)
$$\frac{\partial T}{\partial t} = n[\hat{\alpha}\bar{w} - \frac{\hat{\beta}k}{(1-t)^2}].$$

If the government imposes lump-sum taxes, tax revenues are an increasing function of the tax rate. In this case, there will be no "Laffer-curve". The reason can be found in equation (22) which states that the individuals will choose a longer working time under this regime.

If the government makes transfer payments, the effect cannot be determined unambigiously. The first term on the RHS of (24) is positive. It reflects the fact that a higher proportion of the individual before-tax income accrues to tax collections. On the other hand, the second term is negative for $k > 0$ because of an increased incentive for the individuals to lower their working time and, thereby, their gross income.

Correspondingly, the amount of public goods alters in response of a change in the tax rate. This effect is given by

$$(25) \qquad \frac{\partial G}{\partial t} = \frac{\partial T}{\partial t}.$$

Obviously, the overall effect on tax revenues depends upon three variables: the individual valuations of private consumption and leisure, the tax rate and the transfer payments. We will confine ourselves to the latter two of these variables as the relevance of individual preferences has already been analysed in detail [see e.g. Fullerton (1982)].

At first, one can recognize that

$$(26) \qquad \frac{\partial^2 l_i}{\partial t \partial k} = \frac{\partial^2 l_i}{\partial k \partial t} = - \frac{\hat{\beta}}{(1-t)^2 w_i} < 0.$$

This relationship indicates that the effect of one variable depends on the magnitude of the other. The higher the transfer payments the more alters the labour supply in response of changing the tax rate and vice versa.

This effect also becomes clear if one restricts the analysis to positive transfer payments. In this case, the tax rate can be determined as that value at which both effects offset each other. The solution additionally gives the tax rate t^{max} that maximizes tax revenues,

$$(27) \qquad t^{max} = 1 - (\beta k / \alpha \bar{w})^{1/2}$$

It can be seen that the revenue maximizing tax rate depends heavily upon the transfer payments. As

(28) $$\frac{\partial t^{max}}{\partial k} = \frac{(\beta k/a\bar{w})^{1/2}}{2k} < 0,$$

this tax rate is a decreasing function of k. The reason for this behaviour is that an increase in transfer payments induces the individuals to lower their working time. Equation (26) states that the magnitude of this effect increases with the tax rate. If one postulates that the tax rate imposed on individual gross income is smaller than the revenue maximizing one then the magnitude of the transfer payments restrict the range for determining the tax rate.

The interpretation of this restriction is two-fold. Let us assume that the amount of public goods is fixed. Then the equations (19) and (22) make clear the conflict between equity and efficiency. A more equal distribution of after-tax incomes can only be achieved by increasing the transfer payments. These additional expenditures have to be financed by increasing the tax rate. Because both policies lower the individual supply of labor, equation (27) can be thought of as the limit to redistribution.

Alternatively, for given transfer payments, equation (27) defines the restriction imposed on the government in designing the tax rate. Therefore, the transfer payments determine the maximum amount of public goods that can be provided.

4. Majority Voting

We assume that the individuals decide upon the parameters of government policy by majority voting. Recall that even though there are three variables, the problem is reduced to a two-dimensional choice by equation (18). In order to utilize the majority voting rule, each individual is asked to state his preferences. In this choice, he has to take into account not only public goods and transfer payments but also the effects of government policy on labour supply.

To arrive at the optimum choice, the indirect utility function v_i of individual i has to be formed. Employing (4), (5), (8) and (18), it follows that

(29) $$v_i(k,t) = A[1\text{-}t]^{\alpha\text{-}1}[(1\text{-}t)w_i + k]^{\alpha+\beta}[\hat{\alpha}t(1\text{-}t)\bar{w}\text{-}(1\text{-}\hat{\alpha}t)k]^{\gamma}$$

where $A = [\hat{\alpha}]^{\alpha}[\hat{\beta}]^{\beta}[n]^{\gamma}[w_i]^{-\beta}$. Differentiating (29) with respect to k and t and equating the partial derivatives to zero results in two equations for k and t from which the optimum values can be determined. Thus,

$$\frac{\partial v_i}{\partial k} = 0$$

leads to

(30) $$k_i = \frac{1-t}{1-\hat{\alpha}t}[\alpha t - \gamma(1-\hat{\alpha}t)r_i]\bar{w}$$

where $r_i = w_i/\bar{w}$ is the relative ability of individual i and the index i indicates that k_i is the optimum value of k for individual i. Differentiating k_i with respect to r_i yields

(31) $$\frac{\partial k_i}{\partial r_i} = -\gamma(1-t)\bar{w} < 0$$

as $t < 1$ by (7). Thus, the most preferred transfer payments are a decreasing function of individual ability. As one could have presumed, a person with greater ability prefers lower transfer payments. From (30), it follows that k_i is positive as long as

(32) $$r_i < \frac{\alpha t}{\gamma(1-\hat{\alpha}t)}$$

This relation depends heavily upon the tax rate. For $t = 0$, everyone recommends lump-sum taxes since this is the only way of financing the provision of public goods. For $t \rightarrow 1$, the optimum transfer payments tend to zero regardless of the individual ability.

The second problem is to determine the optimum tax rate. By inserting equation (30) into (29), the relationship

$$\frac{\partial v_i}{\partial t} = 0$$

leads to

(33) $$\hat{a}(a+\gamma)(1-r_i)t_i^2 - [(1+\hat{a})(1-r_i) + \beta r_i]t_i + [1-r_i] = 0.$$

Again, t_i designates the optimum tax rate for individual i. The expression (30) for the optimum transfer payments is used to derive equation (33). This is the reason why (33) determines the optimum tax rate only in the case that the transfer payments are at the optimum level, too.

In order to analyse the change in the most preferred tax rate in response to an alteration of individual ability, we form the inverse function

(34) $$r_i = \frac{\hat{a}(a+\gamma)t_i^2 - (1+\hat{a})t_i + 1}{\hat{a}(a+\gamma)t_i^2 - (1+\hat{a})t_i + 1 + \beta t_i}.$$

It follows that

(35) $$\frac{\partial t_i}{\partial r_i} = \frac{1}{\partial r_i / \partial t_i} < 0 \text{ for } t_i^2 < \frac{1}{\hat{a}(1-\beta)}$$

It should be noted that the equation (33) has no solution for an r_i that is greater than

(36) $$\tilde{r} = \frac{2\sqrt{\hat{a}(1-\beta)} + 1 + \hat{a}}{2\sqrt{\hat{a}(1-\beta)} + 1 + a - \beta} > 1.$$

The value $\tilde{r}$ is determined by $\tilde{t} = -\sqrt{1/\hat{a}(1-\beta)}$. If one takes into account that $1/\hat{a}(1-\beta) > 1$, the range $-1 \leq t_i < 1$ is admissible in every case. The constraint $t_i < 1$ imposes no restriction on the most preferred tax rate as the relative ability must be negative to result in the choice of $t_i = 1$.It follows that the most preferred tax rates are given by

$$(37) \qquad t_i = \begin{cases} \text{solution to (33)} & \text{for } r_i \leq \tilde{r} \\ \tilde{t} & \text{for } r_i > \tilde{r} \end{cases}$$

If t_i and k_i are known, the optimum supply of public goods follows from equation (18),

$$(38) \qquad G_i = n[\hat{\alpha} t_i \bar{w} - \frac{1 - \hat{\alpha} t_i}{1 - t_i} k_i].$$

In this equation, G_i indicates the optimum value of G for individual i. In general, it cannot be determined how this optimum provision of public goods depends on relative ability,

$$(39) \qquad \frac{\partial G_i}{\partial r_i} = n \left[\hat{\alpha} \bar{w} - \frac{\hat{\beta} k_i}{(1 - t_i)^2} \right] \frac{\partial t_i}{\partial r_i} - \frac{1 - \hat{\alpha} t_i}{1 - t_i} \frac{\partial k_i}{\partial r_i}.$$

The expression in square brackets is positive as long as the tax rate is below the revenue maximizing one defined by equation (27). In this case, the first term on the RHS of (39) is negative because of (35). This finding is due to the fact that individuals with greater ability prefer lower tax rates. For given transfer payments, tax revenues are thus reduced. This relationship induces the provision of public goods to decline. On the other hand, the second term on the RHS of (39) is positive due to equation (31). Individuals with higher ability prefer lower transfer payments. Therefore, the proportion of government expenditures used for the provision of public goods increases. It cannot be said whether the overall effect is positive or not.

We now consider which tax rates and transfer payments the individuals prefer. At first, the individual with mean ability endeavours the tax rate to be zero. In his opinion the provision of public goods is to be financed solely by lump-sum taxes,

$$(40) \qquad r_i = 1 \rightarrow \begin{cases} t_i = 0 \\ k_i = -\gamma\bar{w} < 0 . \end{cases}$$

Of course, this result is due to the fact that our assumptions imply two things [see also Romer (1975)].

- First, that the individual with mean ability has the mean gross income, too, and
- second, that this individual will pay a tax that is equal to his share in the amount of public goods, regardless of the tax rate and the transfer payments.

These are the reasons why he wants the public good to be financed in a way that avoids distortions.

Individuals with an ability above the average are in favour of lump-sum taxes, that are used first to finance the provision of public goods and, second, to pay an addition to individual gross incomes,

$$(41) \qquad r_i > 1 \rightarrow \begin{cases} t_i < 0 \\ k_i < 0. \end{cases}$$

The reason for this behaviour is obvious. By choosing these parameters, these individuals pay taxes that are below the average. The tax schedule they want leads to a redistribution from the poor to the rich.

On the other hand, people with below-average ability recommend a positive income-tax rate,

$$(42) \qquad r_i < 1 \rightarrow \begin{cases} t_i > 0 \\ k_i \begin{cases} < 0 & \text{for } r_i > \alpha t_i/[\gamma(1-\hat{\alpha} t_i)] \\ = & \qquad = \\ > & \qquad < \end{cases} \end{cases}$$

But, in general, it cannot be determined, whether they prefer transfer payments, too. There will always be individuals which vote for lump-sum taxes even though their ability is below the average. For them, the advantage of a progressive tax schedule is so small that they prefer the marginal conditions to be distorted only to a little extend.

Let us now turn to the voting process. Under majority voting, the individual whose ability is the median of the distribution of abilities is the decisive voter. If we assume that the distribution of abilities is skewed to the right, then

(43) $$r_m < 1$$

where the index m denotes the median of the distribution of abilities. This assumption ensures that the tax rate is positive but it is not a sufficient condition for the transfer payments to be positive.

A very important problem in the context of majority voting relates to cyclical majorities [see also Parks (1979)]. It is a well-known argument that if individual preferences are single-peaked, they avoid cyclical majorities. In our case, each individual has to take a two-dimensional decision. Thus, the ordinary concept of single-peakedness as elaborated by Black [1958] cannot be applied. Instead, Plott's [1967] pairwise symmetry condition takes this place. Assuming that there is an odd number of voters, for any point to be an equilibrium under majority voting it requires two conditions to be fulfilled. First, exactly one voter is at his ideal point, and second, all the other voters can be divided into two groups of equal number so that each member of one group has exactly one counterpart in the other group whose preferences are just the opposite. Or, to quote Enelow and Hinich [(1983), p. 317] "all nonzero utility gradients at the equilibrium must be divisible into pairs that point in opposite directions."

In order to ensure that these conditions are satisfied, we assume that the number of individuals is odd and that in (1)

(44) $$\ldots w_{m-1} < w_m < w_{m+1} \ldots$$

holds. This assumption means that there is exactly one individual at the median position. Furthermore, the assumption (43) ensures that the optimum tax rate for the median is given by the solution to (33).

In order to show that the second part of Plott's pairwise symmetry condition is fulfilled we have to form the directional derivative of the indirect utility functions at that point which the median prefers denoted by (k*, t*). It follows that

(45) $$(\partial/\partial t)v_i(k^*,t^*) = c_i[\hat{a}t\bar{w} - \gamma(1-\hat{a}t)w_m][w_m - w_i]$$

and

(46) $$(\partial/\partial k)v_i(k^*,t^*) = c_i[1-\hat{a}t][w_m - w_i]$$

where $$c_i = [\hat{a}]^{\alpha}[\beta]^{\beta}[n]^{\gamma}[w_i]^{-\beta}[1-t]^{\alpha}[(1-t)w_i + k]^{-\gamma} \cdot [\hat{a}t(1-t)\bar{w} - (1-\hat{a}t)k]^{\alpha+\beta}[\gamma] \quad > 0.$$

Now it becomes clear that the slope of the directional derivative given by

(47) $$[(\partial/\partial t)v_i(k^*,t^*)] / [(\partial/\partial k)v_i(k^*,t^*)] = k^*/(1-t^*)$$

is independent of the individual under consideration. It is solely determined by the parameters of the tax system that are preferred by the median. Additionally, the expressions (45) and (46) show that the directional derivatives point into opposite directions for two individuals, whose abilities are above and below the median, respectively. As, by definition, the number of voters, whose abilities are above the median, is equal to the number of voters with abilities below the median, Plott's pairwise symmetry condition is fulfilled. The level of government policy, preferred by the median, defines an equilibrium under majority voting. There will be no cyclical majorities.

5. A Numerical Example

To illustrate our results, we consider the case in which the distribution of abilities can be approximated by a lognormal distribution. This case has attracted considerable interest in the literature since the work of Lydall [1968] and Mirrlees [1971]. In particular, Mirrlees took the parameters of the associated normal distribution to be $\bar{\mu} = -1$ and $\sigma = 0.39$ leading to $\bar{w} = 0.3964$ and $r_m = 0.9268$. His alternative assumption was $\sigma = 1$ resulting in $\bar{w} = r_m = 0.6065$. Using the first assumption, Mirrlees found marginal tax rates that were rather low. This fact caused him to state "that I had expected the rigorous analysis of income-taxation in the utilitarian manner to provide an argument for high tax rates. It has not done so" [Mirrlees (1971), p. 207]. But, if the dispersion of the distribution is widened ($\sigma = 1$), his model leads to tax rates that are considerably higher. These calculations suggest that the tax rate is very sensitive with respect to the dispersion of the distribution of skills.

In the context of our model, figure 1 illustrates the optimal government policy depending on the relative ability of the median. By (1) and the assumption that the distribution of abilities is skewed to the right, the feasible range of r_m is bounded by $0 < r_m < 1$. The figure uses values of $\alpha = 0.5$ and $\beta = \gamma = 0.25$.

In order to normalise the results, we put $\tilde{G} = G/(n\bar{w})$ and $\tilde{k} = k/\bar{w}$. Figure 1 clearly shows that especially in the "realistic" range of $0.6 < r_m < 0.95$ the sensitivity of the tax rate with respect to the ability of the median is strongly pronounced. Small changes in the position of the median within the distribution of abilities lead to great changes in the tax rate. Therefore, the assumption concerning the distribution of abilities can be regarded as the most important one for determining the optimum marginal tax rate under majority voting.

On the other hand, the optimum provision of public goods nearly stays constant. This leads to the conclusion that the dispersion of the distribution of abilities has not a very strong impact on the provision of public goods. Of course, the transfer payments play an intermediate role due to the government's budget constraint.

In a second example, we analyse the effect that results from a change in the individual evaluation of public goods. To this end, we vary the parameter γ. In table 1, the optimum values of government policy are shown. They are calculated using two alternative assumptions concerning

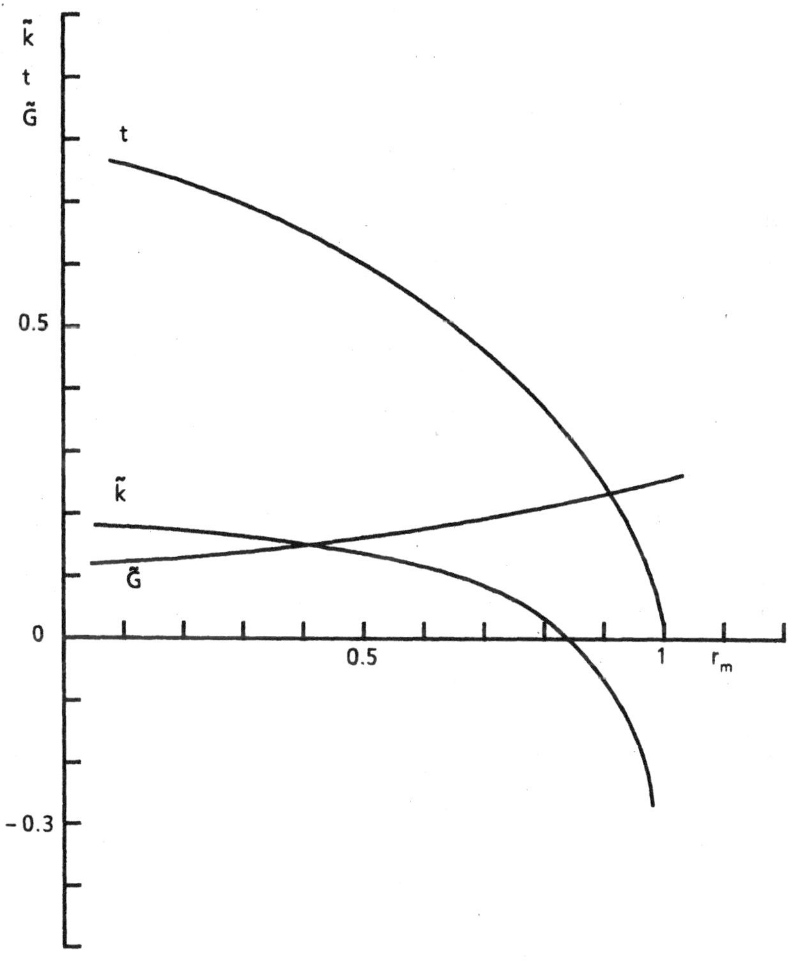

Figure 1: Government policy and median ability

- the relative median ability and
- the individual evaluation of private consumption and leisure.

Concerning the relative median ability, we use the two specifications of Mirrlees ($r_m = 0.9268$ and $r_m = 0.6065$) mentioned above. The second problem is connected with the individual evaluation of private consumption and leisure. Referring to Stern [(1976), p. 140], we assume that if there was no government policy ($t = 0$, $k = 0$) the individuals would work 2/3 of their time. This assumption results in $\alpha = 2\beta$. As this figure for working time seems to be rather high, we carried out alternative calculations for $\alpha = \beta$. This relation held if, under the conditions above, the individuals worked 1/2 of their time.

Table 1 again shows the values of $\tilde{k}$ and $\tilde{G}$ that result from the choice of the median. Moreover, $\bar{l} = l(\bar{w})$ is the optimum working time of the individual with mean ability and $\bar{x} = x(\bar{w})/\bar{w}$ is his normalized consumption of private goods. Finally, s gives the relative size of the government, measured as the ratio of tax revenues to aggregated before-tax incomes.

Table 1 shows that the individual evaluation of private consumption and leisure has not a very strong impact on the optimum supply of public goods. This becomes clear if one compares the first with the second as well as the third with the fourth section of this table. But, increasing the evaluation of private consumption leads to increasing tax rates and transfer payments. As, by assumption, the median ability is below the mean one, the median takes an advantage from the government redistribution policy that is in favour of the poor. If his evaluation of private consumption increases he prefers the tax schedule to be more progressive.

In general, it can be established that the main determinant for the optimum provision of public goods is its evaluation by the individuals. This is true because the changes within each section of the table are much greater than those between them. If the median prefers an increased provision of public goods, this also alters the way in which the public good is financed: it results in decreasing transfer payments and increasing tax rates. Therefore, the median wants both instruments to be used to finance the additional supply of policy goods.

α	γ	t	$\tilde{k}$	$\tilde{G}$	$\bar{l}$	$\bar{x}$	s
		$\alpha = 2\beta$; $r_m = 0.9268$					
0.60	0.10	0.186	0.028	0.094	0.655	0.562	0.186
0.57	0.15	0.194	-0.010	0.140	0.671	0.531	0.209
0.53	0.20	0.202	-0.048	0.187	0.687	0.500	0.273
0.50	0.25	0.212	-0.086	0.234	0.703	0.469	0.333
0.47	0.30	0.222	-0.122	0.281	0.719	0.438	0.391
		$\alpha = \beta$; $r_m = 0.9268$					
0.45	0.10	0.140	-0.022	0.093	0.513	0.419	0.182
0.43	0.15	0.146	-0.061	0.140	0.536	0.396	0.261
0.40	0.20	0.153	-0.101	0.186	0.559	0.373	0.333
0.38	0.25	0.161	-0.139	0.233	0.583	0.350	0.400
0.35	0.30	0.170	-0.177	0.280	0.606	0.327	0.462
		$\alpha = 2\beta$; $r_m = 0.6065$					
0.60	0.10	0.532	0.203	0.075	0.522	0.488	0.532
0.57	0.15	0.542	0.179	0.112	0.537	0.424	0.542
0.53	0.20	0.553	0.155	0.150	0.551	0.401	0.553
0.50	0.25	0.565	0.131	0.189	0.566	0.377	0.565
0.47	0.30	0.578	0.108	0.227	0.581	0.354	0.578
		$\alpha = \beta$; $r_m = 0.6065$					
0.45	0.10	0.485	0.117	0.070	0.386	0.316	0.485
0.43	0.15	0.497	0.096	0.106	0.405	0.299	0.497
0.40	0.20	0.509	0.075	0.141	0.424	0.283	0.509
0.38	0.25	0.522	0.054	0.177	0.443	0.266	0.522
0.35	0.30	0.536	0.035	0.214	0.463	0.249	0.536

Table 1: Median abilities, preferences, and the supply of public goods

6. Summary

Our considerations are based on the assumption that individuals have identical tastes but differ in abilities. They have to decide upon the extent of government policies with regard to the imposition of a constant marginal income tax rate, transfer payments, and the provision of public goods. It is shown that the problem of determining the optimum values of these variables can be reduced to a two-dimensional one because the public budget has to be balanced. Given the tax revenues, the government expenditures are also fixed.

Therefore, we concentrate our analysis on the income tax rate and the transfer payments as instruments of government policy. At first, their economic effects on labour supply are investigated. As a result, we get the following interaction: the greater the value of one instrument, the greater the disincentive effect of the other, with the amount of transfer payments determining the limits of designing the tax rate and vice versa.

In this environment, the individuals state their preferences. As one could have presumed, low individual abilities increase the most preferred tax rate and also the transfer payments. The individual with mean ability favours a zero marginal tax rate and positive lump-sum taxes to finance the provision of public goods.

It seems to be consistent with reality to assume that the distribution of abilities is skewed to the right and, consequently, that the ability of the median is smaller than the average one. In this case, the median individual prefers the marginal tax rate to be positive. The question whether he prefers transfer payments or lump-sum taxes cannot be answered in general. This will depend upon his evaluation of private consumption, public goods, and leisure as well as upon his position in the distribution of abilities.

Within the framework of majority voting, it is shown that the tax rates and the transfer payments favoured by the median voter define an equilibrium. Thus these values are stable against majority voting and there will be no cyclical majorities.

References

Black, D. (1958), *The Theory of Committees and Elections*, Cambridge

Bowen, H.R. (1943), "The interpretation of voting in the allocation of economic resources", *Quarterly Journal of Economics* 58, 27-48

Brito, D.L., and Oakland, W.H. (1977), "Some properties of the optimal income-tax", *International Economic Review* 18, 407-423

Enelow, J.M., and Hinich, M.J. (1983), "On Plott's pairwise symmetry condition for majority rule equilibrium", *Public Choice* 40, 317-321

Feldstein, M. (1973), "On the optimal progressivity of the income tax", *Journal of Public Economics* 2, 357-376

Fullerton, D. (1982), "On the possibility of an inverse relationship between tax rates and government revenues", *Journal of Public Economics* 19, 3-22

Gevers, L., and Proost, S. (1978), "Some effects of taxation and collective goods in postwar America. A tentative appraisal", *Journal of Public Economics* 9, 115-137

Lydall, H.F. (1968), *The Structure of Earnings*, Oxford

Mirrlees, J.A. (1971), "An exploration in the theory of optimum income taxation", *Review of Economic Studies* 38, 175-208

Moreh, J. (1983), "Optimal taxation and public goods", *Public Finance Quarterly* 11, 181-201

Moreland, K. (1984), "Public goods and optimal income taxation", *Public Finance Quarterly* 12, 197-212

Parks, R.P. (1979), "Comments on "Some effects of taxation and collective goods in postwar U.S.A. A tentative appraisal", *Journal of Public Economics* 12, 263-265

Plott, Ch.R. (1967), "A notion of equililbrium and its possibility under majority rule", *American Economic Review* 57, 787-806

Romer, Th. (1975), "Individual welfare, majority voting, and the properties of a linear income tax", *Journal of Public Economics* 4, 163-185

Samuelson, P.A. (1954), "The pure theory of public expenditure", *Review of Economics and Statistics* 36, 386-389

Sheshinski, E. (1972), "The optimal linear income-tax", *Review of Economic Studies* 39, 297-302

Stern, N.H. (1976), "On the specification of models of optimum income taxation", *Journal of Public Eonomics* 6, 123-162

Majority Decisions on Regional Environmental Quality and Interregional Pollution*

by

Ferdi Dudenhöffer

1. Introduction

The problem of interregional pollution (transfrontier pollution) has been discussed in the literature within two institutional settings. The first approach argues that transfrontier pollution requires a national government to reach an efficient allocation. The second approach asserts that regional authorities yield optimal bargaining solutions if property rights are explicitly defined. Both approaches do not take into consideration intraregional decision problems assuming regional welfare functions.[1] In this paper more emphasis has been placed on intraregional decision problems and we discuss an institutional arrangement that solves inter- and intraregional decision problems simultaneously.

As far as intraregional decisions on environmental allocation are concerned, we assume that in each region consumers decide directly by majority vote on regional environmental quality. Acceptance of losses of environmental quality are compensated by payments to consumers. Thus a decentralized mechanism determines "demand" for pollutants ambient in each region. Pollutants are generated by waste producing firms. Wastes generated in an upstream region will deteriorate environmental quality in upstream as well as in downstream region. A solution to this interregional allocation problem must take into consideration these spillovers. We assume that there is an environmental authority that levies a charge on wastes in both regions but charges for upstream wastes take into account their transfrontier pollution effect. The existence of such an environmental authority could be interpreted as a common consent or a mutual agreement between both

* This paper results from a research program on federal environmental policy in the Sonderforschungsbereich 5 at the University of Mannheim. It has been presented at the 24th European Congress of the Regional Science Association in Milan (Italy), August 1984.

1) Compare e.g. Siebert (1975), (1983), Dudenhöffer (1979).

regions and is therefore motivated by the above mentioned approaches to the transfrontier pollution problem.

In the next section we specify our model and study efficiency of equilibria. In section 3 we concentrate on the topic of uniform emission charges for both regions and show some asymmetry in regional concentration of production. Applying a comparative static analysis we elaborate in section 4 impacts of alternative densities of population and distribution of wealth on regional allocation.

2. The Model

Assume that there are two regions, an upstream region 2 and a downstream region 1. In both regions price taking firms produce an interregionally tradeable consumption good y_j by using the input l_j and generating emissions e_j as joint products. We assume that the regional production function G^j, defined as

$$y_j = G^j(l_j, e_j) \qquad j = 1,2$$

is a linear homogenous and differentiable function. Further marginal product of input l_j and of emissions e_j are strictly positive and decreasing.[2)]

In our economy total amount of factor l is given as a stock L and is perfectly mobile between both regions. Therefore we have a common factor market for both regions with a common price p_l and factor market equilibrium is given by

(1) $$L = l_1 + l_2$$

In our economy a tax is charged for generating emissions e_j. Each firm in each region has to pay a regionalized price p_{ej} (sometimes called emisson tax) per unit of emission. The price p_{ej} can be interpreted as the price of an emission licence that a firm in region $j = 1,2$ has to pay for the right to emit one unit of wastes.

2) Of course, the domain of the production function could be further truncated to exclude conflicts with the material balance approach. However, as far as our analysis here is concerned nothing could be gained by such a generalization. For a generalized approach compare e.g. Dudenhöffer (1983), chapter 2.

Since the consumption good y_j is interregionally tradeable, there is a common market and one price p for this good. Profit maximization of the firm leads to optimal production plans where factor prices are equal to the marginal value product (MVP) of each factor. Hence we obtain

$$(2) \qquad p_l = pG_1^{\,1}(l_1, e_1) = pG_1^{\,2}(l_2, e_2)$$

$$(3) \qquad p_{e_1} = pG_2^{\,1}(l_1, e_1)$$

$$(4) \qquad p_{e_2} = pG_2^{\,2}(l_2, e_2)$$

where $G_1^{\,j} \equiv \partial G^j / \partial l_j$ and $G_2^{\,j} \equiv \partial G^j / \partial e_j$ for $j = 1,2$.

In each region the regional environmental system is the receptor of wastes and emissions will result in regional environmental damages. We quantify this damage by a real number s_j that measures the level of pollutants ambient in the regional environment. Since we concentrate on the upstream-downstream case the following functional relationship between emissions e_j in region $j = 1,2$ and pollutants ambient in regional environment s_j holds

$$(5) \qquad s_1 = Z_1(e_1, e_2) = e_1 + \alpha e_2 \qquad \text{where } 0 < \alpha < 1$$

$$(6) \qquad s_2 = Z_2(e_2) = (1 - \alpha) e_2$$

For the sake of simplicity a linear relationship between pollutants ambient in regional environment s_j and total emissions e_j generated in region j is assumed. Of course, one can generalize the diffusion function Z_j and assume any monotonous, increasing, convex and continous function [Dudenhöffer (1983), chapter 2].

Up to now, we have explained the firms' demand for emission licences and therefore their demand for the factor emission as well as the corresponding pollutants for both regions. We will assume that consumers in each region will be compensated for pollutants ambient in their regional environment. The consumer sector of each region obtains a compensation payment of p_{sj} per unit of pollutants. Thus in our model we have two types of payments. On the one hand there is revenue received from selling licences to waste generating firms and on the other hand compensation payments to consumers. Suppose there is a clearing office that handles both payments and call this clearing office the environmental authority. The authority will conduct its business along the lines of a competitive firm. For given prices p_{ej}, p_{sj} and given diffusion functions Z_j the authority's task is to select combinations of emissions e_j and pollutants s_j that maximize its profits. Since the authority's revenues stem from selling emission licences to firms and its cost consists of payments to consumers, the optimization problem of the authority can be described as

$$\text{(P1)} \qquad \max_{e_j, s_j} \sum_{j=1}^{2} (p_{ej} e_j - p_{sj} s_j) \qquad \text{s.t. (5), (6)}$$

Since in (5), (6) we have assumed linear diffusion functions Z_j , an interior solution $(e_1, e_2, s_1, s_2) > 0$ to problem (P1) must fulfill

$$\text{(7)} \qquad p_{e1} = p_{s1}$$

$$\text{(8)} \qquad p_{e2} = \alpha \, p_{s1} + (1 - \alpha) p_{s2}$$

Equation (7) and (8) show that interregional externalities are internalized. The emission of one unit of waste in region 1 is taxed by p_{e1}. This is exactly the amount that all consumers in region 1 receive for one additional unit of pollutant. A firm in region 2 is taxed by p_{e2} per unit of emission. Since α gives us the additional environmental disruption in region 1 caused by one additional unit of waste emitted upstream, one component of p_{e2} is the amount all consumers in region 1 receive for one additional emission in region 2. Since the emission of one unit of waste in region 2 leads to $(1-\alpha)$ additional pollutants in this region, the other component of p_{e2} is the compensation $(1-\alpha)p_{s2}$ to consumers in region 2.

By now it is clear how pollutants s_j in each region are connected to regionalized emission prices p_{ej} and compensation payments p_{sj}. Hence the supply of pollutants is determined. In the following we characterize the regional demand for pollutants. The distinctive attribute of pollutants is their local public-bad character. Hence the individual demands for pollutants will differ, in general, if in each region each consumer receives some fixed positive share $\beta_i \varepsilon (0,1)$ of total compensation for pollutants ambient in his regional environment. We will assume that the decision between the different demands for pollutants is taken by majority vote. In both regions consumers are interregionally immobile and decide directly by majority vote on their regional environmental quality. That means, consumer i determines a real number s_i that quantifies his desired level of pollutants ambient in his regional environment. If $i = 1, \dots, n_1$ consumers live in region 1 and $i = n_1 + 1, \dots, n$ consumers live in region 2 we can formalize the i-th consumer's decision problem at voting as[3]

$$\text{(P2)} \qquad \max\ u_i(x_i, s_i) \ \text{ s.t. } \ px_i - \beta_i p_{sj} s_i \le I_i$$

with $j = 1$ for $i = 1, \dots, n_1$ and $j = 2$ otherwise. (P2) tells us that for any given prices p, p_{sj}, shares β_i and income I_i the decision problem is to select an utility maximizing bundle of the private good x_i and public bad s_i. The following Figure 1 clarifies the optimization problem.

Assume that the utility functions u_i are strictly quasi-concave and differentiable; the private good is always desirable, i.e. $\partial u_i / \partial x_i > 0$ and pollutants are always non-desirable, i.e. $\partial u_i / \partial s_i \le 0$. Under these assumptions we can show that the indirect utility function

$$v_i(s_i) = \max_{x_i} u_i(x_i, s_i) \ \text{ s.t. } \ px_i = I_i + \beta_i p_{sj} s_i$$

is single-peaked.[4] Therefore applying Black's (1958) result on majority voting,

---

3) Here we assume that consumers in region 1 have no interest in the environmental quality of region 2 and vice versa. For a generalization, assuming pollutants in region 2 as an argument in the utility function of consumers in region 1 compare Dudenhöffer (1983), chapter 6.

4) Notice that for $p > 0$ the indirect utility function can be written as $v_i(s^i) = u_i[I_i / p + \beta_i p_{sj} s_j / p, s^i]$. Let (s, x), $(\tilde{s}, \tilde{x})$ such that $v_i(s) \ge v_i(\tilde{s})$. It is fairly clear that $(s^\lambda, x^\lambda) \equiv (\lambda s + (1-\lambda)\tilde{s}, \lambda x + (1-\lambda)\tilde{x})$ fulfills the budget constraint for any $\lambda \in (0,1)$, i.e. it is a feasible plan. As u_i is strictly quasi-concave, we have $v_i(s^\lambda) > v_i(\tilde{s})$ i.e. v_i is a strictly quasi-concave function. Therefore we get only one maximum on a compact, convex domain and establish single peakness.

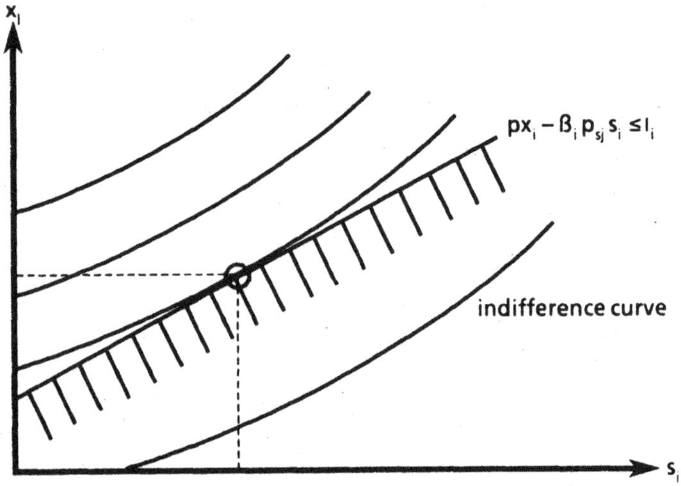

Figure 1: Consumer's decision problem

we can compute the majority-vote decision on regional environmental quality by selecting the median demand for pollutants. Thus the demand s_j for pollutants in region j is

(9) $$s_1 = \text{median}\,[S^1(\beta_1 p_{s1}, p, I_1), \ldots, S^{n1}(\beta_{n1} p_{s2}, p, I_{n1})]$$

(10) $$s_2 = \text{median}\,[S^{n1+1}(\beta_{n1+1} p_{s2}, p, I_{n1+1}), \ldots, S^n(\beta_n p_{s2}, p, I_n)]$$

where the demand $S^i(\beta_i p_{sj}, p, I_i)$ for pollutants of consumer i maximizes his indirect utility function v_i and is therefore a solution to problem (P2) and

$$\sum_{i=1}^{n_1} \beta_i = \sum_{i=n_1+1}^{n} \beta_i = 1$$

holds. Under the above assumptions on consumer preferences the demand function of each consumer is continuous and the "median" is an upper semi-continuous correspondence [Dudenhöffer (1983), p. 199f].

In our model the i-th consumer's income is given as his share $\lambda_i \in (0,1)$ on total factor endowment L. Therefore we obtain[5)]

(11) $$I_i = \gamma p_l L \quad \text{and} \quad \sum_{i=1}^{n} \gamma_i = 1$$

Observe that the consumer's problem to determine his demand x_i for the private consumption good degenerates if a certain level of pollutants s^*_j is determined. In that case the demand for private goods x_i is given by $px_i = I_i + \beta_i p_{sj} s^*_j$ and an equilibrium of the private-goods market satisfies

(12) $$y_1 + y_2 = \sum_{i=1}^{n} x_i$$

Now our model is fully specified. Three types of agents acting as price takers on four markets can be distinguished. The environmental authority acts on the market for emission licences as supplier and on the markets for pollutants as buyer. Firms demand emission licences and factor l and are supplier on the market for the consumption good. Consumers act on the market for pollutants and the markets for factor l as suppliers and demand consumption goods. A price vector $(p^*, p^*_l, p^*_{e1}, p^*_{e2}, p^*_{s1}, p^*_{s2}) > 0$ and an allocation $(l^*_1, l^*_2, e^*_1, e^*_2, s^*_1, s^*_2) > 0$ that satisfy equations (1), (2), (3), (4), (5), (6), (7), (8), (9), (10) constitute an equilibrium of the economy. Observe that at such a state the markets for pollutants, emission licences and factor l are cleared. Thus by Walras' law the market for the consumption good will be balanced too, i.e. equation (12) holds.

Now let us review some important properties of our model.

---

5) As we have assumed linear-homogeneous production functions G^j and linear diffusion functions Z_j there are zero profits and income does not contain profits. Dudenhöffer (1983), chapter 2, presents a more general model allowing for positive profits.

Proposition 1: Given the assumptions of section 2, an equilibrium exists.

Proof: Dudenhöffer (1983).

Proposition 2: In general, the equilibrium does not constitute a Pareto-Optimum.

Proof: Dudenhöffer (1983).

The second property seems pretty clear. As the individual shares β_i are exogenously fixed we cannot expect the familiar Samuelson-condition

$$(p_{s1}/p) = \sum_{i=1}^{n_1} \left(-\frac{\partial u_i}{\partial s_i}\right) / \frac{\partial u_i}{\partial x_i}$$

to hold. Thus we identify a lack of intraregional adjustment as source of inefficiency. Clearly if we extend our model and integrate a mechanism that generates Lindahl prices $\beta_i\, p_{sj}$ we are confronted with the well-known free-rider problem. On the other hand we can state that the lack of intraregional adjustment is the only source of inefficiency, i.e. the transfrontier-pollution problem itself has an efficient solution. To prove this assume that in each region identical consumers live with compensation shares $\beta_i = 1/n_1$ for $i = 1, ..., n_1$ and $\beta_i = 1/(n-n_1)$ for $i = n_1+1, ..., n$. Under this assumption one can easily show that equilibria of the above model are Pareto-Optima.[6]

6) Under the above assumptions Pareto optima can be determined by maximizing the Lagrangian

$L = n_1 u_1(x_1, s_1) + (n-n_1) u_2(x_2, s_2) + \lambda_1 [L - \ell_1 - \ell_2] + \lambda_2 [\Sigma^2_{j=1} G^j(\ell_1 e_j) - n_1 x_1 - (n-n_1) x_2]$
$+ \lambda_3 [s_1 - e_1 - \alpha e_2] + \lambda_4 [s_2 - (1-\alpha) e_2]$.

Assuming interior solutions a Pareto optimum is characterized by

$n_1(-u_{s1}/u_{x1}) = \partial G^1/\partial e_1$; $\alpha n_1(-u_{s1}/u_{x1}) + (1-\alpha)(-u_{s2}/u_{x2})(n-n_1) = \partial G^2/\partial e_2$.

The same relationship holds at the equilibrium of the above model.

3. Uniform Emission Taxes, Transfrontier Pollution and Regional Concentration

An interesting question might be the relationship between regional emission taxes. Can we expect them to be uniform for both regions or do they differ? This question shows some analogy to the factor-price equalization theorem of the Heckscher-Ohlin Model and has been discussed between Stein (1971), Peltzman and Tideman (1972) and others in the American Economic Review. In our model this question seems of interest because we have assumed a fixed interregional diffusion parameter α and interregionally immobile consumers. If emission prices for both regions are the same, all factors in all regions have the same MVP and no further adjustment strategy like high stack policy or consumer mobility can improve welfare.[7] On the other hand, suppose $p_{e1} < p_{e2}$ holds. If we allow for higher stacks to be built upstream ($d\alpha > 0$) we obtain from (8) $dp_{e2} = (p_{s1} - p_{s2})\, d\alpha$. Since we know from equation (7) and (8) that $p_{e1} < p_{e2}$ implies $p_{s1} < p_{s2}$ emission prices in both regions move toward equalization. Thus it is possible to exploit differing MVP and improve welfare by higher stacks.

3.1 Different production functions

Suppose that the production functions differ between both regions in that upstream production is more intensive in its use of the factor "emission" than downstream production. Since production functions for both regions are linear homogenous cost functions are linear. Hence marginal cost curves of production in region j, denote by $MC_j(p_1, p_{ej})$ can be drawn as in Figure 2.

Figure 2 shows that at point A marginal costs are the same if the emission prices p_{ej} are equal in both regions. Thus production in both regions (incomplete concentration) and uniform emission taxes for both regions are only possible at

7) A high stack policy would imply that the parameter α could be increased parametrically by building higher stacks upstream and therefore transporting a greater part of the waste from that region to the downstream environmental system.

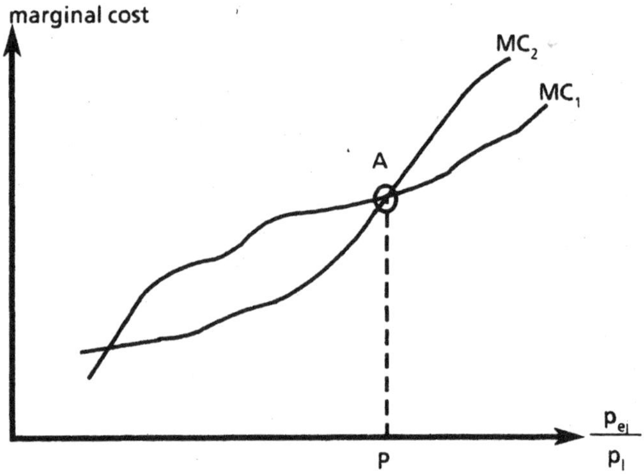

Figure 2: Marginal cost curves for different production functions

price ratio P. Otherwise incomplete concentration requires different emission prices for both regions. Suppose that the emission price ratio P is given. Then the production possibilities of the economy can be depicted as in Figure 3.

Since the economy is endowed with a total amount L of the interregionally mobile factor l all production possibilities for a given factor-price ratio $p_e / p_l = P$ are given as combinations along the line AB in Figure 3. If production is completely concentrated in region 1, point A in Figure 3 shows that emissions e_1^{max} are produced. If we shift part of the production to the upstream region, we move from A to point C where e_1^c and e_2^c indicate emissions generated in downstream and upstream, respectively. Since all feasible production plans in Figure 3 are linearly dependent and diffusion functions Z_j are linear too, the transformation curve for the economy corresponding to Figure 3 can be drawn according to Figure 4.

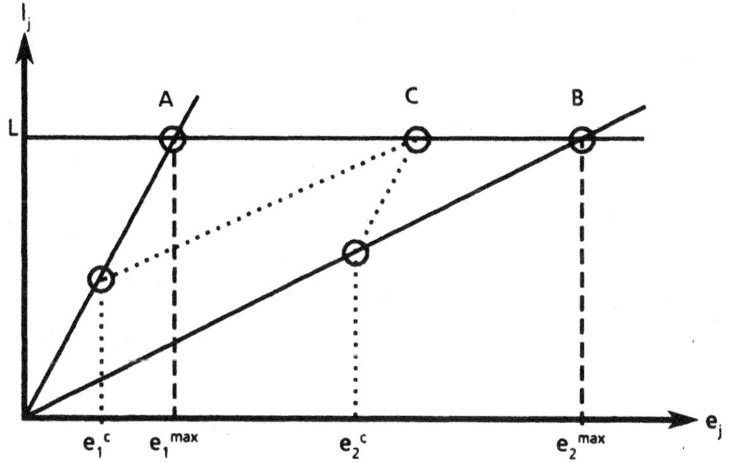

Figure 3: Production possibilities for given factor-price ratio

Thus uniform emission taxes for both regions constitute an equilibrium only if the plans of consumers in both regions are compatible with some point on the transformation curve drawn in Figure 4. But this will not hold in general. To prove this, suppose we have an equilibrium with uniform emission taxes such that points D and D' describe pollutants and national product. This implies that consumers in region 1, for example, vote at given equilibrium prices for s_1^D pollutants. Now assume we add one consumer to region 1 who has no endowment of factor l at all. Thus the total endowment of factor l remains constant but since this "new" consumer receives the right to vote the share β_i of all consumers in region 1 will decrease. That is equivalent to saying that the price $\beta_i\, p_{s1}$ of pollutants for each consumer in region 1 and therefore the demand for pollutants will change, i.e. we get $s_1 \neq s_1^D$ and $s_2 = s_2^D$. Hence uniform emission taxes cannot constitute an equilibrium any more and we can conclude:

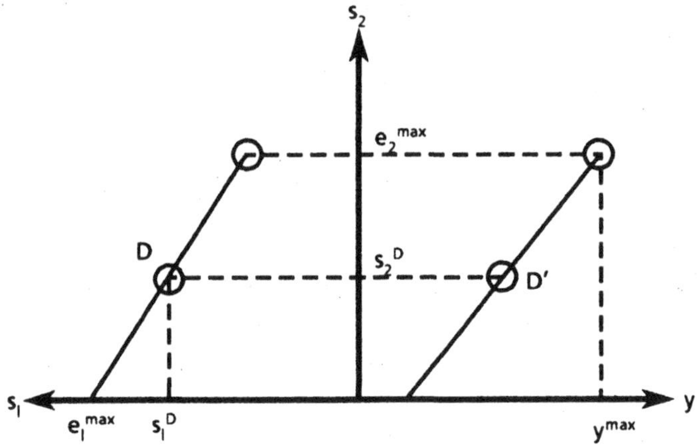

Figure 4: Transformation curve

Proposition 3: If production functions differ between regions equilibrium emission taxes differ too, in general.

3.2 Identical production functions for both regions

Suppose that no regional advantage in production can be observed, i.e. production functions are the same for both regions. This implies identical marginal cost curves $MC_1 \equiv MC_2$ for both regions. Therefore it will be fairly clear that any equilibrium must fulfill $p_{e1} = p_{e2}$ if production takes place in both regions. Put in another way, only at complete concentration emission prices can differ.

Studying the pattern of regional concentration one finds some interesting asymmetries. If we assume that very low levels of pollutants do not affect the well-being of any individual, i.e. small numbers of s_i are imperceptible, a complete concentration of production in region 1 is impossible whereas complete concentration in region 2 is not excluded. Notice, this implies that $p_{e1} < p_{e2}$ can be ruled out but $p_{e1} > p_{e2}$ may be possible at equilibrium. The diffusion parameter α plays the crucial role in explaining the asymmetry. The smaller the parameter α the sooner we can exclude $p_{e1} > p_{e2}$ and with higher values of α the probability of $p_{e1} > p_{e2}$ rises. Let us proceed to prove the above claims and propose a definition of imperceptibility of small pollutant quantities s.

Definition (Imperceptibility of small s)
If for any $p_{sj} > 0$ the demand for pollutants of each consumer of region $j = 1,2$ is not zero $(s_j \neq 0)$ low levels of pollutants are said to be imperceptible.

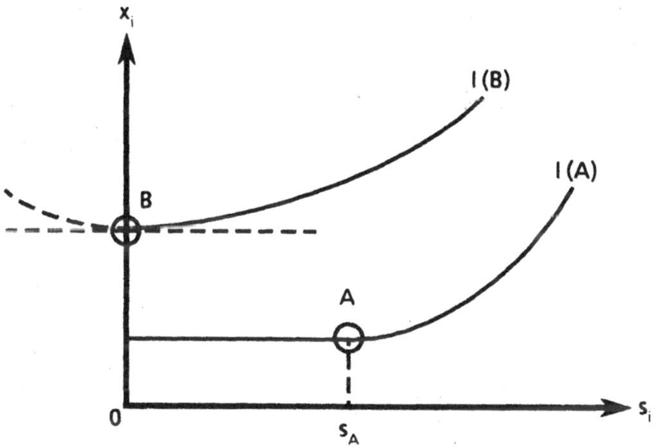

Figure 5: Imperceptibility of small number of pollutants

Figure 5 illustrates the idea behind the definition. It shows two indifference curves of consumers for whom small s is imperceptible. If consumer A whose indifference curve is I(A) is confronted with pollutants smaller than s_A his well-being is not influenced. For consumer B whose indifference map is I(B) this is only valid at ε neighbourhood of $s = 0$. Now we can state

Proposition 4: If production functions do not differ between regions and low levels of pollutants are imperceptible for the majority, then complete concentration of production in downstream region 1 cannot occur. In particular, $p_{e2} > p_{e1}$ cannot constitute an equilibrium.

Proof: Suppose $y_1^* > 0$ and $y_2^* = 0$ constitutes an equilibrium. Hence we have $e_2^* = s_2^* = 0$. Since we have assumed imperceptibility this implies $p^*_{s2} = 0$. Using equation (8) we get $p_{e2}^* = \alpha p_{s1}^* = \alpha p_{e1}^*$ and $p_{e2}^* < p_{e1}^*$ is implied for $\alpha < 1$. This clearly contradicts $y_2^* = 0$ as cost functions are identical.

Put it in another way, if there is no advantage in producing downstream a complete concentration of production in the downstream region can be ruled out but a complete concentration in the upstream region cannot be excluded. The following example illustrates this claim.

Example: Suppose that only one consumer lives in each region. Preferences are described by the following utility functions

$$u^1(x_1, s_1) = x_1 - \bar{a}(s_1)^2 \qquad \text{and} \qquad \bar{a} > (1-\alpha)/\alpha$$
$$u^2(x_2, s_2) = x_2 - (s_2)^2$$

The slope of the indifference curves at equilibrium are given as (i) $dx_1 / ds_1 = 2\bar{a}s_1 = p_{s1}/p$ and (ii) $dx_2/ds_2 = 2s_2 = p_{s2}/p$. Notice that imperceptibility is assumed for both consumers. Further the diffusion functions (5), (6) imply $s_1 \geq [\alpha/(1-\alpha)]/s_2$ or in other words (iii):

$$\frac{(1-\alpha)}{\alpha} s_1 < s_2$$

Now suppose we have an equilibrium at which $p^*_{s1} \leq p^*_{s2}$ holds. From (i), (ii) then follows $[(1-\alpha)/\alpha]\, s^*_1 < \bar{a}s^*_1 \leq s^*_2$ which contradicts to (iii). Hence $p_{s1} > p_{s2}$ implying $p_{e1} > p_{e2}$ must hold at any equilibrium for the example and production is completely concentrated in the upstream region.

The example explains further the crucial role of the diffusion parameter α. Let α decrease, i.e. interregional spillovers decline, then $(1-\alpha)/\alpha$ will rise and the inequality $\bar{a} > (1-\alpha)/\alpha$ may reverse. This clearly implies that emission prices in both regions will equalize, i.e. $p_{e1} = p_{e2}$ and no complete concentration either upstream or downstream can occur if imperceptibility prevails.

4. Impacts of Interregional Distribution of Population and Wealth on Regional Allocation

In this section we analyze how different interregional distributions of population and wealth affect regional concentration and environmental quality. To get clearcut conclusions we do not take into account different production technologies in both regions. Hence locational advantages can only arise from differences in consumer preferences, population densities and differences in wealth of consumers in both regions. In particular, we assume throughout this section that for each region we can identify two types of consumers: the majority type mj and the minority type $\bar{m}j$ for regions $j = 1,2$. Of course the minority group in each region could be made up of a number of rather different types whereas the majority group is assumed to be homogenous. Thus the model considers the case of a large "middle class" with smaller "upper and lower classes" in each region, an empirical characteristic of many societies.[8] Note that in our model we assume that minority has no direct influence on the decision concerning regional environmental quality. Thus redistribution of wealth and changes in density of regional population affect the patterns of allocation only if the characteristic of the majority class of one region will be altered. For region $j = 1,2$ the parameters γ_{mj} and β_{mj} measure the share of the total endowment of factor l and of the compensation for pollutants of one consumer of majority class, respectively. Thus wealth distribution is explained by γ_{mj} and population density of the regions is directly reflected in β_{mj}. We now proceed by studying changes in these parameters.

From our assumption of equal production functions for both regions it follows that equilibria with incomplete concentration of production imply uniform emission

8) Notice that the assumption of a homogeneous majority class for each region helps to manage comparative static analysis If we did not apply this assumption we would have had to specify the complete characteristic of each individual to identify a median voter. In addition it would then be possible for the median function to exhibit kinks and therefore not be differentiable on the whole range

prices $p_{e1} = p_{e2} = p_e$. Taking this into consideration and applying the "∧" calculus to equations (1), (2), (3), (4) we get [9] [10]

$$\sigma(\hat{p}_e - \hat{p}_l) - \lambda_a(\hat{y}_2 - \hat{y}_1) + \hat{e}_2 = \hat{L} \tag{14}$$

where σ denotes the elasticity of substitution and $\lambda_a \equiv l_1 / L$ denotes the share of factor l used for production in region 1.[11] Equation (14) gives us a complete description of the supply side for private goods in our economy.

Differentiating equations (5), (6) we obtain the reaction of the environmental authority to exogenous changes as

$$\hat{s}_1 = \varepsilon\hat{e}_1 + (1-\varepsilon)\hat{e}_2 \tag{15}$$

$$\hat{s}_2 = \hat{e}_2 \tag{16}$$

where $\varepsilon \equiv [\partial Z_1 / \partial e_1] | [e_1 / s_1] = e_1 / (e_1 + \alpha e_2)$ is defined as pollutants elasticity of emissions in region 1. Thus $\varepsilon \in [0,1]$ gives us a measure for the intensity of transfrontier pollution. Small values of ε indicate that additional emissions in region 1 do not seriously affect pollutants downstream or in other words: most pollutants downstream are generated upstream. As we have $p_{el} = p_{e2} = p_e = p_{sl} = p_{s2}$ all prices change in fixed proportion and the comparative-static analysis is completed by determining the reaction of the majority's demand for pollutants in each region.
Define $p_Z \equiv p_s / p$ and $p_L \equiv p_l / p$. As the consumer's demand for pollutants is homogenous of degree 0, we can denote the demand for pollutants of the majority class in region j by $s_j = S_{mj}(\beta_j p_Z, I_{mj} / p)$. Applying the "∧" calculus we obtain

$$\hat{s}_j = \eta_{pj} [\hat{\beta}_{mj} + \hat{p}_Z] + \eta_j [\hat{y}_{mj} + \hat{p}_L + \hat{L}] \tag{17}$$

9) The derivation of (14) is given in an appendix.

10) A "∧" over a variable indicates the relative change in that variable, i.e. $\hat{y}$ is dy/y.

11) Note that $l_2 / L = 1 - \lambda_a$

where $\eta_p^j \equiv \hat{s}_{mj} / (\widehat{\beta_{mj}\, p_z})$ and $\eta^j \equiv \hat{s}_{mj} / \hat{I}_{mj}$ denote the price elasticity and income elasticity of a typical consumer of the majority in region j = 1,2, respectively.

If we rearrange (14), (15), (16), (17) and consider equation (5d) of the appendix we get the following system

$$(18)\quad \begin{bmatrix} -\varepsilon & -d_1 & 1 \\ 0 & d_2 & 1 \\ -\lambda_a & 0 & 1 \end{bmatrix} \begin{bmatrix} (\hat{y}^2 - \hat{y}^1) \\ (\hat{p}_e - \hat{p}_l) \\ \hat{e}_2 \end{bmatrix} = \begin{bmatrix} \eta^1 (\hat{L} + \hat{\gamma}_{m1}) + \eta_p^1 \hat{\beta}_{m1} \\ \eta^2 (\hat{L} + \hat{\gamma}_{m2}) + \eta_p^2 \hat{\beta}_{m2} \\ \hat{L} \end{bmatrix}$$

where $d_1 \equiv \eta_p^1 \theta_a - \eta^1 \theta_e$, $d_2 \equiv -(\eta_p^2 \theta_a - \eta^2 \theta_e)$. Further $\theta_a \equiv p_l \ell_j / p\, y_j$ and $\theta_e \equiv p_e e_j / p\, y_j$ denote the share of factor ℓ and e on total value of production in region j. The following table summarizes the multipliers of (18)

	$(\hat{y}_2 - \hat{y}_1)/r$	$(\hat{p}_e - \hat{p}_\ell)/r$	$\hat{e}_2/r$	$(\hat{s}_2 - \hat{s}_1)/r$
$r = \hat{\gamma}_{m1}$	$\eta^1 (d_2 - \sigma)\Delta$	$-\eta^1 \lambda_a \Delta$	$\eta^1 \lambda_a d_2 \Delta$	$\eta^1 \lambda_a [d_1 + d_2]\Delta - n^1$
$r = \hat{\lambda}_{m2}$	$\eta^2 (d_1 + \sigma)\Delta$	$\eta^2 (\lambda_a - \varepsilon)\Delta$	$\eta^2 (\lambda_a d_1 + \varepsilon\sigma)\Delta$	$\eta^2 \varepsilon (d_1 + \sigma)\Delta$
$r = \hat{\beta}_{m1}$	$\eta_p^1 (d_2 - \sigma)\Delta$	$-\eta_p^1 \lambda_a \Delta$	$\eta_p^1 \lambda_a d_2 \Delta$	$\eta_p^1 \lambda_a [d_1 + d_2]\Delta n_p^1$
$r = \hat{\beta}_{m2}$	$\eta_p^2 (d_2 + \sigma)\Delta$	$\eta_p^2 (\lambda_a - \varepsilon)\Delta$	$\eta_p^2 (\lambda_a d_1 + \varepsilon\sigma)\Delta$	$\eta_p^2 \varepsilon (\sigma + d_1)\Delta$

$\Delta \equiv [d_2 (\lambda_a - \varepsilon) + \lambda_a d_1 + \varepsilon\sigma]^{-1}$

Table 1: Multipliers of comparative statics

To obtain information about the sign of the multipliers listed in table 1 we must further specify consumers' preferences. Let us assume that pollutants in each region are inferior and no Giffen goods:

<u>Assumption U:</u> $\eta_p^j \geq 0$ and $\eta^j \leq 0$ hold for j = 1,2.

Using assumption U it is fairly clear that $d_1 \geq 0$ and $d_2 \leq 0$ hold. Furthermore it can be proved that $\Delta > 0$ holds.[12] With this in mind, we are able to determine the signs of the multipliers of table 1. They are listed in table 2.

	$(\hat{y}_2 - \hat{y}_1)/r$	$(\hat{p}_e - \hat{p}_\ell)/r$	$\hat{e}_2/r$	$(\hat{s}_2 - \hat{s}_1)/r$
$r = \hat{\gamma}_{m1}$	+	+	+	+ if $\lvert d_2\rvert > \lvert d_1\rvert$
$r = \hat{\gamma}_{m2}$	–	+	–	–
$r = \hat{\beta}_{m1}$	–	–	–	– if $\lvert d_2\rvert > \lvert d_1\rvert$
$r = \hat{\beta}_{m2}$	+	–	+	+

Table 2: Results of comparative statics

<u>4.1 Different distribution of wealth</u>

In this section we study impacts of the distribution of wealth. The first two rows of table 1 analyze these impacts. We have already noted above that changes in the distribution of wealth will only have impacts on the allocation if the majority's position is affected. Suppose the downstream region's majority becomes wealthier and the upstream region's majority wealth position remains constant. This could be the case when the downstream or upstream minority suffers a decline in wealth, i.e. $\hat{\gamma}_{m1} > 0$ and $\hat{\gamma}_{m2} = 0$. The first row of table 1 shows the allocational impacts. If $\hat{\gamma}_{m1} > 0$ holds income $I_{m1} = \gamma_{m1} p_1 L$ of each member of the downstream majority class will rise. As the income elasticity η^1 is negative the demand for pollutants ambient in region 1 declines. This decline in the demand for pollutants must be accompanied by a rise in the price of emission licences so that firms substitute the environmental factor by the factor l. As an increase of the price of emission licences will lead to a rise of compensation prices p_z the upstream majority demands more pollutants according to their price elasticity

12) From the definition of Δ we have $\Delta > 0$ if $\lambda_a < \varepsilon$. Let us check that $\lambda_a < \varepsilon$ is valid. First the definition implies $(l_1 / L) < e_1 / (e_1 + \alpha e_2)$. If we rearrange this inequality we arrive at $(l_2 / e_2) > \alpha\,(l_1 / e_1)$. As we assumed identical production functions the intensities l_j / e_j must be the same for both regions. Hence $1 > \alpha$ is fulfilled.

$\eta_p{}^2$. Thus two effects can be distinguished: First, a substitution effect in production and second, a dislocation effect in the upstream region. The multipliers in the first row of table 1 show that the dislocation effect dominates the substitution effect, i.e. $\hat{e}_2 \mid \hat{\gamma}_{m\ell} > 0$. As part α of the emission generated upstream will deteriorate environment downstream it cannot be excluded that $(\hat{s}_2 - \hat{s}_1) \mid \hat{\gamma}_{m1} < 0$ holds.

On the other hand, if we analyze the impacts of a relatively rich majority upstream ($\hat{\gamma}_{m2} > 0$), a comparison of rows 1 and 2 in table 1 shows that the effects listed above are valid for the upstream region, i.e. a dislocation effect to downstream region $(\hat{y}_2 - \hat{y}_1) < 0$, a substitution effect in production $(\hat{p}_e - \hat{p}_a) > 0$ and an unambigous shift of pollutants to the downstream region $(\hat{s}_2 - \hat{s}_1) < 0$ will result.

Now we investigate the impact of different distributions of wealth in both regions. Suppose an increase in wealth of the upstream majority results in a decline in wealth of the downstream majority, i.e. we have

$$\hat{\gamma}_{m1} = - \frac{\hat{\gamma}_{m2}}{\hat{\gamma}_{m1}} \hat{\gamma}_{m2}$$

with $\hat{\gamma}_{m2} > 0$. It is fairly clear that this result summarizes the effects discussed above, i.e. the relatively rich region has a relatively clean environment and will dislocate production to the poorer region. Thus we can conclude:

Propositon 5: Suppose that production functions are the same for both regions and environmental damages are inferior but no Giffen goods. Under these assumptions unique relationships between wealth, location of production and regional environmental quality can be established: the greater the difference in the distribution of wealth, the greater will be the concentration of production and the lower the environmental quality in the relatively poor region.

4.2 Density of population and allocational patterns

In this last section we study the trade-off between density of population and concentration of production. We assume that total population is fixed to n and compensation shares within each region are equal for all consumers, i.e. for each consumer of the majority class holds

$$\beta_{m1} = \frac{1}{n_1} \quad \text{and} \quad \beta_{m2} = \frac{1}{n_2}$$

where n_1 and n_2 are the number of consumers in each region, respectively and $n = n_1 + n_2$. Hence variations in regional density directly result in changes in β_{m1}, β_{m2}. If $\hat{n} = 0$ we get

$$\hat{\beta}_{m1} = \frac{n_2}{n_1}\hat{n}_2 \quad \text{and} \quad \hat{\beta}_{m2} = -\hat{n}_2$$

Therefore combining rows 3 and 4 in table 1 we obtain the allocative impact of different densities of population. Suppose that population increases in the upstream region $(\hat{n}_2 > 0)$ and that in both regions the wealth of each consumer in the majority class does not change, i.e. $\hat{\gamma}_{m1} = \hat{\gamma}_{m2} = 0$. Under our assumptions this will lead to a higher concentration of production in the relatively sparsely settled downstream region $(\hat{y}^2 - \hat{y}^1) < 0$ and to better environmental quality in the upstream region $\hat{e}_2 < 0$. As far as the substitution effect in production is concerned we cannot give an unique answer. If n_2 / n_1 is rather large, i.e. most people live in region 2 we can expect that $(\hat{p}_e - \hat{p}_a) / \hat{\beta}_{m1} + (\hat{p}_e - \hat{p}_a) / \hat{\beta}_{m2}$ is dominated by the first term of the sum and pollution licences become cheaper. Thus we can conclude:

Proposition 6: If production functions are the same for both regions and environmental damages are inferior but no Giffen goods, then production will concentrate in the sparsely settled region.

5. Conclusions

In this paper we have studied equilibria of a model which assumes that pollutants ambient in regional environment are directly determined by regional majority vote. We proposed an institutional arrangement of an environmental authority that solves the transfrontier pollution problem by applying the Polluters-Pay Principle. We have shown that our solution to the transfrontier pollution problem is a best one but efficiency losses are caused by a lack of intraregional coordination. The simple majority-vote mechanism applied to our environmental problem does not in general adjust MRS among consumers such that the familiar Samuelson condition will hold.

Using our assumption of imperceptibility of small quantities of pollutants we were able to show that undirectional transfrontier pollution will cause asymmetric structures of regional concentration in production. If both regions are equipped with identical production functions a complete concentration of production in the downstream region cannot occur. On the other hand, complete concentration of production in the upstream region may constitute an equilibrium. In addition, the model has been used to analyze in which way regional population density and interregional distribution of wealth influence regional concentration in production and regional patterns of environmental quality. If locational advantages are caused by differences in consumers' preferences or different regional population densities or different wealth distributions then trade-offs could be estabilished. Assuming ambient pollutants to be inferior but no Giffen goods we showed that production will concentrate in the poorer region, and that sparsely settled regions attract production.

6. References

Black, D. (1958), *The Theory of Committees and Elections*, Cambridge University Press, Cambridge

Dudenhöffer, F. (1979), "Umweltpolitik in einem föderativen System. Ein Vergleich alternativ institutionalisierter Umweltpolitik", Beiträge zur angewandten Wirtschaftsforschung, No. 134-79, Universität Mannheim

Dudenhöffer, F. (1983), *Mehrheitswahl-Entscheidungen über Umweltnutzungen*, Lang-Verlag,Frankfurt, Bern, New York

Greenberg, J. (1980), "Consistent majority rules over compact sets of alternatives", *Econometrica* 47, 627-637

OECD (1973), *The Mutual Compensation Principle: An Economic Instrument for Solving Certain Transfrontier Pollution Problems*, Paris

Peltzman, S., and Tideman, T.N. (1972), "Local versus national pollution control: Note", *American Economic Review* 62, 959-63

Siebert, H. (1975), "Regional aspects of environmental allocation", *Zeitschrift für die gesamte Staatswissenschaft* 131, 496-513

Siebert, H. (1984), "Spatial aspects of environmental economics", in: Kneese, A. V., and Sweeny, J.L. (eds.), *Handbook of Resource and Energy Economics* (forthcoming)

Siebert, H., Walter, I., and Zimmermann, K. (1980), *Regional Environmental Policy. The Economic Issues*, New York University Press, New York

Stein, J.L. (1971), "The 1971 report of president's Council of Economic Advisers: Microeconomic aspects of public policy", *American Economic Review* 61, 531-37

Appendix

Derivation of equation (14)

If we differentiate equation (1), (2), (3) and take $p_{e1} = p_{e2} = p_e$ into account we arrive at

(1d) $$\lambda_a \hat{l}_1 + (1 + \lambda_a)\hat{l}_2 = \hat{L} \qquad \text{where } \lambda_a \equiv y_1 / L$$

(2d) $$\hat{p}_A = \frac{\theta_e}{\sigma}(\hat{e}_j - \hat{l}_j) \qquad j = 1,2$$

(3d) $$\hat{p}_E = \frac{-\theta_a}{\sigma}(\hat{e}_j - \hat{l}_j) \qquad j = 1,2$$

where $\theta_a \equiv p_l l_j / py_j$ and $\theta_e \equiv p_e e_j / py_j$.

Notice that $\hat{p}_E - \hat{p}_A = \hat{p}_e - \hat{p}_a$. Hence (2d), (3d) imply

(4d) $$(\hat{p}_e - \hat{p}_a) = \frac{-1}{\sigma}(\hat{e}_j - \hat{l}_j)$$

Differentiating the production function G_j and considering (2), (3), (4) yields

(0) $$\hat{y}_j = \theta_a \hat{l}_j + \theta_e \hat{e}_j \qquad j = 1,2$$

Combining these four equations we get equation (14). Notice that (2d), (3d), (4d) imply

(5d) $$\hat{p}_A = -\theta_e (\hat{p}_e - \hat{p}_a) ; \qquad \hat{p}_E = \theta_a (\hat{p}_e - \hat{p}_a)$$

Environmental Policy with Pollutant Interactions

by
Alfred Endres

1. Introduction

Alternative means of environmental policy are usually analyzed in economics within the framework of a set of pollution standards serving as targets for environmental quality:
"On the basis of evidence concerning the effects of unclean air on health or of polluted water on fish life, one may, for example, decide that the sulfur-dioxide content of the atmosphere in the city should not exceed x percent, that the oxygen demand of the foreign matter contained in a waterway should not exceed y, or that the decibel (noise) level in residential neighborhoods should not exceed z, at least 99 percent of the time. These acceptability standards, x, y, and z, then amount to a set of constraints that society places on its activities. They represent the decision maker's subjective evaluation of the minimum standards that must be met in order to achieve what may be described as "a reasonable quality of life."[1]

Environmental policy instruments as charges, direct controls and tradeable pollution permits are discussed as the means to attain these standards.
The standards are "admittedly somewhat arbitrary"[2], reflecting the difficulty to calculate a socially optimal level of pollution, environmental policy could aim at.

The problem to be dealt with in this paper is generated by the fact that acceptability standards for several pollutants should not be defined independently from each other. Generally, the environment does not provide special sub-capacities for the assimilation of each pollutant. Several pollutants rather draw upon the same capacity of the environment simultaneously. Moreover, they often react chemically. In these cases their mixtures generate an environmental impact

---

1) W.J. Baumol, W.E. Oates (1975), p. 137.

2) W.J. Baumol, W.E. Oates (1975), p. 134.

different from the sum of the impacts that each individual pollutant would have in the absence of the others. Synergisms among pollutants are an example for this type of an interaction.

Below, any pair of pollutants X_i, X_j is called "interactive" if the acceptable level of X_i depends upon how much of X_j is discharged[3].

Even though the main body of the environmental economics literature (often implicitely) assumes that different pollutants can be regulated independently from each other, some authors allow for environmental quality to be determined by interactive pollutants[4]. However, there has not been much effort to answer the question of how the properties of alternative means for environmental policy are affected by the existence of pollutant interaction[5].
In this paper effluent charges and marketable pollution permits are compared regarding their efficiency and accuracy in the presence of interactive pollutants. Direct controls are mentioned in passing.
For all policies it is assumed that the environmental policy makers know the nature of pollutant interaction but can only estimate the polluters' marginal abatement cost functions. There is some focus in the analysis below, to the question of how the policy makers' knowledge of the marginal abatement costs changes in the process of applying alternative environmental policy instruments.

It is assumed below, that a single indicator "I" exists which relates the quantities of n pollutants (X_1,...,X_n) to "load units" of this medium. (The higher the index value the lower the quality of the environmental medium). This indicator is assumed to take care of the problems of simultaneous environmental capacity use and chemical reactions.

---

3) This is a wide definition of the term "interaction", adopted from the literature of fn. 5). A narrower definition might use this term only if the marginal environmental impact of one pollutant depends upon the emission level of another one.

4) See e.g. K.G. Mäler (1974), R. Pethig (1979).

5) Notable exceptions are B. Beavis, M. Walker (1979), H. Bonus (1970).

Here, the target of environmental policy can be defined in terms of a predetermined level $\bar{I}$ of this index. It should be noted that this type of a target definition is compatible with indefinitely many combinations of n pollutant quantities.

Of course, it cannot be said in general terms what properties the environmental constraint, defined for the economic process by setting the target $\bar{I}$, might have. If the indicator would take the linear additive form of $I = a_1X_1 + \ldots\ldots + a_nX_n$ where the a_i are constant "load-parameters", the pollutants could be substituted against each other at a constant rate for each given level $\bar{I}$. This very simple type is called "linear interaction", below.

Of course, the marginal rate of substitution among pollutants $-(dX_j / dX_i)_{dI=0}$ may decrease (convex interaction) or increase (concave interaction) or take non-monotone forms (non-convex/non-concave interaction)[6]. It is even possible that pollutants are complements rather than substitutes. Here, the detrimental effects of different pollutants compensate each other. This case, however, will not be discussed below.

Following Sprague (1970) these types of interactions are illustrated in figure 1 for the case of two pollutants denoted X and Y.

Henceforth, the existence of a regulatory agency is supposed, aiming at a decrease of the environmental load in its control region from the unregulated level I* to a predetermined target level $\bar{I}$. There are n pollutants supposed to be generated by n regional industries, one pollutant by each. The unregulated equilibrium pollution levels are denoted $X^*_1,\ldots,X^*_n$. The emissions reduced from their unregulated levels $X^*_1,\ldots,X^*_n$ to any level $\hat{X}_1,\ldots,\hat{X}_n$ are denoted $\hat{x}_1,\ldots,\hat{x}_n$. Since $\bar{I}$ can be met with many combinations of pollutant quantities it is to be decided which combination the agency is to aim at.

6) Taking the toxicity to fish as an indicator of the environmental load caused by a combination of pollutant concentrations, J.B. Sprague (1970) found high evidence for linear pollutant interaction.
From the four air quality indices surveyed by A.E.S. Green et al. (1980), three take the linear interactive form. In the Soviet Union, interactive ambient air quality standards are used. They all take the form of linear interaction. See F.J. Dreyhaupt (1971), p. 66.
Of course, the use of linear indicators in biology and other sciences is no proof of the underlying environmental structure being a linear one. Indicators are only proxies, after all. Their quality cannot be assessed by the author, a simple economist only.

It is supposed that the agency is trying to find the pollutant allocation $(X^{*}_{1}{}^{*},\ldots,X^{*}_{n}{}^{*})$ which meets the environmental constraint $\bar{I}$ at minimum cost.

Simultaneously with the problem of finding $(X^{*}_{1}{}^{*},\ldots,X^{*}_{n}{}^{*})$ the agency of course has to solve the problem of assigning each industry pollutant quantity $X^{*}_{i}{}^{*}$ to the individual generators of pollutant i. Since the latter problem is extensively treated in the literature using independent targets for the pollutants[7], it is ignored henceforth.

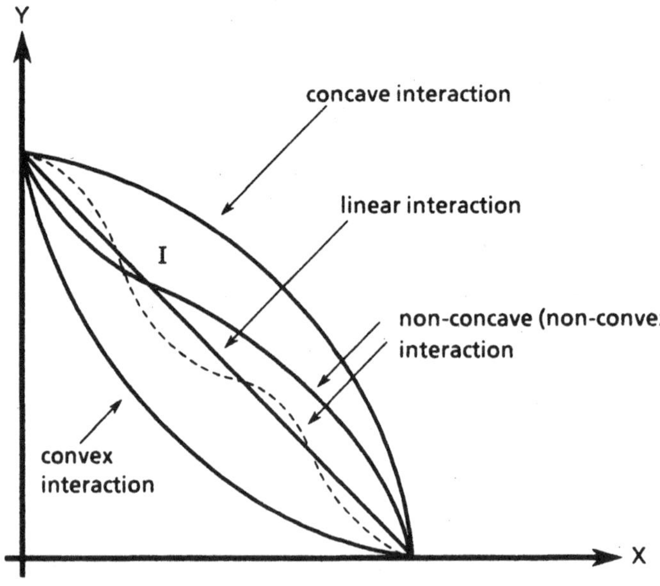

Figure 1: Types of interaction among pollutants

7) See e.g. W.J. Baumol, W.E. Oates (1975), P. Burrows (1979), A. Endres (1985), H. Siebert (1981).

2. Properties of the Optimum

Before analyzing the ability of alternative policies to meet $\bar{I}$ at minimum cost the nature of the optimum allocation is to be elaborated. The problem of the environmental agency is one of constrained cost minimization. The objective function is

$$C = \sum_{i=1}^{n} C^{(i)}(x_i), \tag{1}$$

where C is the aggregated abatement cost of all polluters, $C^{(i)}$ is the abatement cost of the industry generating pollutant i and x_i is the abatement quantity of this pollutant[8].

$\partial C^{(i)}/\partial x_i > 0$, $\partial^2 C^{(i)}/\partial x_i^2 > 0$ is supposed to hold for any pollutant i. The first constraint for the cost minimization is the environmental standard to be met, i.e., $\bar{I} - I(x_1,...,x_n) \geq 0$, where $\partial I/\partial x_i < 0 \quad \forall i \varepsilon \{1,...,n\}$.

Moreover, you cannot clean up more mess than generated. Thus, for each abatement activity an "upper boundary condition"

$X^*_i - x_i \geq 0 \quad \forall i \varepsilon \{1,...,n\}$

holds, where X^*_i is the unregulated "status quo ante" euqilibrium quantity of pollutant i.

Finally, the levels of pollution abatement are non-negative, i.e., $x_i \geq 0 \quad \forall i \varepsilon \{1,...,n\}$ holds[9].

The Lagrangean function for this constraint minimization problem is

$$Z = C(x_1, ..., x_n) + \mu(I(x_1, ..., x_n) - \bar{I}) + \sum_{i=1}^{n} \lambda_i (x_i - X^*) \tag{2}$$

---

8) The index (i) in $C^{(i)}$ is dropped, below, where no confusion seems to be possible.
As mentioned above, the problem of assigning the maximum allowable emission level for each industry to the members of this industry is not analyzed in this paper. It is therefore assumed that within each industry, the pollution allowances are distributed in a manner minimizing intra-industry abatement cost.
The reader familiar with the traditional environmental economics literature will notice that this assumption is warranted in the case of the effluent charges and transferable permits policy, but excessively favourable in the case of a command and control policy.

9) A more general model might allow for activities simultaneously generating $x_i < 0$, $x_j > 0$ if the effect of the latter one upon the environmental quality index overcompensates the effect of the former

The Kuhn-Tucker Conditions are

(3) $\partial C/\partial x_i + \mu \partial I/\partial x_i + \lambda_i \geq 0$ $\quad x_i \geq 0 \quad$ $x_i(\partial C/\partial x_i + \mu \partial I/\partial x_i + \lambda_i) = 0$

$\forall i \varepsilon \{1,...,n\}$

(4) $I(x_1,...,x_n) - \bar{I} \leq 0$ $\quad \mu \geq 0 \quad$ $\mu(I(x_1,...,x_n)-\bar{I}) = 0$

(5) $(x_i - X^*_i) \leq 0$ $\quad \lambda_i \geq 0 \quad$ $\lambda_i(x_i-X^*_i) = 0 \quad \forall i \varepsilon \{1,...,n\}$

According to the Arrow-Enthoven Theorem, these conditions are necessary and sufficient for a global solution of our cost minimum problem, given the constraint qualification is met, the objective function $C(x_1,...,x_n)$ is differentiable and quasiconvex and the constraint function $I(x_1,...,x_n)$ is differentiable and quasiconcave. (The condition that $\exists i \varepsilon \{1,...,n\}$ such that $\partial C/\partial x_i > 0$ at the solution, is met anyway, in the problem analyzed here). The Kuhn-Tucker Conditions allow for interior and corner solutions. In the case of an interior solution ($0 < x_i < X^*_i, \forall i$), for the reduction of any pair of pollutants i, $j \in \{1,...,n\}$ it follows that

$$\partial C/\partial x_i = - \mu \partial I/\partial x_i$$
$$\partial C/\partial x_j = - \mu \partial I/\partial x_j$$

(6) $$\rightarrow -(dx_j / dx_i)_{dC=0} = -(dx_j / dx_i)_{dI=0}$$

Condition (6) indicates that in the solution the marginal rate at which the two pollutants can be substituted against each other at the predetermined index level $\bar{I}$ (their marginal rate of substitution) equals the marginal rate at which the two pollutants can be substituted against each other at a given level of aggregate abatement cost (their marginal rate of transformation). Thus, given the above requirements are met, an interior solution can be illustrated as follows, for the case of two pollutants X and Y.

In Fig. 2, $\hat{C} < \bar{C} < \bar{\bar{C}}$ show alternative levels of aggregate abatement cost and $\bar{I}$ shows the predetermined environmental constraint. The size of the "box" in Fig. 2 represents the non-negativity and upper boundary conditions. The solution is given by P**(x**,y**) where an iso-abatement-cost curve is tangent to the constraint curve.

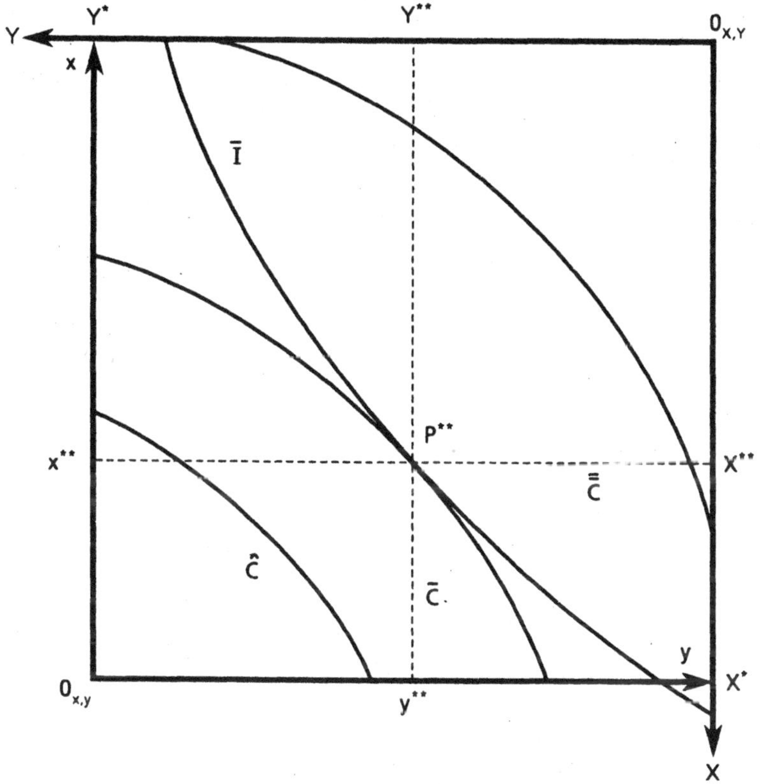

Figure 2: Meeting the target at minimum cost - the interior solution

It should be noted that since x = X* - X and y = Y* - Y, the solution in terms of abatement levels (x**, y**) corresponds to a solution in terms of emission levels (X**, Y**) still generated after abatement is done. Moreover, a curve which is concave (convex) towards the x, y-origin is convex (concave) towards the X,Y-origin.

Corner solutions can turn up in two kinds of forms.

First, in the nonnegativity condition(s) of one (several) variable(s) the strict equality sign may hold, second in the upper boundary condition(s) of one (several) variable(s) the strict equality sign may hold (or both).

To give an example for the first type, suppose that in the solution, $0 < x_i < X^*_i$ $\forall i \varepsilon \{1,...,j-1, j+1,...,n\}$ and $0 = x_j < X^*_j$ hold.

Then,

$$\frac{\partial C/\partial x_i}{\partial C/\partial x_j} \leq \frac{\partial I/\partial x_i}{\partial I/\partial x_j},$$

i.e.,

(7) $$-(dx_j / dx_i)_{dC=0} \leq -(dx_j / dx_i)_{dI=0} \text{ holds.}$$

This is shown in Fig. 3 for two abatement activities x (for x_i) and y (for x_j) (and the strict unequality holding in (7)):

For the second type of a corner solution, the case of $0 < x_i = X^*_i$ and $0 < x_j < X^*_j$, $\forall j \varepsilon \{1,...,i-1, i+1,...,n\}$ is illustrative. Here,

$$\frac{\partial C/\partial x_i}{\partial C/\partial x_j} = \frac{-\mu \partial I/\partial x_i - \lambda_i}{-\mu \partial I/\partial x_j},$$

i.e.,

(8) $$-(dx_j / dx_i)_{dC=0} \leq -(dx_j / dx_i)_{dI=0} \text{ holds.}$$

This is shown in Fig. 4 for two abatement activities x (for x_i) and y (for x_j) (and the strict unequality holding in equation (8)).

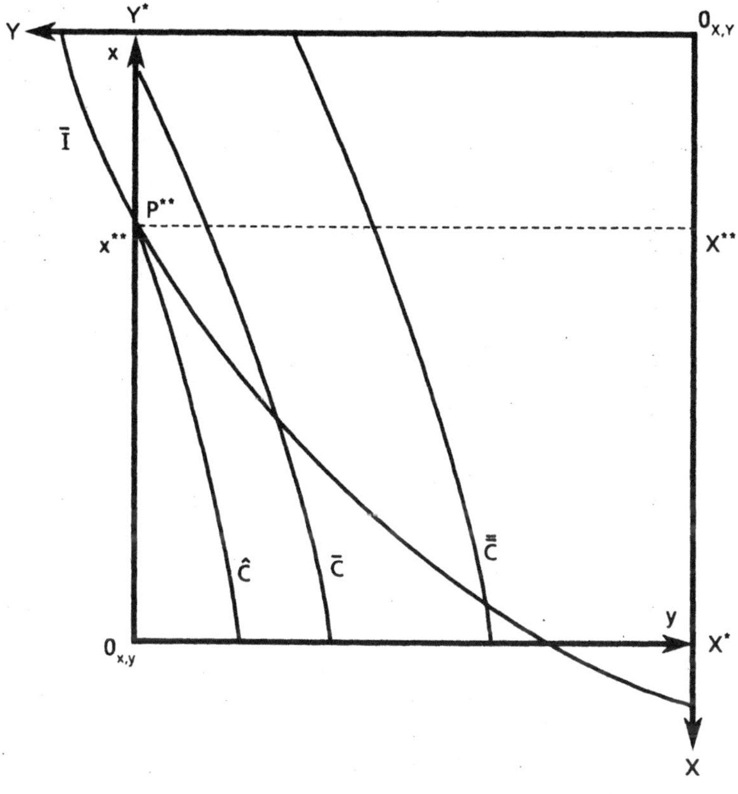

Figure 3: Meeting the target at minimum cost - corner solution I

The properties of the solution of the cost minimization problem under environmental restrictions have been established. How about the chances to arrive at this optimum by applying alternative environmental policies? Discussing this question, the cases of linear, concave and nonconcave interaction in the environmental target constraint are separately dealt with, below.

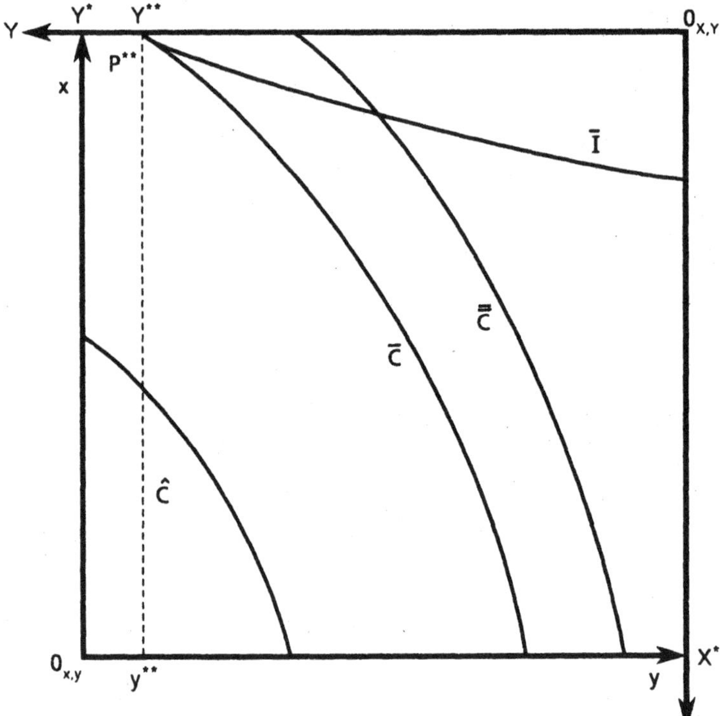

Figure 4: Meeting the target at minimum cost - corner solution II

3. Linear Interaction

3.1 Effluent charges

Suppose, the regulatory agency is to use effluent charges as a means to achieve the predetermined interactive quality standard $\bar{I}$ [10].

To decide which of the indefinitely many combinations of the n pollutants compatible with $\bar{I}$ it is to aim at, the regulatory agency has to make a guess on the marginal abatement costs of the n polluting industries. On the basis of this estimate and the agency's knowledge of $I(X_1,...,X_n)$, the n pollutant target levels $(\bar{X}_1,...,\bar{X}_n)$, are defined. These levels are the ones the agency takes to meet the environmental restriction $\bar{I}$ at minimum cost.

The estimate of thc abatement cost functions is also needed for another purpose: It provides the basis for a guess on how the n polluting industries will adjust their discharges to alternative levels of tax rates $t_{X_1},...t_{X_n}$, just as in the case of no pollutant interactions: Consider any polluter A in any i-polluting industry wanting to minimize his burden of environmental policy $B_A = t_{X_i} \cdot X^{(A)}_i + C^{(i)}{}_A\ (x^{(A)}_i)$. The first term indicates the firm's emission tax bill and the second term its abatement cost. Under the above mentioned condition of increasing marginal abatement cost, the burden is minimized for

$$(9) \qquad t_{X_i} = \partial C^{(i)}{}_A / \partial x^{(A)}{}_i .$$

Thus , under an effluent charge law each polluter will reduce emissions until the marginal abatement cost equals the tax rate, as is well known in the literature. Using this information and having assessed the marginal abatement cost, the regulatory agency tries to set tax rates $t_{X_1},...,t_{X_n}$ equal to (its guess of) the marginal abatement cost of the polluting industries in the target situation $(\bar{X}_1,...,\bar{X}_n)$.

If the target situation is not attained after the industries' adjustment to the taxes, the tax rates have to be revised. It is hoped that a solution will be attained after

---

10) Henceforth, it is assumed that discharges of any pollutant X_i decrease (increase) when the respective tax rate t_{X_i} increases (decreases).
Of course, there are exceptions from this rule. See e.g. R. Pethig (1979), pp. 135 f.

an iterative process of trial and error [11].

Fig. 5 illustrates this "pricing and standards" technique for the case of linear interaction, the existence of an interior solution and two pollutants X, Y.

The first quadrant of fig. 5[12] depicts the situation of the X-industry. The unregulated equilibrium emission quantity of that industry is X*. C(x) is the total, $\partial C/\partial x(x)$ the marginal abatement cost curve.

Of course, it is highly unlikely that the regulatory agency's estimate of the abatement cost of the X-industry (and any other industry) would be correct. Therefore, in the first quadrant of fig. 5, the agency's estimates $C^e(x)$ and $\partial C^e/\partial x(x)$ are distinguished from the true curves C(x), $\partial C/\partial x(x)$. The second quadrant depicts the situation of the Y-industry, analogously.
The solution of the constraint cost minimization is graphically derived in the third quadrant[13]. P**(X**,Y**), where an iso-cost curve C** derived from the true abatement cost curves is tangent to the target line $\bar{I}$ represents the genuine optimum. $\bar{P}(\bar{X},\bar{Y})$, where an iso-cost curve $\bar{C}^e$ derived from the agency's estimate of the abatement costs is tangent to the target line represents the optimum as assessed by the agency.

Under these circumstances the regulator will set tax rates $t_X^{(1)} = \partial C^e/\partial x(\bar{x})$, $t_Y^{(1)} = \partial C^e/\partial y(\bar{y})$, which he expects to induce abatement activities $\bar{x}$, $\bar{y}$ to bring emissions down from X*,Y* to the targent levels $\bar{X},\bar{Y}$.

The firms adjust to these taxes by reducing emissions up to the point where their marginal abatement costs equal the tax rates. However, the costs calculated by the firms in their adjustment are the genuine abatement costs [14], rather than the

11) See W.J. Baumol, W.E. Oates (1975), Ch.10.

12) The quadrants are counted counterclockwise, beginning with the upper right hand quadrant.

13) The third quadrant of fig. 5 shows what the box in fig. 2 has shown. For simplicity, in fig. 5 and the following figures, the bottom and the left hand side of the box have not been drawn. It should be kept in mind, however, that each level of X(Y) in the third quadrant corresponds to a level of x(y) on the left hand side (bottom) of the box.

14) It is assumed that each firm is aware of its own marginal abatement cost function.

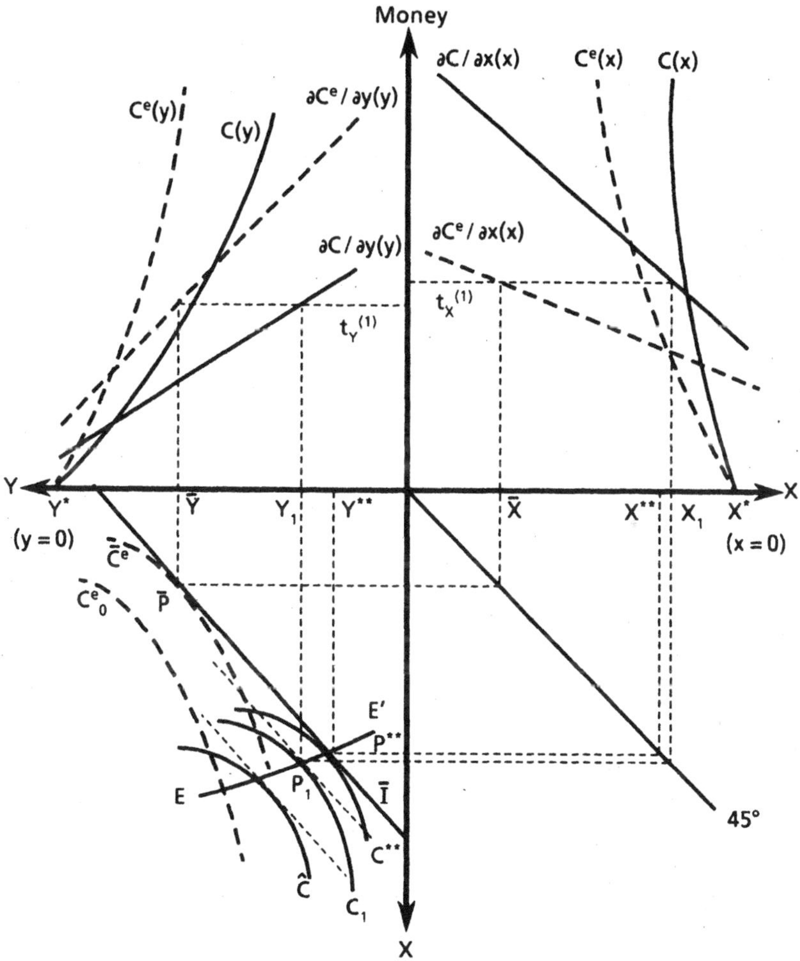

Figure 5: Effluent charges with linear interaction

marginal abatement costs, as estimated by the agency.
Thus, the post tax emission equilibrium is X_1, Y_1 with $t^{(1)}_X = \partial C/\partial x(x_1)$, $t^{(1)}_Y = \partial C/\partial y(y_1)$.
This equilibrium is illustrated as P_1 in fig. 5, missing the target $\bar{P}(\bar{X},\bar{Y})$.
Therefore, the tax rates have to be revised.
In the process of restructering tax rates the regulatory agency can rely upon the following informations, given interaction is linear:
The agency knows from (6) that in the cost minimum situation (X**,Y**)

(6a) $\quad -(dy/dx)_{dC=0}\,(X^{**},Y^{**}) = -(dy/dx)_{dI=0}\,(X^{**},Y^{**})$ holds.

From (9) it is known that

(9a) $\quad (t_X/t_Y) = -(dy/dx)_{dC=0}\,(X^{**},Y^{**})$ holds.

The agency concludes that

(10) $\quad (t_X/t_y) = -(dy/dx)_{dI=0}\,(X^{**},Y^{**})$ holds[15].

Thus, the regulatory agency can take it for granted that in the optimum it is struggling for, realized as emission tax equilibrium, the relative tax rate for the two pollutants equals the marginal rate of pollutant substitution, evaluated in the solution.

Since $I=I(X,Y)$ is known to the agency and the marginal rate of pollutant substitution does not depend on the levels of pollutants in the case of linear interaction, the agency knows the term $-(dy/dx)_{dI=0}$ in (10) without knowing where the solution lies. Therefore, the agency is aware of the relative optimum tax rates without having complete information on the polluting industries marginal abatement costs.

15) For the case of n variables the equations are

(6) $-(dx_j/dx_i)_{dC=0}(X^*{}_1{}^*, \ldots, X^*{}_n{}^*) = (dx_j/dx_i)_{dI=0}(X^*{}_1{}^*,\ldots,X^*{}_n{}^*)$, $\forall i,j \varepsilon \{1,\ldots,n\}$

(9b) $t_{x_i}/t_{x_j} = -(dx_j/dx_i)_{dC=0}(X^*{}_1{}^*, \ldots, X^*{}_n{}^*)$, $\forall i,j \varepsilon \{1,\ldots,n\}$

(10a) $t_{x_i}/t_{x_j} = -(dx_j/dx_i)_{dI=0}(X^*{}_1{}^*, \ldots, X^*{}_n{}^*)$, $\forall i,j \varepsilon \{1,\ldots,n\}$

In the abatement equilibrium attained after the agency's first tax rate estimation (P_1) the condition $t^{(1)}_X / t^{(1)}_Y = -(dy/dx)_{dI=0}$ holds. Thus, all the agency has to do after realizing that the environmental restriction is not met, in P_1, is to raise the absolute value of the tax rates leaving relative taxes as they are. In fig. 5, this would correspond to a move of the equilibrium allocation along the line EE' from P_1 towards P**.

Even though it is well known that restructering tax rates may be difficult in practice[16] (with or without pollutant interaction) it is interesting to note that in the case of linear interaction the agency's strive for optimality is not more complicated than in the case of regulating a single pollutant. The simple decision rule is:

If the load on the environment after adjusting to the tax rates set in the first place is above the target level $\bar{I}$, all tax rates have to be raised in the same proportion, until $\bar{I}$ is met. If the load falls short of the level aimed at (contrary to what is shown in fig. 5) all tax rates may be reduced by the same percentage amount.

In the cases of corner solutions (not shown in fig. 5) the procedure of tax restructering would be basically the same. Consider the example of a corner solution at $X^{**}, Y=0$. Here, increasing tax rates in the same proportion starting from an initial situation P_1, violating the constraint $\bar{I}$, would result in a situation $X^0, Y=0$, with $X^0 \geq X^{**}$. If $X^0 > X^{**}$ (as shown in fig. 5a), still violating $\bar{I}$, both tax rates could be increased, as in the case of an interior solution, until $\bar{I}$ is met. Alternatively, having attained $X^0, Y=0$, t_Y could be left constant, increasing t_X only, until $\bar{I}$ is met.

3.2 Transferable discharge permits

Suppose the regulatory agency is using transferable discharge permits as a means of environmental policy. Then, a quantity of permits is issued by the agency guaranteeing that the environmental target level $\bar{I}$ is met. The agency has the option of auctioning the permits off, or giving them away free of charge to the polluters. In both schemes permits can be resold. Moreover, the permits may be

16) See W.J. Baumol, W.E. Oates (1975), Ch 10.

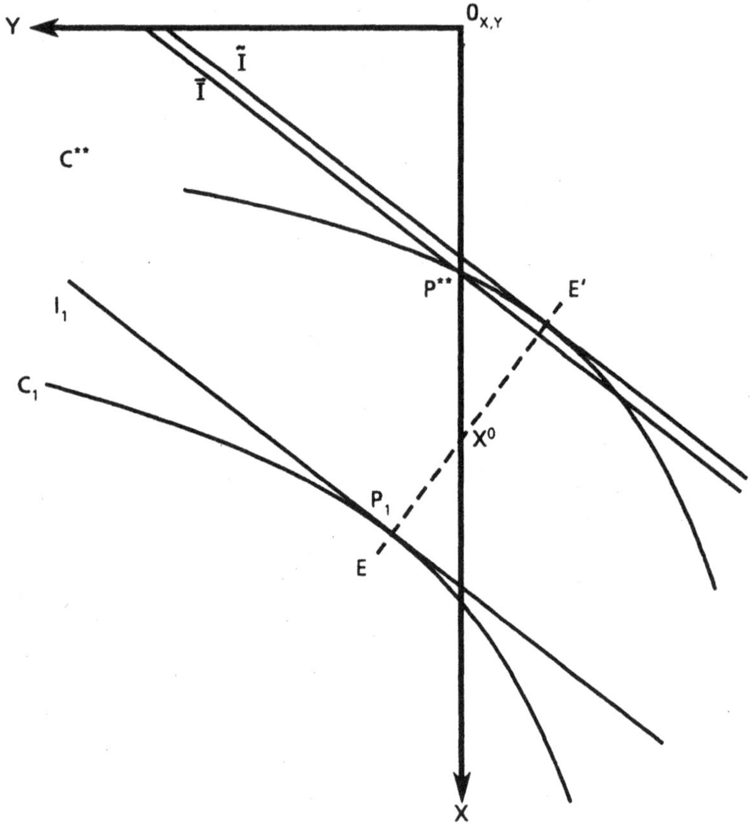

Figure 5a: Effluent charges with linear interaction - a corner solution

designed as separate emission rights, one type of a right for each type of a pollutant, or they may be written in the form of "load-permits" (L-permits), allowing the generation of load-units in terms of the indicator I. Shaping L-

permits, it would be convenient to use one of the pollutants (say, j) as a numeraire. Then, the permits would be written out in units of pollutant j. One L-permit would certify the right of discharging one unit of pollutant j or, alternatively, the quantity of pollutant i, equivalent to a unit j in terms of the index I. In the case of linear interaction, it follows from the definition of I that the quantity of pollutant i equivalent to one unit of j is $1/(a_i/a_j)$ units. The coefficient a_i/a_j shows the adverse effect of pollutant i relative to the adverse effect of the numeraire pollutant, i.e., the marginal rate of pollutant substitution.
Consider the properties of a L-permit policy with free initial distribution:
If the regulatory agency is aiming at a set of emissions $(\bar{X}_1,...,\bar{X}_n)$, as outlined above, it may assign the permits as follows: A number of $\bar{X}_j$ L-permits are given to the j-industry (discharging the numeraire pollutant). Each firm k in the j-industry may be assigned a quantity of $X^{(k)}{}_j^* \bar{X}_j/X^*_j$ permits (where $X^{(k)}{}_j^*(X^*_j)$ is firm k's (industry j's) unregulated emission level), leaving the emission share of each firm within the industry at its pre-regulatory level[17].

Each i-industry $(i \in \{1,...,j-1, j+1,...,n\})$ may be assigned a quantity of L-permits certifying the right to discharge $\bar{X}_i$ pollutant units, i.e., $a_i/a_j \bar{X}_i$ permits. Analogously to what has been said for the members of the j-industry, each firm k in the i-industry may receive $a_i/a_j \cdot X^{(k)}{}_i^* \cdot \bar{X}_i/X^*_i$ permits. If this initial distribution of permits put into effect by the agency would not be modified by trade among firms of different industries, the agency's environmental target $(\bar{X}_1,...,\bar{X}_n)$ would be realized and maintained.
Of course, the procedure outlined above is just an example of determining the initial allocation of rights. If the agency is not afraid of the permit market process getting caught in a local optimum between the initial distribution of rights and the global optimum it might just assign a quantity of permits to each industry i proportional to its pre-regulatory emission level X^*_i.
If in the pre-regulatory equilibrium $I^* = a_1X^*_1 + ... + a_nX^*_n$ holds, each industry might be granted the right to pollute $X^*_i \cdot \bar{I}/I^*$ pollutant units leaving the interindustry distribution of emission quantities at its pre-regulated form and

17) The problem of firms producing higher unregulated emission levels to secure a higher endowment of permits is ignored here

confining the index to the target level $\bar{I}$. In this case, each industry i would be assigned $a_i/a_j X^*_i$ $\bar{I}/I^*$ L-permits.The latter procedure would be very attractive because the agency would not have to worry about estimating the marginal abatement costs of the polluting industries at all. Thereby, the permit policy would achieve an important advantage compared to the effluent charge policy. Nevertheless, $(\bar{X}_1,...,\bar{X}_n)$ will be used as a starting emission allocation below, for better analytical comparability of the charges and the permits policies.

How about the incentives to modify the initial distribution of pollution rights? Suppose the cost to abate an additional amount of pollutant i equivalent to a unit of the numeraire pollutant j differs from the cost to abate an additional amount of pollutant k equivalent to a numeraire unit, in the starting situation. Then, there are potential gains from permit trade between the i-and k-industry. If the marginal abatement cost for a j-equivalent in industry i are higher (lower) than the marginal abatement costs for a j-equivalent in industry k, then, a L-permit can be traded from the k-(i-)industry to the i-(k-)industry to their mutual advantage. Of course, given the above assumption on the slope of the marginal abatement cost curves, these costs of the industry supplying (demanding) permits rise (fall) in the process of trading since more (less) pollutants are abated. The competitive equilibrium occurs where the marginal abatement costs in terms of numeraire equivalents of the two industries have adjusted to each other in the transaction process. With equal marginal abatement costs across the industries in terms of j-equivalents, all gains from trade are exhausted[18].

Figure 6 illustrates the market for discharge permits for two pollutants X and Y in the case of perfect competition. Y serves as the numeraire pollutant.
The initial permit assignments of the two industries are indicated as $\bar{Y}$ and $a \cdot \bar{X}$ in the second and first quadrant, respectively. a stands for a_X/a_Y, the marginal rate of pollutant substitution. Since permits are written in numeraire units, the abscissa in the first quadrant depicting the situation of the X-industry has been rescaled into Y-units. Thus, the marginal abatement cost curve of the X-industry,

18) The analogy to the traditional analysis without pollutant interaction should be noted. Here, an optimal intra-industry distribution is defined by equal marginal abatement costs for all the member firms of the industry. Of course, this condition is still valid in the case of interactive pollutants, in addition to the one explained above.

shown in the first quadrant, indicates the marginal cost of the X-industry to abate pollutant X in terms of Y-equivalent units.
From the definition of I, it follows that $Y = a \cdot X$ units of X in terms of Y-equivalents. Therefore, the marginal abatement cost of X defined for Y-equivalents is $dC(x)/dy = 1/a\ \partial C/\partial x(x)$, shown in the first quadrant[19].

Since in the initial situation, the X-industry is allowed to emit a quantity $\bar{X}$ of its pollutant (i.e., it is forced to abate $\bar{x}$ pollutants) its rescaled marginal abatement cost is $1/a\partial C/\partial x(\bar{X})$, in this situation. Thus, the marginal willingness to pay of the firms in that industry to receive a (small) additional quantity of L-permits would be just that amount of money. If the industry's firms were *offered* that amount they would supply a marginal L-permit. The marginal cost of the Y-industry is $\partial C/\partial y(\bar{y})$ in the initial situation. Thus, this amount of money is the marginal permit supply (demand) price of the firms in that industry. Since in the example given in fig. 6 $\partial C/\partial y(y)$ happens to be smaller than $1/a\partial C/\partial x(x)$, the firms in the Y-industry turn out to be the suppliers in the permit market, the X-firms being their customers. Thus, $\partial C/\partial y$ is the supply curve and $1/a\ \partial C/\partial x$ is the demand curve of the permit market.

To read quantities supplied along the same scale as quantities demanded the supply curve $\partial C/\partial y$ is shifted from the second to the first quadrant in fig. 6 to an extent of $a \cdot \bar{X} + \bar{Y}$. The transformed curve is labeled $\partial C/\partial y^T$. It should be noted that units of Y removed by the Y-industry are read from the left to the right in that quadrant and units of Y-equivalents removed by the X-industry are read from the right to the left.
It is obvious that the initial situation $1/a\partial C/\partial x(x) > \partial C/\partial y(y)$ is no equilibrium in the permit market. The equilibrium will be reached if the X-industry buys Y^*-Y^{**} permits from the Y-industry.
Then, $1/a\ \partial C/\partial x = \partial C/\partial y$ holds, i.e. supply and demand curves intersect.
Since $a = -(dy/dx)_{dI=0}$, in the case of linear interaction, this equilibrium condition is identical to equation (6a), the condition for the minimum cost situation keeping the target $\bar{I}$.

---

19) For total abatement cost, $C = C(x)$ holds. With $X = 1/a\ Y$, $X = X^*-x$ and $Y = Y^*-y$, $dC(x)/dy = 1/a\ \partial C/\partial x$ follows.

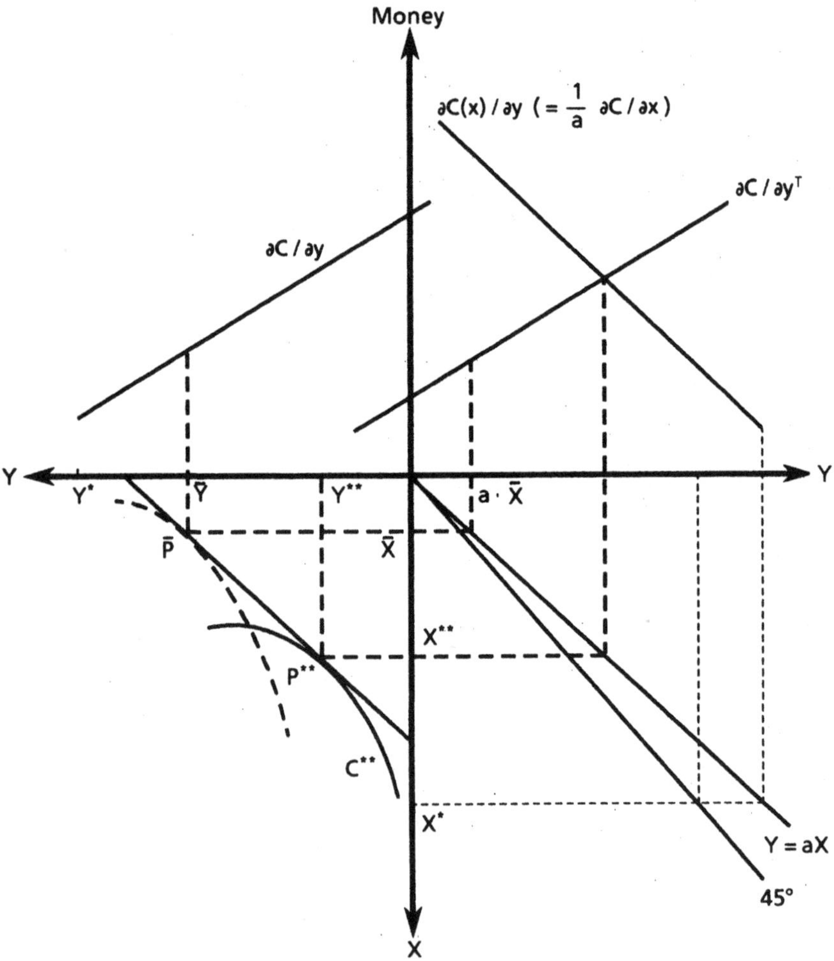

Figure 6: Transferable discharge permits with linear interaction

Since this optimum is unique we can be sure about the permit market equilibrium being identical to the solution of the regulatory agency's problem, (X^{**}, Y^{**}).
It is worth noting that with the permit policy this efficient allocation is achieved without the detour of preliminary allocations which violate the environmental target, as necessary in the effluent charge approach[20].

4. Concave Interaction

4.1 Effluent charges

Analogously to what has been said above, the regulatory agency is aiming at an emission allocation $\bar{X}_1, \ldots, \bar{X}_n$, with the tax rates $t^{(1)}{}_{X_1}, \ldots, t^{(1)}{}_{X_n}$. The rates are set according to the shape of the policy restriction $\bar{I}$ and according to what the agency takes to be the marginal abatement costs in the n polluting industries. The polluters, however, adjust their emission levels to $X^{(1)}{}_1, \ldots, X^{(1)}{}_n$ according to their true marginal abatement costs. If the agency's estimate fails to be accurate, as assumed in this paper, $(\bar{X}_1, \ldots, \bar{X}_n) \neq (X^{(1)}{}_1, \ldots, X^{(1)}{}_n)$ follows, in general[21]. Also, the environmental target is missed $(I(X^{(1)}{}_1, \ldots, X^{(1)}{}_n) \neq \bar{I})$, in general[22].
As in the case of linear interaction, the result of $\bar{X}_i > X^{(1)}{}_i$ $(\bar{X}_i < \bar{X}^{(1)}{}_i)$ is signalling to the agency that it overestimated (underestimated) the marginal abatement cost of the i-industry, in the first place. This will certainly be helpful for a reassessment of the cost functions.

It is important to note, however, that contrary to the case of linear interaction, there is no simple decision rule for the correction of the tax rates misspecified in the first step. Even though conditions (6), (9b), (10a), still hold when interaction is

---

20) It is obvious that in the case of linear interaction a corner solution, say $X^{**}, Y=0$, (not shown in fig. 6) would also be a permit market equilibrium.

21) In the (practically irrelevant) special case, in which the agency's estimate of the marginal abatement cost functions is the same monotonic transformation of the true functions for all industries,
$(\bar{X}_1, \ldots, \bar{X}_n) = (X^{(1)}{}_1, \ldots, X^{(1)}{}_n)$ would hold

22) If, accidentally, $I(X^{(1)}{}_1, \ldots, X^{(1)}{}_n) = \bar{I}$ holds in spite of the agency misjudging the marginal abatement costs, the agency would have to check whether the relative tax rates for all pollutants equal the (inverse) marginal rates of pollutant substitution (see equ. (10)) in this situation. Only then, $(X^{(1)}{}_1, \ldots, X^{(1)}{}_n)$ would meet $\bar{I}$ at minimum cost.

concave (given the solution is an interior one), they are not much of a help in this case. The reason is that the marginal rate of pollutant substitution is no longer constant. Thus, in (10a) the marginal rate of pollutant substitution calculated in the cost minimum situation $(X^{*}{}_{1}{}^{*},...X^{*}{}_{n}{}^{*})$ is not known to the agency even though the shape of the policy restriction $I = I(X_1,...,X_n)$ is known because the agency does not know the values $X^{*}{}_{1}{}^{*},...,X^{*}{}_{n}{}^{*}$. Thus, equation (10a) does not provide a compass for the revision of the tax rates.

All the agency can do when the industries do not react as expected to the effluent charges is to reassess the marginal abatement costs of the polluting industries and to try out a new set of tax rates.

Thus, the simple process of trial and error in the linear interactive case turns into a complex one when interaction is concave. In this process, not only the absolute levels of the tax rates but also the relative rates are questionable to the agency.

The problem is illustrated in fig. 7 for two pollutants X and Y, and the case of an interior solution.

Industries' adjustment to the initial set of tax rates $t^{(1)}{}_{X}$, $t^{(1)}{}_{Y}$, leads to the situation $P_1(X_1,Y_1) \neq \bar{P}(\bar{X},\bar{Y})$, where the constraint $\bar{I}$ is violated. $P^{**}(X^{**},Y^{**})$ again shows the optimum, unknown to the agency.

In P_1 the agency does not know how to change the tax rates. Rising both taxes proportionally until $\bar{I}$ is met, which was all it had to do in the case of linear interaction, would result in a situation on $\bar{I}$ "north east" to P_1 in fig. 7, missing the optimal situation[23].

It can be concluded that the possibility of attaining a predetermined environmental target at minimum cost by the use of effluent charges is hampered by the existence of concave pollutant interaction.

23) The following procedure would be helpful to the agency: Having achieved $\bar{I}$ by proportionally increasing both tax rates, realizing a situation of, say, $\bar{\bar{P}}(\bar{\bar{X}},\bar{\bar{Y}})$, the agency might check whether $t_x/t_Y \gtrless -(dy/dx)_{dI=0}(\bar{\bar{X}},\bar{\bar{Y}})$ holds. It would then conclude whether the solution lies to the right or to the left of $\bar{\bar{P}}$ (i.e , whether $(X^{**} < \bar{\bar{X}}, \bar{\bar{Y}}^{**} > Y)$ or $(X^{**} > \bar{\bar{X}}. Y^{**} < \bar{\bar{Y}})$, hold. Then, taxes would have to be adjusted, accordingly.

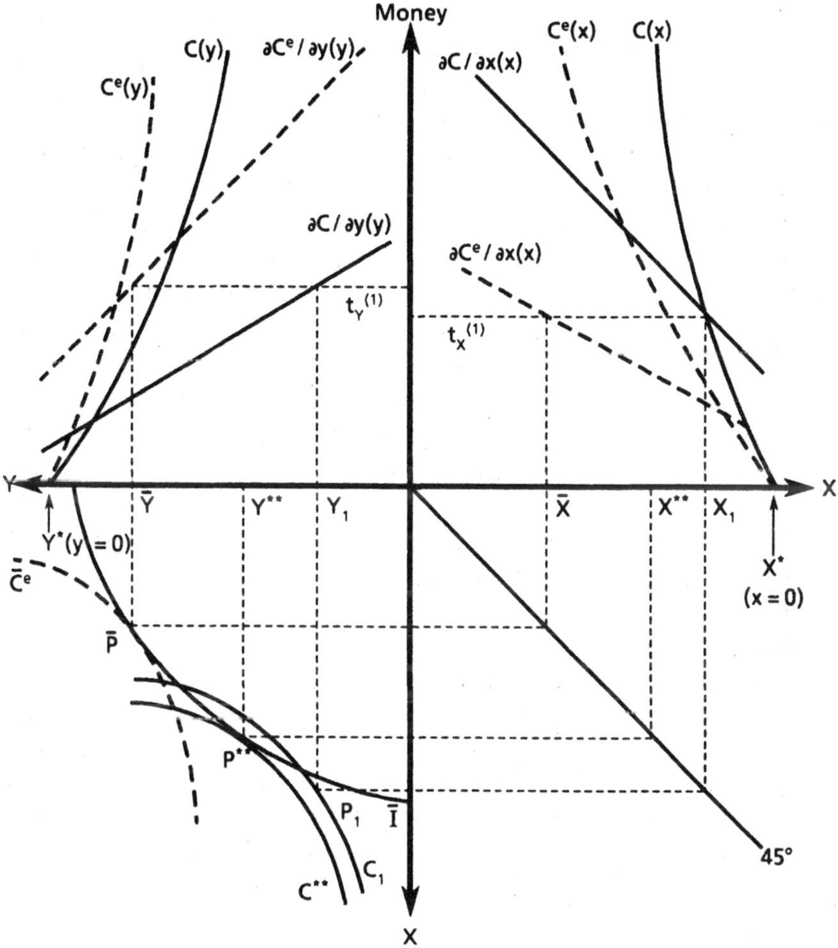

Figure 7: Effluent charges with concave interaction

4.2 Transferable discharge permits

In the case of linear interaction the quantity of i-emissions equivalent to a unit of numeraire emissions j is constant at $1/(a_i/a_j)$, the reciprocal of the marginal rate of pollutant substitution. Thus, one L-permit can be used to discharge $1/(a_i/a_j)$ units of pollutant i, irrespective to the prevailing pollutant combination.
This is no longer true in the case of concave interaction. Since the marginal rate of substitution between the numeraire pollutant j and any other pollutant i depends upon the quantity of pollutants X_i and X_j (and of all other pollutant quantities) discharged, no constant "exchange rate" among the pollutants exists. Thus, for each alternative pollutant distribution, the agency has to set a different exchange rate, corresponding to the marginal rate of pollutant substitution prevailing in this very situation[24].
Apart from this divergency, the permit market equilibrium is defined analogously to the case of linear interaction. It is illustrated in fig. 8 for the case of two pollutants X and Y and an interior solution.

The environmental damage index I is a function monotonely increasing in the quantities of pollutants X and Y. Therefore, the index function $I = I(X,Y)$ can be rewritten as $Y = Y(X,I)$. For any given level of I, say, $\bar{I}$, this function indicates the (maximal) quantity of Y compatible with $\bar{I}$, for any given level of X. With $Y(X=0,\bar{I})$ denoting the quantity of Y meeting the standard $\bar{I}$ when no X is discharged, $Y = Y(X=0,\bar{I}) - Y(X,\bar{I})$ gives the quantity of Y equivalent to X for each given level of the latter pollutant. For the index level $\bar{I}$, considered in this analysis, this function is abbreviated to $Y = I^T(X)$. Graphically it is obtained by shifting the constraint function $\bar{I}$ from the third to the fourth quadrant of fig. 8 transforming $Y(\bar{I},X=0)$ to the origin of that quadrant. At any situation $\hat{X},\hat{Y}$, the additional pollution of a unit of X has to be offset by the reduction of $\partial I^T/\partial X$ units of Y, keeping the standard $\bar{I}$. $\partial I^T/\partial X$ is identical to the marginal rate of pollutant substitution $-(dY/dX)_{\bar{I}}$.

Accordingly, an additional L-permit in the X-industry is the right to a firm A of

24) With perfect competition in the market for permits, no individual polluter's activities do have any effect on this rate. So relative prices of polluting X_i or X_j are given for each firm.

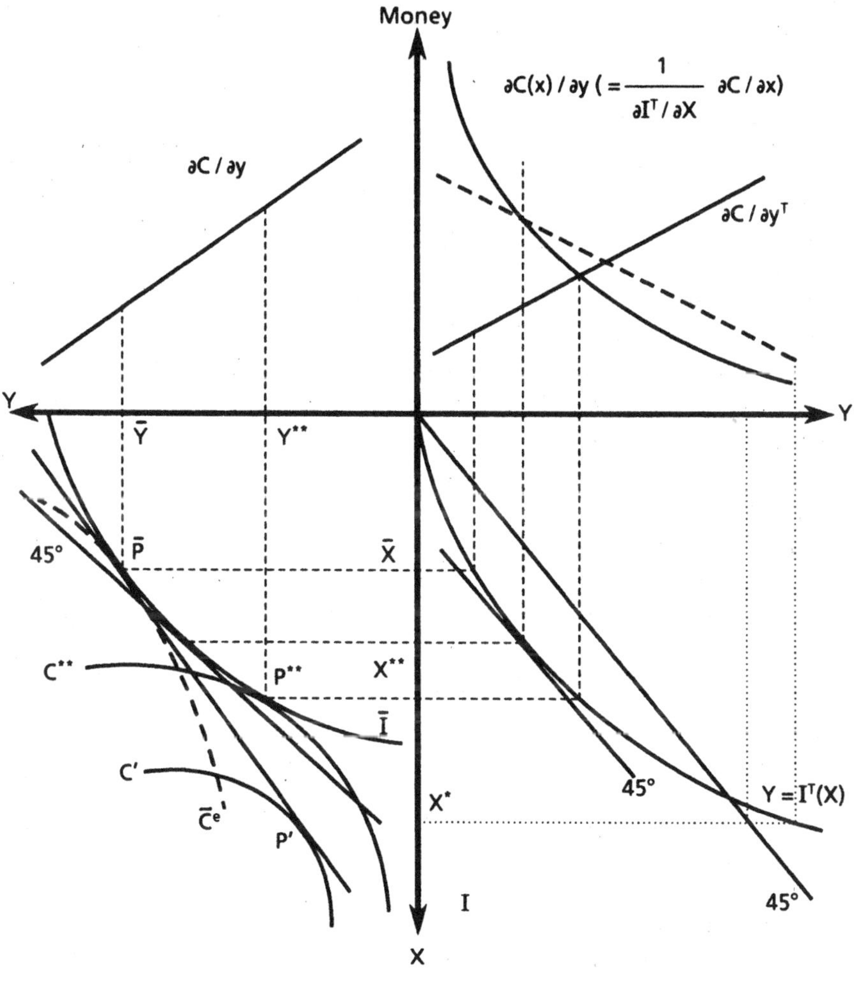

Figure 8: Transferable discharge permits with concave interaction

that industry to pollute $1/(\partial I^T/\partial X)$ additional units. Buying an L-permit in a situation where the pollution distribution is $\hat{X},\hat{Y}$ and the firm already abated $\hat{x}_A$ units, thereby saves abatement costs of

$$\frac{1}{\partial I^T/\partial X}(\hat{X})\partial C/\partial x(\hat{x}_A).$$

So that is the maximum amount the firm would be willing to pay to get hold of an additional permit.

Thus,

$$\frac{1}{\partial I^T/\partial X}(X)\partial C/\partial x(x).$$

is the permit demand function of the firms in the X-industry[25]. The demand curve is shown in the first quadrant of fig. 8 where the abscissa is rescaled to Y units[26]. (The dashed curve ($\partial C/\partial x$) is just serving as a construction line).

The aggregate permit supply function of the Y-industry's firms is not affected by changing from linear to concave interaction since the discharges of this industry serve as the numeraire pollutant. Selling a permit induces additional abatement cost of $\partial C/\partial y$ to a firm in this industry. Thus, $\partial C/\partial y$ is the permit supply function of the firms in the Y-industry. To read quantities demanded and supplied along the same scale the supply curve $\partial C/\partial y$ is shifted from the second quadrant of fig. 8, to $\partial C/\partial y^T$ into the first one, as it was in the case of linear interaction.

Market equilibrium is illustrated by the two curves intersecting with equilibrium pollution quantities X^{**},Y^{**}. The equilibrium condition is

$$\frac{\partial C}{\partial y} = \frac{1}{\partial I^T/\partial x}\frac{\partial C}{\partial x}.$$

Since $\partial I^T/\partial X = -(dy/dx)_I$, the permit market equilibrium condition is identical to the condition for constraint cost minimization, (equation (6a)). Thus, as in the case of linear interaction, the market equilibrium allocation is identical to the solution aimed at by the regulatory agency. This result is plausible by the following reasoning:

Firms of the Y-industry supply permits until their marginal abatement costs are

25) It should be kept in mind that it was assumed above that the problem of cost minimal allocation of abatement activities *within* each industry is solved. Therefore, the marginal abatement costs of all the firms in the X-industry are equal at $\partial C/\partial x$ in the equilibrium.

26) For total abatement cost, $C = C(x)$ holds. With $Y = I^T(X)$, $X = X^*\text{-}x$ and $Y = Y^*\text{-}y$, $dC(x)/dy = 1/(\partial I^T/\partial X)\ \partial C/\partial x$ follows.

equal to the equilibrium price of a permit. Firms of the X-industry demand permits until their marginal abatement costs in terms of Y-equivalents are equal to that very equilibrium price. The marginal abatement costs (in terms of the numeraire pollutant) of the firms in the two industries to be equal is a requirement for a cost minimum allocation.

The consequence of all that is that tradeable emission permits as a means of environmental policy appear to be less sensitive to a change from linear to concave interaction than emission taxes. The trial and error process of the latter becomes much more complicated whereas the nature of the competitive equilibrium in the former case is virtually uneffected[27].

5. Non-Concave Interaction

The case of non-concave interaction comprises a monotonely decreasing marginal rate of pollutant substitution $d(-(dY/dX)_{dI=0})$, $dX<0$ (convex interaction) and all forms of non-monotone changes in this rate.
It should be noted that the Kuhn-Tucker conditions, given in section 2., may not represent the solution of the cost minimum situation in these cases since the condition of quasi-convexity of the constraint function (with respect to the variables X,Y, i.e., quasi-concavity with respect to the variables x,y) is not met. Apart from that, a convex section in the constraint $\bar{I}$ may intersect the axis in a "cusp", possibly violating the constraint qualification.
Below, the example of a target constraint, exhibiting a concave and a convex section, is considered. (See $\bar{I}$ in fig. 9-11).

27) The permit policy would run into trial and error problems, also, if the regulatory agency would persue the following policy, perhaps seeming to be plausible, at first glance: The agency might issue a specific type of a permit for each type of a pollutant assigning a quantity of $\bar{X}$ and $\bar{Y}$ to the polluting industries, according to its guess of the cost minimum. Then, it might allow permit trade at fixed permit prices Z_X, Z_Y with Z_X/Z_Y chosen according to the marginal rate of pollutant substitution in the starting situation (P). Trade among firms of the two polluting industries would result in a situation with
$Z_X/Z_Y = -(dY/dX)_{dC=0}$, as shown at P' in fig. 8.
Here, the target $\bar{I}$ would be missed. Therefore, the relative permit prices would have to be modified. In this procedure, the agency would have to go through an iterative process with uncertain ends, as in the case of the effluent charge policy.

Here, the problem of multiple optima arises: A local optimum occurs at $\hat{P}(\hat{X},\hat{Y})$ where an iso-abatement cost curve is tangent to the target curve $\bar{I}$. The global optimum, however, is in the corner P** with X = X**, Y = 0.
To avoid lenghthy considerations, below, the discussion is confined to the points different from the cases of linear and concave interaction.

5.1 Effluent charges

For the effluent charge policy the problems of the regulatory agency are not much different from the case of concave interaction, in the first place.
Starting in $P_1(X_1,Y_1)$, again, the agency will have to go through a process of "complicated trial and error" restructering the tax rates, as in the previous case. However, the process may end up in a situation $\hat{P}$, satisfying $t_X/t_Y = -(dY/dX)_{dI=0} = -(dY/dX)_{dC=0}$. As mentioned above, this situation may only qualify for a local optimum (and does so in the example of fig. 9). In this situation, there would be no reliable signal inherent to the tax policy indicating to the agency that it could do better than that.
There is, however, a "weak test" the agency may apply to check whether $\hat{P}$ is a global optimum or a local one, only:
If in $\hat{P}$, the tangency to $\bar{I}$ and to the iso-cost curve $\hat{C}$ (tangent to $\bar{I}$ in $\hat{P}$), is a separating line for $\hat{C}$ and $\bar{I}$, then the agency can be sure that $\hat{P}$ is the global optimum, since the iso-cost curves are known to be convex towards the X,Y-origin.
If this tangency does intersect $\bar{I}$, however, $\hat{P}$ may be a local or the global optimum. So meeting the separating line criterion is a sufficient but not a necessary condition for $\hat{P}$ to represent the global optimum.
This is illustrated in fig. 10:
If the constraint takes the form of $\bar{I}_a$, the tangency to $\hat{C}$ and $\bar{I}$ through $\hat{P}$ is a separating line. Therefore, $\hat{C}$ is identical to C**, the minimum cost compatible with the constraint.
If the constraint takes the form of $\bar{I}_b$ or $\bar{I}_c$ the tangency ceases to be a separating line. In the case of $\bar{I}_b$, $\hat{C}$ nevertheless represents the minimum cost compatible with the constraint. In the case of $\bar{I}_c$, however, the corner solution X_c^{**}, Y = 0 meets the constraint at a cost less than $\hat{C}$, making $\hat{P}$ an inferior local optimum.

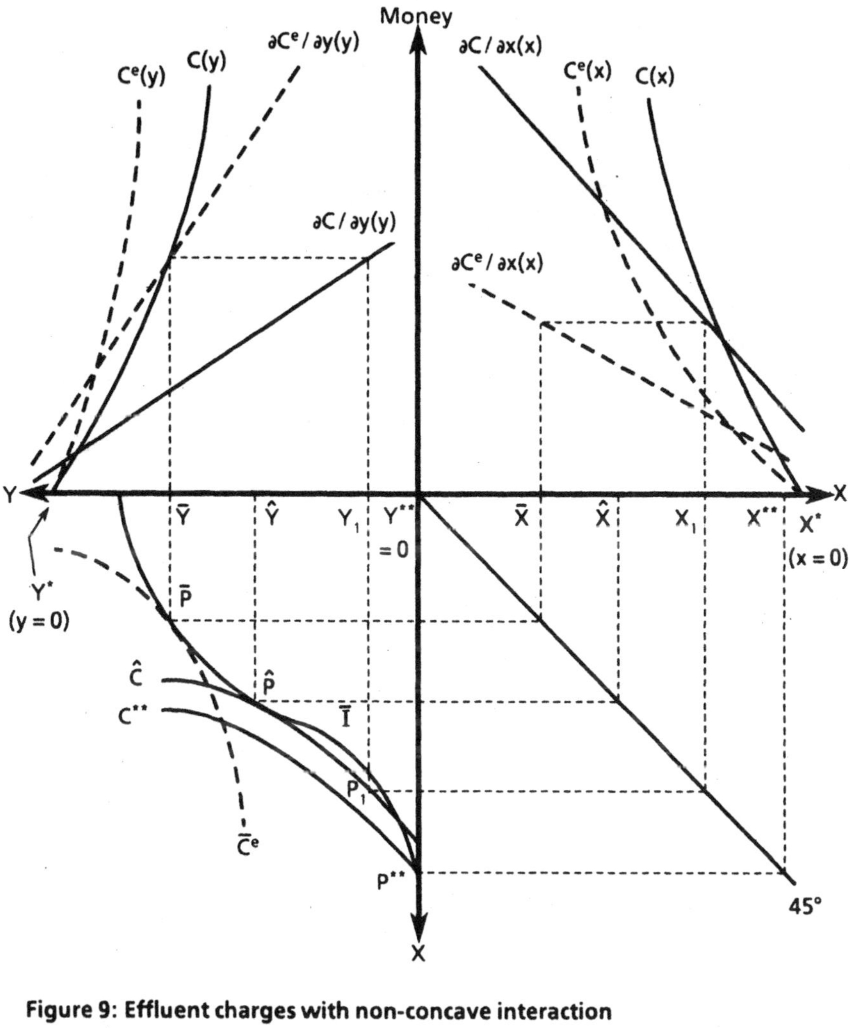

Figure 9: Effluent charges with non-concave interaction

It is interesting to note that it is not impossible to end up in the globally optimal corner solution P** after an iterative process of tax setting: Even though the

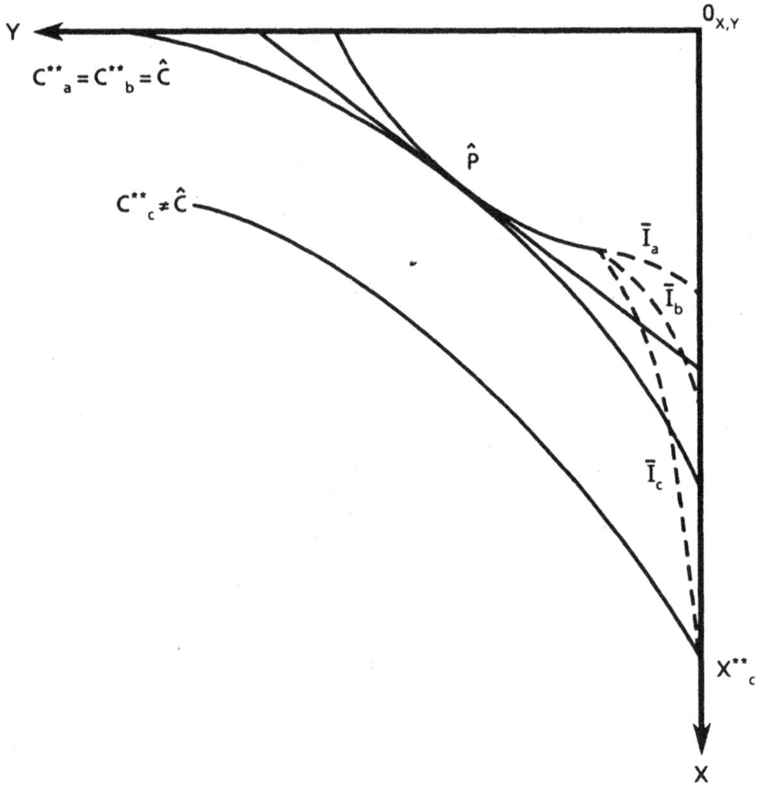

Figure 10: "Weak test" for global optimality

constraint is convex close to P**(X**,Y=0), the situation qualifies for an effluent charge equilibriuim. The appropriate tax rates are $t_Y \geq \partial C/\partial y(y=Y^*)$ and $t_X = \partial C/\partial x(x^{**})$. The reason for that result (perhaps surprising to some) is that marginal abatement costs are monotonely increasing for both industries (i.e., their attainable "emission reduction sets" are convex). In this case, any emission combination can be attained as an effluent charge equilibrium, if only the tax rates are set correctly.

On the other hand,it should be clear that there is no guarantee for the agency to find the global optimum in the process of restructering tax rates. It may well end up at the "wrong" optimum (if at any optimum at all). Finding the right one is the less likely the more local optima there are.

5.2 Transferable discharge permits

Fig. 11 illustrates the permit policy with non-concave interaction for the case of two pollutants X and Y. In the first quadrant of fig. 11, $\partial C/\partial y^T$ is the Y-industry's permit supply curve, as in the cases of linear and concave interactions. The curve

$$\frac{1}{\partial I^T/\partial X} \cdot \frac{\partial C}{\partial x}$$

indicating the permit demand curve in the previous cases, exhibits a downward sloping and an upward sloping part in the case of non-concave interaction as underlying here. The upward sloping part corresponds to the convex part of the constraint curve $\bar{I}$. Here, the amount of X-emissions equivalent to one unit of Y increases (as X increases), i.e. for the first factor of

$$\frac{1}{\partial I^T/\partial X} \cdot \frac{\partial C}{\partial x}, \quad \frac{\partial(1/\partial I^T/\partial X)}{\partial X} > 0$$

holds.

This tends to make the X-industry's marginal willingness to pay for a L-permit increase (as Y decreases (and X increases)). Of course, there is a countervailing effect in the sense of the marginal abatement cost increasing with x (decreasing with X) providing for $\partial^2 C/\partial x \partial X < 0$ for the second factor of

$$\frac{1}{\partial I^T/\partial X} \cdot \frac{\partial C}{\partial x}.$$

In the case considered here, however, the first tendency is supposed to overcompensate the second one. This makes the X-industry's marginal willingness to pay for permits increase with X, i.e

$$\frac{1}{(\partial I^T/\partial X)^2} \cdot \frac{\partial^2 I^T}{\partial X^2} = \frac{\partial C}{\partial x} + \frac{\partial^2 C}{\partial x \partial X} \cdot \frac{1}{\partial I^T/\partial X} > 0,$$

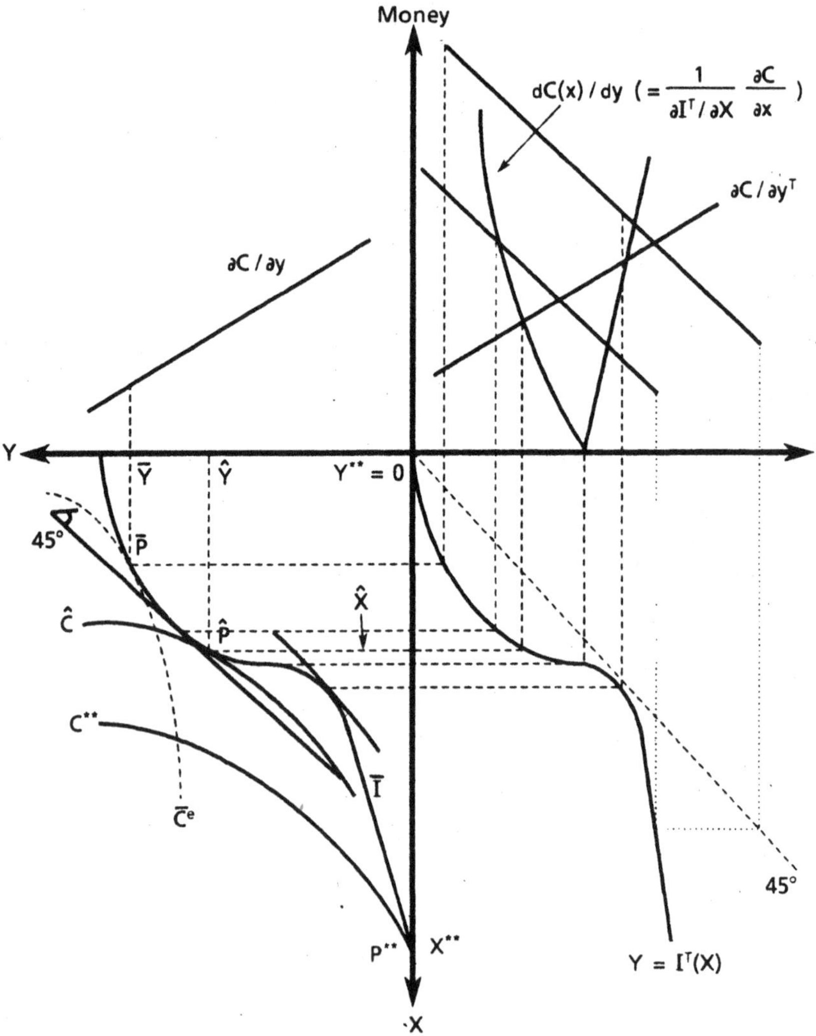

Figure 11: Transferable discharge permits with non-concave interaction

in the relevant section. Of course, the curve

$$\frac{1}{\partial I^T / \partial X} \cdot \frac{\partial C}{\partial x}.$$

represents the permit demand curve of the X-industry only in its downward sloping part. Moreover, to qualify for the demand curve, the points $(z^0 x^0)$ on this curve have to meet the total condition

$$\int_{x=0}^{x^0} \frac{1}{\partial I^T / \partial X} \frac{\partial C}{\partial x} dx \leq z^0 x^0,$$

where z^0 denotes the permit price.
The point, where

$$\frac{\partial C}{\partial y^T} = \frac{1}{\partial I^T / \partial X} \frac{\partial C}{\partial x}$$

holds, is identical to the local constraint cost minimum $\hat{P}(\hat{X},\hat{Y})$ meeting condition (6a). This point may violate the aforementioned total condition. Moreover, the global optimum $(X^{**}, Y=0)$ may not be an equilibrium in the permit market at all.
Therefore, the tradable permit policy possibly fails to attain the solution of the constrained cost minimization problem.

5.3 Command and control policy

So far, the command and control approach to environmental protection has not been mentioned in this paper. Using this policy, the regulatory agency specifies the maximum amount of emissions for each polluting industry. Each firm within each industry is assigned an individual share of the respective amount. There is no trading of emission rights and no charge for the emission units below the firm's limit. With this policy, all the agency can do is to assign the emission quantities $\bar{X}_1,...,\bar{X}_n$, thought to minimize the cost of meeting $\bar{I}$ to the n industries. Each quantity $\bar{X}_i$ would be distributed among the members of the i-industry according to what the agency thinks to be their marginal abatement costs.
By this procedure the agency could be sure that the environmental target $\bar{I}$ would be met. It would be unclear to the agency, however, what the efficiency sacrifices of that policy might be. If the agency would misjudge the marginal abatement costs of the n industries (as assumed for all policy alternatives, above), the environmental target would be attained at excessive cost.

Irrespective of interaction being linear, concave or non-concave, the command and control approach would not provide for any signal to the agency that it does the wrong thing, let alone what kind of a corrective should be taken.
The lack of any incentive for correction is a regretable property of the command and control policy whatever the type of pollutant interaction may be.
Thus, in addition to the general inability to assign efficient pollution limits to the firms within one polluting industry, well known in the literature, the command and control approach will generally be unable to assign efficient pollution limits among different polluting industries drawing upon the same capacity of the environment.

6. Summary

The possibilities to meet an interactive pollutant constraint at minimum cost have been considered. Effluent charges, transferable discharge permits and the (briefly mentioned) command and control strategy have been used to represent the environmental policy options.

It turned out that effluent charges are efficient in the case of linear pollutant interaction. The environmental policy constraint is met in an iterative process not more complicated than in the case of no pollutant interaction, as analyzed traditionally in the literature. Given concave interaction, charges are still efficient but the trial and error process towards meeting the environmental policy target is more complicated than in the linear case. In the case of non-concave interaction providing for the possibility of multiple optima the complicated trial and error process may even end up missing the global optimum. Then, effluent charges would stop being an efficient means of environmental policy.
Tradeable emission permits will always guarantee that the environmental target is met. In addition, they are an efficient means of environmental policy in the cases of linear and concave interaction. With non-concave interaction, however, they may loose the efficiency property.

The environmental target can savely be attained by a command and control strategy. In general, however, this strategy will be inefficient, regardless of the form of pollutant interaction.

References

Baumol, W.J., Oates, W.E.(1975), *The Theory of Environmental Policy*, Englewood Cliffs

Beavis, B., and Walker M. (1979), "Interactive pollutants and joint abatement costs: Achieving water quality standards with effluent charges, "*Journal of Environmental Economics and Management*, 275-286

Bonus, H. (1976), "Möglichkeiten der Internalisierung externer Effekte als Instrument der Koordinierung von Unternehmenszielen und gesellschaftlichen Zielen", *Schriften des Vereins für Socialpolitik*, N.F., Bd. 88, 207-226

Burrows, P. (1979), *The Economic Theory of Pollution Control*, Oxford

Dreyhaupt, F.J. (1971), *Luftreinhaltung als Faktor der Stadt- und Regionalplanung*, Köln

Endres, A. (1985), *Umwelt- und Ressourcenökonomie*, Darmstadt

Green, A.E.S. et al. (1980), "Factors and safety method - Application to air and noise pollution," *Atmospheric Environment*, 327-338

Mäler, K.-G. (1974), *Environmental Economics: A Theoretical Inquiry*, Baltimore and London

Pethig, R. (1979), *Umweltökonomische Allokation mit Emissionssteuern*, Tübingen

Siebert, H. (1981), *Economics of the Environment*, Lexington, Mass.

Sprague, J.B. (1970), "Measurement of pollutant toxicity to fish", *Water Research*, 3-32

Alternative Allocation Procedures for Public Goods: Towards a Comparative Analysis?*

by
Wolfgang Blümel

1. Introduction

The slogan "market versus politics" raises the question whether private or political actions are superior modes of resource allocation. Historically, this issue played a prominent role far beyond the economic profession, and the discussion is still going on. Consider, for instance, the debate on deregulation aimed at revitalizing private market activities or on (re-)privatization of economic activities actually provided through political means. Also the general dispute on the size of government in a market economy points to the above question.

In this paper we do not focus on the broad issue of the "growth of government", but rather on allocation procedures for a set of goods - namely public goods (to be specified below), for which various modes of allocation have been applied, both over time and across countries. There are politicians as well as economists who firmly believe in the superiority of one or the other allocative scheme. We take the view, instead, that comparative merits of allocation procedures cannot be delineated unless one applies systematic economic analysis and general normative criteria. It is the objective of this paper to investigate the contributions of various theoretical approaches and criteria to the normative comparison of alternative allocation procedures for public goods. Is there a well-founded comparative analysis suitable for guiding decision-making in public allocation policy?

* This paper is part of the author's research program of the "Sonderforschungsbereich 5 der DFG: Staatliche Allokationspolitik im marktwirtschaftlichen System" at the University of Mannheim. I am indebted to Rüdiger Pethig for his substantial help. I also wish to thank Oskar von dem Hagen for helpful comments and Sylvelie Hartig for editing the English style. However, all remaining errors are in the author's responsibility.

Since the definition of public goods has led to considerable confusion in the professional literature, the subsequent use of the notion of public goods has to be clarified. Public goods are defined as jointly consumable goods in the sense that the same unit of such a good can be simultaneously consumed by at least two consumers (cf. Blümel/Pethig/von dem Hagen 1984). In our view, joint consumability is the constitutive characteristic of public goods. Moreover, there are accessory attributes generating certain subclasses of public goods such as excludability, congestability, or rejectability. Since market and non-market allocation is to be compared, excludability will be of some interest for our analysis.[1] Observe that the above characterization of public goods means that "publicness" does not imply its non-market provision (institution-oriented definition of public goods, cf. Buchanan 1968). The term "public" refers to what public goods are, but not by which means they are provided. The institution-free definition of public goods is adopted here because it is analytically convenient for an evaluation of comparative merits of alternative allocation procedures.

In what follows, we discuss different lines of economic theory trying to evaluate and to compare markets and political allocation procedures for public goods. In section 2 the well-known Pareto-efficiency concept will be applied for comparative purposes, which is the usual view taken by both new welfare economics and welfare politics. It is shown that markets as well as politics generally fail to allocate public goods in a Pareto-efficient way, thus impeding meaningful economic policy recommendations - at least on an a-priori basis. Section 3 is devoted to even more comprehensive approaches using multiple performance criteria for comparisons. To some extent, we deal with Hurwicz's normative theory of allocation mechanisms which, in many respects, goes beyond new welfare economics. Though this theory leads to some important general insights, it fails to provide concrete and empirically useful results. This directs our attention in section 4 to two recent developments focusing on different, rather special lines of arguments for drawing conclusions about the comparative merits of allocative schemes. First, the theory of property rights is considered as emphasizing the relationship between different property rights assignments, individual incentives, and economic outcomes. Then we examine the theory of

1) For more details as to the various attributes of public goods see Blümel/Pethig/von dem Hagen (1984).

economic institutions, which investigates transaction costs within a framework of contractual relations between agents. Concluding remarks are left to section 5.

2. Pareto Efficiency as the Measuring Rod of Comparison

While new welfare economics studies and evaluates the outcomes of markets, welfare politics and public choice theory analyzes political allocation procedures. The criterion for evaluation is, in general, the ideal scale of Pareto efficiency. Here we do not intend to give a comprehensive overview about this kind of analysis, but with the help of selected examples we will show how markets and politics perform in public-goods provision, if Pareto efficiency is the common measuring rod.

2.1 Private provision of public goods

2.1.1 *Non-exclusive allocation procedures*

Consider a public good, the potential consumer of which cannot be excluded at reasonable costs, or where, for whatever reason, the exclusion principle is not applied. If such a good is to be provided privately, it is difficult to charge a positive price since consumers have a strong incentive to "free ride". It does not follow, however, that zero-provision of that public good is the only conceivable outcome under these conditions. One way to cope with non-coercive allocation of non-exclusive public goods is the so-called "subscription procedure" proposed by Buchanan (1968) and Malinvaud (1972).

Consider an economy with one private and one public consumption good. Let us denote individual i's quasi-concave utility function by $u^i = U^i(x^i, z^i)$, where x^i and z^i are the quantities of the private and public good respectively, consumed by individual i. Each individual has a positive endowment y^i of the private good (income), and the public good is produced and sold at constant marginal costs p_z. Finally, denote by s^i the amount of public good that is bought by individual i. Since the public good is non-exclusive, we have $z^i = z := \Sigma_j s^j$ (for all i), whereas agent i's expenditure on the public good is $p_z s^i$. Depending on the agent's behaviour, this procedure yields different outcomes.

(1) If agent i determines the amount of the public good he wishes to purchase, taking into account the quantity bought by the other individuals, then agent i's decision problem is to maximize $U^i(y^i - p_z s^i,\ \Sigma_{j\neq i} s^j + s^i)$ over s^i for alternatively given s^j $(j \neq i)$. In this case an interior solution satisfies

$$(1) \qquad MRS^i = p_z \qquad (i = 1, \ldots, n),$$

where MRS^i is the marginal rate of substitution between total public-good consumption and the private good or the individual marginal willingness-to-pay for the public good.

Equation (1) holds for every set of strategies s^j $(j \neq i)$, in particular in a Nash equilibrium, called "subscription equilibrium" by Malinvaud (1972) or "independent adjustment equilibrium" by Buchanan (1968). According to (1), each agent selects his expenses by equating his own MRS to p_z, as if the public good were a private good. Summation of (1) over all individuals gives us $\Sigma_i MRS^i = np_z$. As compared with Samuelson's (1954) efficiency condition, it is evident that the subscription procedure implies a Pareto-inefficient provision of public goods. Though it is generally argued that an underprovision occurs (cf. Malinvaud 1972, p. 214), an overprovision is also possible.

(2) Suppose that all consumers' marginal willingness-to-pay is smaller than p_z. Then nobody will voluntarily pay for that good ("no-contribution" behaviour). If, regardless of the other agents's behavior, everybody tries to take a "free-ride" by expecting to consume the public good free of charge, the result is a prisoner's dilemma situation such that the public good is not provided at all. This is, in general, Pareto inefficient ($\Sigma_i MRS^i > p_z$).

(3) If all individuals act according to a special conjectural variation hypothesis, for instance, that each agent behaves as he wants the others to behave ("Kantian behavior"), then under certain qualifications Pareto efficiency through voluntary contributions is achieved (cf. Cornes/Sandler 1984). However, we consider such a behavorial assumption to be implausible so that the general conclusion seems to be that the unfettered market fails to achieve a Pareto-efficient allocation ("market failure").

So far, "market failure" was derived from non-cooperative behavior. It is now a natural question to ask whether the opposite behavioral pattern, namely cooperation, can be expected to improve the voluntary and non-regulated provision of non-exclusive public goods. It is clearly beyond the scope of the present paper to give an adequate review of the relationship between efficiency and bargaining for non-exclusive public goods. However, a few remarks are in order. One approach, centering around but reaching beyond the contribution of Coase (1960), is the optimistic bargaining theorem (Cooter 1982, p.15n.) or, for short, the Pangloss Theorem (cf. Culyer 1984). It asserts, roughly, that all bargaining games reach efficient solutions. To get an idea of "proof", suppose that this proposition is wrong, i.e. that there are mutual gains form bargaining for at least two parties. Then self-interest leads the agents to continue the bargaining process until all mutual advantages are exhausted. The polar opposite is the pessimistic bargaining theorem called Hobbes Theorem by Cooter (1982, p.18).[2] Its thrust is that bargaining games have, in general, non-cooperative and hence suboptimal outcomes, irrespective of transaction costs because the players cannot solve the problem of distributing the surplus resulting from cooperation. In case of non-excludable public goods the distribution problem is essentially the problem of cost sharing which gives rise to the prisoner's dilemma. Probably none of these polar cases comes close to the truth, but, in our view, some degree of allocative inefficiency seems to be inevitable in bargaining for non-exclusive public goods as, for example, Olson's (1965) theory of group formation suggests.

To summarize, voluntary actions without public regulation will generally result in a Pareto-inefficient provision of non-exclusive public goods. The theory leaves us, however, with substantial vagueness as to the degreee of inefficiency.

---

2) See also Buchanan (1984).

2.1.2 Exclusive allocation procedures

Now consider the case of private provision of public goods when exclusion is applicable at negligible costs. Here, too, the literature provides diverse procedures leading to different outcomes. Those suggested by Thompson (1968), Demsetz (1970), and Oakland (1974) are the most prominent and hence will be briefly reviewed in the sequel.

In Thompson's model, exclusive public goods are oversupplied because competitive firms know each consumer's demand function and are able to perfectly price-discriminate between consumers. In Demsetz' model, the firms' informations are slightly different. Each consumer's true marginal willingness-to-pay is known. Thus firms are able to charge individualized (Lindahl) prices for that public good. Hence, Pareto efficiency is achieved. In either case, however, it is open to question how firms manage to have or acquire complete information about strictly private preferences (cf. Head 1977, Endres 1981).[3]

This informational assumption is not applied by Oakland (1974) who assumes the public-good supplier to be incompletely informed about the demand for public goods. In this model, average costs of the public goods, say p_z, are assumed to be constant. Then the pricing rule is such that, if for some amount of the public good there are n consumers whose marginal willingness-to-pay for the last increment of the good is greater than or equal to p_z/n, then this amount is sold to them at $p^i_z := p_z/n$ $(i=1,\dots,n)$ per unit. At this quantity only the (marginal) consumers whose MRS coincides with p_z/n are fully satisfied while the higher-demand consumers would like to buy a larger amount of public good. Consesquently, we have $\Sigma_i MRS^i > p_z$, violating, of course, the condition for Pareto efficiency. The public-good quantity will be raised as long as there are enough agents willing to pay for additional quantities, where the lower-demand agents will gradually be excluded. At equilibrium the provision of exclusive public goods is generally

3) In our view, allocation procedures based on such an informational requirement must be classified as informationally infeasible in the sense of Hurwicz (1972). See also section 3.

suboptimal.[4] The allocative inefficiency is not only manifest in an undersupply of public goods (production inefficiency) but also in an underconsumption by exclusion (consumption inefficiency). In concept, the excluded agents could be admitted to consumption at no extra costs which would make them better off. Hence, a Pareto-superior allocation is attainable, since nobody else suffers a loss in utility.

To sum up, new welfare economics deduces "market failure" in private provision of non-exclusive and exclusive public goods. The methodology is to employ Pareto efficiency as the ideal scale for comparison. The principle barriers to attain allocative efficiency in private provision of public goods are related to both individual incentives and information. Consequently, these causes of market deficiencies may be labeled "failure by signals" (i.e. information) and "failure by incentives" (Bator 1958).

2.2 Political provision of public goods

In contrast to our procedure in section 2.1.2, we restrict our subsequent analysis to non-exclusive allocation procedures in the sense that either non-excludable public goods are allocated, or if we deal with excludable public goods, the procedure is such that the exclusion principle is not applied.[5] The principle reasons for non-exclusion are distributional objectives of policy makers, the avoidance of consumption inefficiencies, or high exclusion costs. Zero-price provision of public goods is tantamount to financing them by tax revenues. Although this bears allocative consequences, they will not be discussed in the present paper.[6] In what follows, we will focus our attention on voting procedures and on bureaucratic allocation schemes.

---

4) Note, a Pareto optimum z^* is attainable if the highest demander's MRS is equal to p_z and if, in addition, the others' MRS is zero. Conversely, if at any given quantity of public good the MRS of the corresponding lowest demander is smaller than the unit price necessary to cover costs, only a zero-provision is feasible. Hence, in Oakland's model the range of public-good allocations is $[0,z^*]$, depending on assumption on preferences and costs (cf. Head 1977).

5) We realize that there is ample evidence for the application of the exclusion principle in political allocation procedures (e.g. public swimming pools, public opera houses etc.), but for comparative purposes, non-exclusion is the more controversial aspect of political provision.

6) For allocative consequences distortionary taxation results in, see Atkinson/Stiglitz (1980), for example.

2.2.1 *Voting on public goods*

The specific problem for voting on public goods is that voters have to decide collectively on the provision of one particular quantity, whereas in the case of private goods everyone can freely choose a quantity representing his best "fit" as to both his preferences and income. The efficiency properties of voting procedures are our major concern. Since efficiency cannot be discussesd unless consistent outcomes are secured, we will subsequently use a framework of analysis guaranteeing the existence of a voting equilibrium. Moreover, we will side-step the strategic aspects of voting for a moment.[7]

Consider an economy[8] in which individuals consume one private and one public good. The public good is produced at constant marginal costs p_z and is financed by levying an income tax with a proportional tax rate t. Each individual's preferences are represented by a quasi-concave utility function $u^i = U^i(x^i,z)$ where x^i and z denote i's consumption of the private and public good respectively. His budget constraint reads $x^i + ty^i \leq y^i$, where y^i is i's predetermined income. The public expenditure on the public good is $p_z z$, so that the government's balanced-budget condition reads $p_z z = tY$ with $Y := \Sigma_i y^i$. We substitute $t = p_z z/Y$ from the government's budget constraint into the individual budget constraint to obtain $x^i + p_z z(y^i/Y) \leq y^i$. Assuming non-satiation, this constraint holds as an equality. Hence x^i is a function of z which makes utility $u^i = U^i[y^i - p_z z(y^i/Y), z]$ a single-peaked function of z alone.[9]

Now consider simple majority voting.[10] It can be shown that a majority voting

---

7) A large bulk of literature has addressed the existence problem of voting procedures (cf. Gaertner 1978) and, moreover, the strategic problems involved (cf. Feldman 1979). Both problems are surveyed in Kramer (1977) and Mueller (1979).

8) For related models including more technical details, see Bernholz/Breyer (1984) and Slutsky (1977).

9) Cf. Bergstrom (1979). In the case of one-dimensional policy spaces, single peakedness is a sufficient conditon for a voting equilibrium to exist.

10) Of course, the simple majority rule is only a special, but widely used, democratic decision rule. The pertaining conditions for the existence of voting equilibria with arbitrary majority sizes are given by Greenberg (1979).

eqilibrium exists which is a public-good proposal unbeaten by any other proposal in simple majority voting. Moreover, this equilibrium allocation coincides with that particular allocation representing the most preferred allocation of the median of all the voters. At this so-called median voter allocation, the first-order condition net of cost reads (m for median)

$$MRS^{m} = p_{z}(y^{m}/Y). \tag{2}$$

Under fairly general conditions (e.g. differences in incomes, preferences, and tax shares among individuals) equation (2) is not satisfied for any individual except for the median voter. Thus, a majority voting equilibrium fails to be Pareto efficient, unless at the equilibrium quantity every voter's utility happens to attain its maximum.[11] However, there is no systematic bias whether public goods are undersupplied or oversupplied (cf. Slutsky 1977, Atkinson/Stiglitz 1980).

Observe that the misallocation results whether or not policy makers try to achieve allocative efficiency. In different informational settings, however, inefficiency may arise from the policy makers' incentive to pursue their own goals which may be manifold. In a particularly interesting case inefficiency, say, oversupply of a group-specific public good, works , in fact, as a transfer for an interest group which turns out to be voting-decisive. In any case, the associated inefficiency will be classified as "political failure".[12]

---

11) A Pareto optimum would also be achievable if one imposes a special symmetry assumption as to the distribution of the MRS. Cf. Bergstrom (1979) and section 2.3 below. Shubik (1968) claims that Pareto-efficient voting equilibria could be attained if the assumption of uniform tax rates across individuals is dropped. Bernholz/Breyer (1984, pp.279-281) show, however, that with individualized tax rates on income voting equilibria do not exist any more. Therefore Shubik's result is empty.

12) The literature on "political failure", "government(al) failure", "public (sector) inefficiency", and "non-market failure" is a still growing field of economic research. As compared to "old-fashioned" reasonings on "market failure", the deduction of "political failure" is rather new. For more comprehensive details the reader is referred to:
McKean (1965), McKean /Browning (1975), White (1976), Recktenwald (1978, 1983), Rowley (1978), Weisbrod (1978), Wolf (1979), Peacock (1980), Haveman (1980), Rosenschon (1980), Hanusch (1982, 1983), Blümel (1983), Brennan/Buchanan (1983), Wille (1983), Frey (1983), Wellicz/Wilson (1984).

2.2.2 Implementation of voting outcomes

Once a public-good platform is accepted by majority vote it must be implemented. The literature on voting presupposes voting outcome to be executed automatically, in an unmodified way, and without cost (cf. Mueller 1979). Such an assumption is naive in that it overlooks various sources of malperformance arising in the implementation process itself. To a large extent, the public choice literature focuses specifically on the problem of how a public bureaucracy uses its discretion in order to pursue its own objectives which do not necessarily support the implementation of the voting outcome (cf. Blankart 1975, Orzechowsky 1977, Roppel 1979).

Consider a public administration that is assigned to provide the economy with some amount of a public good. From the board of trustees the bureau receives a budget B to cover its production costs $c = C(z)$. The cost function is specified as follows: $C(0) = 0, C_z > 0, C_{zz} > 0$.[13] The trustees are supposed to know the voters' total benefit (or willingness-to-pay) $u = U(z)$ with $U(0) = 0, U_z > 0, U_{zz} < 0$.[14]

Firstly suppose that the trustees are perfectly informed about the bureau's cost function. Then they choose z such that the social net benefit (consumers' surplus) $U(z) - C(z)$ is maximized, and assign the budget $B = C(z)$ to the bureau. The straightforward result is that the public good is efficiently provided. In this setting the head of the bureau or the chief-administrator has no influence on the outcome whether his objectives coincide with those of the board of trustees or do not.

However, now consider the case where no information about the production costs of the public good is available outside of the bureau. In such a setting the chief-administrator's objective function is obviously crucial for the outcome. As in Migué/Bélanger (1974), suppose that the chief-administrator has a quasi-concave

13) Partial derivatives are denoted as follows: $\partial C/\partial z := C_z, \partial^2 C/\partial z^2 := C_{zz}$ etc.

14) This assumption is made for simplicity and should be appropriately relaxed in more realistic models to reflect private information on preferences.

utility function $u = V[B-C(z), z]$ with positive partial derivatives.[15] In other words, the greater the budget surplus and the greater the output of his bureau, the better off is the bureau's head. Therefore the chief-administrator's decision problem is to maximize his utility over B and z subject to $B \leq U(z)$. For an interior solution the first-order conditions yield

$$(3) \qquad U_z < C_z,$$
$$(4) \qquad B = U(z).$$

Due to equation (4) the chief-administrator selects a budget which leaves the voters without any consumer surplus. He appropriates the entire surplus for both an oversupply of public goods as shown by equation (3) and a budget surplus.[16] In this way the production becomes X-inefficient. If the rather extreme and hence implausible assumption on asymmetric information is relaxed, the bureaucratic outcome is likely to remain Pareto inefficient, but the inefficiency may be slightly reduced (Spencer 1980). This allocative deficiency clearly constitutes "political failure" in a broad sense. Since it is associated with some malfunctioning of public bureaucracies it is properly denoted as "bureaucratic failure" (cf. e.g. Frey 1983).

In summary, "welfare politics" or "mathematical politics" (Samuelson 1967b) in conjunction with public choice theory puts forward various lines of argument diagnosing "political failure" in the provision of public goods. As in the welfare economic analysis of market procedures, here too, Pareto efficiency is the ideal measuring scale.

For the theory of public goods it is convenient to think of "political failure" and "market failure" as complementary pieces of theory because rather similar

15) Of course, the chief-administrator's utility function can be specified quite differently. The most prominent model of bureaucracy is that of Niskanen (1971). Here the chief-administrator's objective function is $u = V(z)$. As a result, the largest budget is spent, the public good is oversupplied, but cost-efficiently produced. Another polar case is the management-slack model of Williamson (1963), in which the objective function reads $u = V[B-C(z)]$. Though a Pareto-efficient level of the public good is produced, the allocation is cost-inefficient due to X-inefficiency. For more details see Blümel/Pethig/von dem Hagen (1984).

16) It is implicitly assumed that the chief-administrator will use all his surplus for non-productive, but utility-generating expenses such as overstaffing, furniture, the reduction of working effort, etc.

barriers for efficiency arise in either case (cf. Blümel 1983). The first reason for "political failure" is due to the monopoly-like position policy makers and public bureaucracies are endowed with (cf. Arrow 1969, Mueller 1979). In Bator's (1958) terminology this phenomenon is called "failure by structure". In addition, there is "failure by information". One aspect of this failure is that simple majority voting does not provide all information necessary for Pareto efficiency (cf. Slutsky 1977). Moreover, due to the costs associated to voting and information processing, too small a level of information is made available (cf. Weisbrod 1978). Finally, there is "failure by incentives" due to weak (or lacking) individual incentives to reveal their true preferences (cf. Green/Laffont 1979). As a result, preferences are misrepresented and this, in turn, causes informational distortions.

2.3 Deviations from Pareto efficiency - what is the message?

Which are the consequences public allocation policy should draw from market and political "failures"? On the one hand, there are welfare theorists, most notably Musgrave (1959), for whom "market failure" provides the dominant justification for allocating public goods through political means. On the other hand, there are economists, in particular some of those working in the field of public choice, for whom "political failure" is considered a sufficient reason to shift an economic activity completely from the political into the market sector. Since each group recommends just the opposite allocation procedure to the remedy for observed or derived inefficiency, one is obviously committing a fallacy. The failure of one procedure is erroneously taken as a sufficient conditon for the comparative advantage of the other. According to Stigler (1975) this fallacy is the same as that of a Roman emperor who was judging a musical contest between two musicians and declared the second player the winner, after having only heard the first.

This kind of normative conclusion has been criticized by various economists in different contexts (cf. Little 1957, Coase 1964, Kapp 1965, Demsetz 1969). In particular, the welfare economic recommendations due to "market failure" have been definitely rejected. The reproach was that welfare economics, denoted as "deductive criticism of markets", involves an "a-priori bias toward political interventionism" (Windisch 1980), and that it almost unconditionally favours political allocation procedures. Demsetz (1969) expressed his objections by blaming welfare economics for employing a "nirvana approach" (p.1). In our view this criticism is valid as far as it refers to the argument that political allocation is superior because market allocation falls short of Pareto efficiency. However, the normative recommendations deduced from "political failure" are questionable, too. In fact, the "deductive criticism" of political allocation schemes may just create an "inverse nirvana approach", thus providing an "a-priori bias" toward unregulated market activities.

How can one avoid this dilemma or confusion without loading an undue share of the blame upon welfare economics and the neoclassical line of reasoning? The answer is that it is not the theoretical concept for the evaluation of allocation procedures, but the erroneous normative conclusions which are correctly - and/or should be - subject to the preceding criticism. Pareto inferiority of one procedure only constitutes a necessary condition for its comparative inefficiency. Once any "failure" is diagnosed, alternative procedures have to be scrutinized, which may or may not turn out to be less inefficient.

One may suggest calling an allocation procedure for public goods comparatively Pareto efficient if its outcome is either Pareto efficient or if there is no other Pareto-inefficient procedure whose outcome is Pareto superior. Such a definition seems to be unsatisfactory, however, because in a world of second best many Pareto-inefficient procedures may be Pareto incomparable and hence comparatively Pareto efficient. Moreover, the theoretical frameworks used to deduce "market failure" and "political failure" respectively, are, in general, far too diverse as to draw conclusions about whether an inefficient market allocation is Pareto superior to an inefficient policy allocation.

Whenever a common theoretical basis is available, efficieny comparisons are viable, at least conceptually. For illustrative purposes, let us try to determine the comparative efficiency of the private subscription equilibrium and the political median voter allocation.[17)] Therefore recall the marginal conditions represented in equations (1) and (2) and compare them with Samuelson's efficiency condition ($\Sigma_i MRS^i = p_z$). We argued in section 2.1.1 that, since equation (1) implies $\Sigma_i MRS^i = np_z$, an inefficient supply of the public good occurs. Now suppose that in the

17) A related comparison is realized by Bernholz/Breyer (1984).

economy under consideration the preference and the income distribution are such that the median of individuals' MRS and their incomes respectively equals the mean. Then summing equation (2) over all individuals gives us $\Sigma_i MRS^i = p_z$, thus a Pareto-efficient voting allocation (cf. Bergstrom 1979, p.218; Green/Laffont 1979, p. 253). Hence voting is the comparatively and absolutely Pareto-efficient allocation procedure.[18] Of course, due to the extremely restrictive assumptions our comparison is definitely a special case hard to generalize. One may conjecture that gradual relaxation of the above assumptions will leave the corresponding voting outcome probably closer to Pareto efficiency than the subscription equilibrium.[19] However, we do not know of any rigorous investigation in the literature that confirms such a conjecture or, more generally, that derives an unambigous Pareto-efficiency ranking of market and political schemes with public goods for a reasonably large class of economies.

On the conceptual level one would like to have a metric scale that allows us to determine and hence to compare the "distance" of two Pareto-inefficient allocations from Pareto efficiency. Compensation criteria or test are one way of doing this; Bergsonian welfare functions are another "solution". However, we do not consider these two formal approaches for "solving" distributional questions helpful for efficiency comparisons. So what are we left with if we stick to Paretian welfare economics? Apparently we cannot make conclusive policy recommendations for allocation procedures with public goods. A-priori arguments neither determine the governmental role - as Samuelson (1967a) already emphasized - nor do they assign a well-founded role to markets. It seems that the only way to support political decision-making is by means of case studies on the basis of applied welfare economics or cost-benefit analysis (cf. Haveman 1980, Buchanan 1983, Vogelsang 1983).[20]

---

18) Observe that the pareto-inefficient voluntary-adjustment allocation need not be Pareto inferior to the Pareto-efficient voting allocation. In this case, on its introduction the voting procedure would not be unanimously accepted in a constitutional vote.

19) This result still holds true when a zero-provision is achieved by private activities.

20) Observe, however, that cost-benefit analysis is bound to deal with distributinal issues either explicitly or implicitly, and thus it has a closer affinity to the welfare-function approach than to Paretian welfare economics.

3. Performance Comparisons by Means of Multiple Criteria

In order to overcome the inconclusiveness of the Pareto-efficiency concept as shown in the preceding section and in order to escape the fallacy of nirvana-like conclusions, in the sequel we will try to give a description of a "multiple-criteria concept of comparison" in the sense of a more comprehensive comparative analysis of alternative allocation procedures with public goods. For years several economists (e.g. McKean 1965, Tullock 1970) have asked for such an analysis called "comparative institution approach" by Demsetz (1969, p. 1). More recently, this demand has been renewed and reinforced, for example, by Slutsky (1977), Blankart (1980), Haveman (1980), Frey (1981), Hauser (1981), Hanusch (1981), Vogelsang (1983), Buchanan (1983), and McCaleb (1983).

The theory of resource allocation mechanisms as developed by Hurwicz (1972), in particular, may be viewed as a fairly adequate "multiple-criteria comparison" for alternative allocation procedure. Hurwicz aims at extending new welfare economics which is preoccupied with efficiency statements about the outcome of allocative schemes. He proposes, instead, to direct attention to allocation procedures themselves [21] and to evaluate and to compare them with respect to four distinct properties (desiderata): Pareto-satisfactoriness, operational costs [22], informational feasibility (or informational efficiency), and (indiviudual or group) incentive compatibility.[23] Performance in the sense of relative efficiency of outcomes is but one of these properties, and not necessarily the most important one.

There is no doubt that such a "multiple-criteria approach" promises to be more adequate for comparative analysis than the isolated "old-fashioned" Pareto

21) Quite appropriately, this extended normative theory of economic systems has been called "(new)"^{2} welfare economics" by Reiter (1977).

22) Analytically Hurwicz (1972) makes some brief remarks about transaction costs as a crucial property of allocative schemes. However, they are not the central point in his analysis.

23) This is, of course, a subjective selection of desiderata. Other important aspects of allocative schemes may be the speed and accuracy of the informational processing system, economic growth, full employment, individual liberty, distributional justice and so forth. Observe, however, that with a rising number of performance criteria a comparative general survey becomes more and more difficult.

criterion. In order to be more specific about Hurwicz's framework of analysis, consider an economy in which agents are characterized by their preferences, technologies, and initial endowments. Since preferences are strictly private information, the agents must communicate in order to coordinate their economic activities. If information exchange comes to an end (equilibrium), the final set of messages is translated into an outcome which represents, in the context of the present paper, a public-good allocation. Technically, an allocation mechanism or procedure in our terminology is a triple composed of a message space, a response function, and an outcome function.[24]

In what follows, we will consecutively discuss the proposed four distinct desiderata from the perspective of a comparative analysis.

(1) Pareto satisfactoriness. At the cost of some simplification an allocation procedure is said to be Pareto satisfactory if its outcome is Pareto efficient. This concept is clearly not innovative since the Pareto criterion that evaluates allocations is simply translated to become a property of allocation procedures. Previously we have already been working on the Pareto-efficiency concept in great detail, and we have shown its inconclusiveness with regard to comparative efficiency. Thus, this issue needs no further elaboration here. There is, however, a crucial relationship between the efficiency of allocation procedures and the costs required to operate the procedures, which has to be explained next.

(2) Operational costs. The extention to Pareto satisfactoriness would be by no means trivial if the specific "running costs" (Arrow 1969) or "operational costs" (Hurwicz 1972) of alternative procedures received explicit analytical consideration. Conceptually, this can of course be done within Hurwicz's framework, but the main body of allocation theory still proceeds with the implicit or explicit assumption of zero transaction costs.[25] Unfortunately, transaction

24) Cf. Hurwicz (1972), Reiter (1977). For a compact review of these concepts, see Seidl (1978) and Pethig (1979, pp.137-151).

25) Transaction costs broadly conceived "represent resource losses due to lack of information" (Dahlman 1979, p.148). This includes search and information costs, bargaining and decision costs, policing and enforcement costs.

costs are often thought of as a verbal appendix to otherwise formal theories. There is clearly a wide consent as to the necessity of considering operational costs. However, there does not seem to be an easy way to incorporate them into the analysis.

These kinds of specific resources required to operate the allocation procedure of course reduce the consumption possibilities in an economy, thus affecting the individuals' well-being. Conceptually, an allocation procedure can be viewed as a production process (cf. Reiter 1977) whoses inputs are traditional productive factors as well as procedure-specific resources which produce the output for "substantive purposes". It follows that in an economy with a given endowment of resources and technologies, the comparative efficiency of alternative allocation procedures is determined by the respective ranking of the consumption allocation associated to their outcomes. But note that increasing operational costs do not logically imply Pareto-inferior consumption allocations. It is conceivable that low operating costs of a procedure coincide with a severe misallocation of public goods so that the advantage of low running costs could be overcompensated by foregone public-good consumption.

In order to get an idea of the difficulty of comparing operational or transaction costs, let us choose a much less abstract level of analysis and try to compare the "running" costs for the market provision of an exclusive and positively priced public good with the costs of operating tax-financed and zero-priced political provision of the same public good. Market provision causes exclusion costs, taking the form of resources needed for both technological devices to prevent non-purchasers from consuming that public good (e.g. fences) and for enforcement activities (e.g. supervisory persons). Exclusion costs depend on various, rather complex institutional, technical, and economic factors. Thus sometimes they are small; but medium or high at other times.

While free political provision of public goods involves no exclusion costs, it causes various kinds of administrative costs. For example, administrative expenses are due to voting and to tax collection and they depend on voting schemes as well as the modes of taxation.[26] It is obvious from the preceding sketchy comparison of

26) If, moreover, public goods are congestible and if there is non-satiation, zero-price political provision may lead that public good to be congested or crowded. Since congestion shrinks the quality of that public good, consumers get a loss in utility. See Blümel/Pethig/von dem Hagen (1984).

transaction costs that no clear-cut efficiency judgement can be made on an a-priori basis. At the first glance, an unambiguous market advantage seems to be deducible if one assumes that in each case the same amount of public good is supplied and that exclusion costs are negligible, whereas administrative costs in the case of public provision are not. But even under these rather special qualifications, the respective consumption allocation may not be Pareto comparable. On the one hand, there is clearly a reduction in private-good consumption due to administrative costs, but on the other hand, some individual suffer under market provision by being excluded from public -good consumption.

Operating costs may also take the form of excessive production costs as suggested by the economic theory of bureaucracy in the case of public production. This X-inefficiency arises from the bureaus' informational advantages and monopoly-like position, freeing them from competitive pressure towards cost-minimization. If private markets of public goods satisfy the model of perfect competition, political provision would be clearly inferior. However, markets are not necessarily competitive and private manager-firms are not perfectly monitored (cf. Marris/Mueller 1980). To the degree that there is also market X-inefficiency, the comparative merit of markets is offset or even reversed.

(3) Informational feasibility. Since information on individual preferences is considered private information, a procedure in which some agent or policy maker is assumed to be perfectly informed is said to be informationally infeasible. Particularly a political procedure based on an omniscient (and benevolent) dictator as well as a market procedure in which producers are assumed to know (a priori) each agent's marginal willingness-to-pay for public goods must be rejected because of informational infeasibility. Loosely speaking, an allocation procedure is considered informationally feasible (i) if primary information is dispersed in such a way that each agent's characteristic is private information, and (ii) if the process of communications is somewhat restricted. In particular, it is required that no agent can gain all information about the economy. Once two allocation procedures qualify as informationally feasible, they may be compared as to the "number and the thickness of communication channels" or, in other words, with respect to informational efficiency. Recently Sato (1981) has shown that the Lindahl process requires the smallest information capacity among a certain class of allocation procedures for public goods. Thus, within the qualifications of Sato's

investigation, the Lindahl process is the informationally most efficient procedure. However the Lindahl process can be interpreted both as a market and a political procedure.[27] Thus we cannot discriminate between political and market provision of poublic goods with resprect to informational efficiency as far as the Lindahl process is concerned.

(4) Incentive compatibility. Gibbard (1973) and Satterthwaite (1975) prove that under fairly general conditions it is impossible to design cheatproof social decison mechnisms. The implication of this theorem for (the design of) allocation procedures with public goods is that under the qualification of the Gibbard-Satterthwaite Thorem no non-dictatorial procedure exists which induces individuals to reveal their preferences truthfully (cf. Green/Laffont 1979). One cannot hope to find incentive compatible procedures in which, by definition, it is not to the individuals' advantage to misrepresent their demand for public goods. The lack of incentive compatibility as a particular issue in allocating public goods was already recognized by such public-finance economists as Wicksell (1896). The modern social choice theory can be viewed as a rigorous restatement of the free-rider hypothesis or the prisoner's dilemma. But this new development also produces the paradox result that incentive compatibility is not only a problem in public-good allocations, most notably for the Lindahl-allocation scheme (Ledyard/Roberts 1974), but also for the competitive allocation mechanism with private goods only (Hurwicz 1972). Does free riding constitute a public-good specific phenomenon, after all? Roberts/Postlewaite (1976) and Roberts (1976) are able to answer this question in the affirmative by showing that in economies without public goods the individuals' advantages from preference misrepresentation tend to vanish with increasing numbers of individuals, whereas this result turns out not to hold true in the case of public goods.

The Gibbard-Satterthwaite Theorem is closely related to Arrow's Theorem on preference aggregation both in its generality and spirit. Since there are several escape routes from Arrow's impossibility result, as reviewed, e.g., by Gaertner

27) Sato's analysis is restricted to a single private producer. However, one may also consider the government as being the producer. Then the result on information efficiency still holds.

(1978), one may wonder whether restrictions can be found yielding incentive compatibililty. Concerning public-good allocation procedures, there are, in fact, a few escape routes suggested in the literature, among them, most notably, the Groves mechanism and the voting procedure (cf. Green/Laffont 1979).

The Groves mechanism develops its incentive property with the help of a sophisticated money transfer scheme implying that truth is each agent's dominant (!) strategy if and only if the domain of admissible preferences is restricted to quasi-linear utility functions. The voting procedure is individually incentive compatible, only if the policy space is one-dimensional and, of course, if the economy is such that a voting equilibrium exists. The latter condition again implies certain restrictions on the domain of preferences as required for single-peakedness.

Intuitively, one may be inclined to maintain that exclusive private provision of a public good is superior to non-exclusive political provision of the same good as to its incentive properties. In the former case, exclusion may induce a better preference revelation while in the latter case, due to non-exclusion, agents have strong incentives to free-ride. As argued in the preceding paragraph, however, this incentive problem in political allocation is "removable" so that the conjectured comparative incentive-merit of exclusive private provision may be offset or even overcompensated. We will return to the relationship between exclusion and incentives (or efficiency) below.

The preceding discussion of various evaluation criteria showed, first of all, that for comparing complex allocation procedures such an approach is more adequate than the one-dimensional efficiency comparison. The question remains, however, how to select the "best" out of a given set of allocation procedures by means of such a multi-criteria comparison. Conceptually, this would be easy to accomplish if one could find a dominant procedure, in the sense that it is at least as good as any other scheme with respect to every single evaluation criteria. Unfortunately, any detailed investigation for dominant procedures is discouraged by a negative result due to Hurwicz (1972), Ledyard/Roberts (1974).[28] These authors roughly show that under general conditions there is no informationally feasible allocation procedure that is simultaneously (i) individually rational[29], (ii) Pareto satisfactory, and (iii) individually incentive compatible.

Observe, for example that the Groves procedure and the voting scheme that have high scores as to incentive compatibility generally yield Pareto-inefficient allocations. On the other hand, the Lindahl-allocation mechanism would imply Pareto efficiency if all agents were indoctrinated ("Kantian") truth tellers. But since this procedure is not incentive compatible it may be considered utterly irrelevant to know that Pareto efficiency would be achieved if all individuals abstain from strategic behavior. Information is needed on the outcome of the Lindahl procedure if strategic behavior or misrepresentation of preferences is allowed for. To the best of our knowledge the literature does not provide this kind of information. Therefore it is not possible to argue that the apparent trade-off, say, between Pareto efficiency and incentive compatibility can be settled by attaching to each allocation procedure an evaluation indicator that is somehow constructed as a weighted average of its various achievements.[30]

To sum up the results so far: The theory of resource allocation mechanism offers no sound arguments for either procedure to be at a comparative advantage in public-good provision. In addition to the arguments given above, this is also attributed to the complexity and abstraction of the analysis which actually prevents operational and more concrete comparative studies. However, to further develop the comparison in this direction, one cannot avoid raising normative problems that are involved in comparing alternative allocation schemes or related outcomes. An unambiguous comparative evaluation with the aim to select from among various allocation procedures is only possible if one takes some kind of social welfare function as the basis for comparison. However, such an approach might be rejected on methodological grounds. Thus there are several reasons

28) For details see Pethig (1978).

29) A procedure is said to be individually rational if its outcome is preferable to the initial situation (status quo) for all individuals.

30) It is obvious that informational feasibility cannot be traded against any other desideratum.

pointing to the infeasiblity of a fairly general comparative analysis of alternative allocation procedures, even if comparisons are restricted to efficiency as the only performance measure. Despite this rather pessimistic assessment as to the scope and prospects of a comparative analysis, we do not consider theoretical comparisons to be entirely useless, as will be shown subsequently.

4. Recent Developments in Comparing Allocation Procedures

Recent developments in comparative economics centered around at least two approaches that are not mutually incompatible, namely the theory of property rights and the theory of economic institutions. Though either approach focuses on quite different aspects of comparative analysis, it is important to emphasize that both of them once again examine the determinants of comparative efficiency of economic systems. In particular, they are very similar in their focus on transaction costs. In this section we wish to investigate the role and relevance of property rights and eonomic institutions within a comprehensive theory of allocation mechanisms for public goods.

4.1 Property rights and comparative efficiency

Within the theory of property rights one central point is the study of the efficiency impact of differences in both assignments and "quality" of property rights.[31]) In the present context a question of particular interest is in which way private and collective property rights[32]) affect the relative allocative efficiency of markets and political allocation procedures. "Private property [right, W.B.] means that an individual's right to the use of the resources he owns are exclusive and voluntarily transferable" (DeAlessi 1983, p.66), while collective property rights are characterized by both non-exclusiveness and non-transferability (cf. Alchian 1979). The basic hypothesis of the property-rights theory is that "different

31) For comprehensive reviews see Furubotn/Pejovich (1972), Buhbe (1980), and Schüller (1983).

32) Collective property rights are also known as common or public property rights.

systems of property rights present decision makers with different structures of incentives, resulting in different alignments of resources and different input-output mixes" (DeAlessi 1983, p. 67). More specifically, as compared to other right assignments, private property rights are said to involve the most favourable structure of incentives in order to achieve allocative efficiency. This proposition follows from the comparative advantage of private property rights in directing individual behavior towards efficiency via a special penalty-reward incentive system, that is, "residual claimancy" (Alchian/Demsetz 1972). Since private property rights play a dominant role in markets, while the structure of property rights is mainly collective in the political sector, market resource allocation is said to be more efficient than political allocation.

When alternative property-rights arrangements are discussesd in the property-rights literature, however, the specific problems posed by public goods are rarely addressed. Since these peculiarities are at the core of the present investigation, we will direct our attention to the particular relationship between property rights and public goods. In the following, this relationship is specified by several important observations.

(1) Consider the set of non-exclusive goods defined as those goods for which either no exclusive property rights are established or, if so, enforcement of exclusive rights is incomplete thus leaving the owners with attenuated exclusive rights. Non-exclusive goods may be either jointly consumable, which makes them public goods, or they may be private goods. As far as non-exclusive private goods are concerned, the property rights doctrine has forceful efficiency arguments in favour of establishing exclusive rights, and hence markets, even though the enforcement of these rights may turn out to be difficult in some cases.[33]

Turning now to the set of non-exclusive public goods, one may distinguish those goods which are excludable, but for which the exclusion principle is not applied, for whatever reasons, and those goods which are not excludable. However, we find it more convenient to take the view that, on a conceptual level, private (i.e.

33) A well-known example in this case is the so-called common pool problem. See, e.g., Pethig (1984b).

exclusive) property rights can be assigned to each and every good, notably to all public goods. Of course, the formal assignment of private property rights and the enforcement of these rights are quite different things. Law enforcement may be imcomplete and costly.[34] Hence, for each public good, we are led to compare market allocation with costly exclusion on the one hand, and provision by means of a non-exclusive political allocation procedure on the other. Consider first the two polar cases of free exclusion and of prohibitively high exclusion costs.

In terms of our comparative analysis, the latter statement means that for the particular public good under consideration market allocation combined with private property rights is unambiguously less efficient than non-exclusive political provision. There is wide agreement in the literature that only a few public goods, such as national defense or the legal system, belong to this category. Suppose now that exclusion costs are negligibly low. Then we know from recent developments in the "price theory" of excludable public goods that the pertinent market allocation typically fails to be Pareto efficient. Hence we are left whith the a-priori inconclusiveness of comparing two Pareto-inefficient procedures that has already been discussed in section 2 of the present paper.

There are good reasons to argue that for a large number of public goods, such as parks, lakes, and the public good "information", the enforcement of exclusive property rights is (or would be) associated with significant, though less than prohibitive, exclusion costs.

It is important to realize that the market allocation of public goods is affected by changing exclusion costs or varying propensities to illegal consumption.[35] Suppose some given public good is privately provided by a monopolist and exclusion costs are initially low. If it becomes more and more difficult for the monopolist to prevent non-purchasers from consuming the public good, then, of

34) Exclusion costs particularly consist of costs for defining, specifying, and enforcing private property rights in order to achieve effective exclusion. See also section 3(2) above.

35) Illegal consumption of the excludable public good "information" contained in an information carrier (book), for example, is made easier if the costs of copying are increasingly reduced by new copy technologies.

course, the monopolist's business becomes less profitable. Under standard assumptions he will also reduce the quantity supplied until profit maximization eventually requires him to close down the market (Pethig 1984a). This observation shows that even if a public good is "marketable" it may be heavily undersupplied due to costly exclusion.[36]

The critical question is whether private and public goods are significantly different with respect to exclusion. This issue already played a certain role in the well-known controversy between Arrow (1962) and Demsetz (1969) about the allocative peculiarities of the public good "information". On the basis of his welfare economic approach, Arrow concludes that price exclusion creates substantial difficulties. Demsetz maintains, on the other hand, that private property rights for information do not cause "special and unique" problems as compared to those of private goods, e.g. automobiles. Suppose that unauthorized public-good consumption is illegal and that somebody consumes the good illegally. Then, by the definitorial property of joint consumability, this "theft" does not detract from anybody's authorized consumption of that public good.[37] Even though there is a thief, nobody is missing anything. This fact clearly marks a unique difference between private and public goods which, in our view, causes "special and unique" problems to enforce private property rights for public goods.

(2) It is important to (re)emphasize that, whenever the enforcement of exclusive property rights raises insurmountable difficulties due to prohibitive exclusion costs, common property rights turn out to be a quite appropriate assignment of property rights (cf. DeAlessi 1983). Over time, this constellation may gradually change due to both technical progress reducing exclusion costs and increasing commercial value of the associated resource (good) making exclusion more profitable. Note that even in the case of common property rights the presumed positive impact of exclusive rights can be used. This is possible by imposing institutional constraints which act as surrogates for private ownership rules, such

36) A similar result of market weakness occurs when an exclusive public good could be retraded on a "second-hand" market (cf. Endres 1980).

37) The situation differs, however, if the excludable public good becomes crowded or congested.

as hunting and fishing seasons, catch quotas, and other conditions and controls (cf. DeAlessi 1983). However, these restrictions of free access are costly and can prove ineffective. Thus an allocative improvement cannot always be guaranteed if property rights become more exclusive.

(3) Another important observation refers to changes in property-right assignments. Suppose, for example, common ownership rules are heavily ineffective so that exclusive rights are preferred. However, the shift in the assignment of rights must not be advantageous. The discounted efficiency gains due to the change may fall short of the adjustment costs associated to this shift. Thus, common property rights, though inefficient, are retained (cf. Anderson/Hill 1983).

(4) Now consider the production process of market-supplied public goods. The property-rights school conceives of private producers of public goods as being constrained by (i) competitive pressure, (ii) monitoring incentives of residual claimants, and (iii) other internal and external monitoring schemes (e.g. markets for corporate control, market for managers; cf. Manne 1981). It is argued that these constraints force private producers to be cost efficient in order to survive in the market. From the property-rights point of view residual claimancy is crucial. The right of claiming the residual (profit) is derived from the exclusive ownership of productive factors, and - as is well-known - cost minimization is a necessary condition for profit maximization.

In contrast, political production of public goods is considered to be weakly constrained due to common property rights. Since, by definition, common ownership is both non-transferable and non-exclusive, the incentive for effective control of public sector production is rather small. There is usually no "residual claimant" monitoring bureaucratic production, and while the benefits resulting from a person's controlling activity are distributed among many individuals, the costs are borne by the controller. In this respect, private production of public goods is obviously more efficient than political production. However, suppose there are some imperfections of "residual-claim" incentives, say, due to non-separable team-production (cf. Marris/Mueller 1980) or, for example, some efficiency-enhancing incentives in bureaucratic production such as "job property rights" (cf. Dobra 1983). Then the a-priori efficiency comparison between less-than-perfect market and political allocation may again become ambiguous.

(5) Even if one accepts the existence of a deductive efficiency advantage of private property rights as suggested by the property-rights doctrine, its order of magnitude and its empirical relevance has not yet become clear. The empirical literature (cf. Caves/Christensen 1980, Pommerehne 1983, Borcherding/ Pommerehne/Schneider 1982, Blankart/Pommerehne/Schneider 1984) provides some evidence that as compared to other efficiency-determining factors, property rights are not as decisive as put forward by property-rights theorists. On the contrary, its impact is insignificant relative to factors such as competitive pressure and controlling activities. These factors not only offset, but usually exceed the defects due to attenuation in private property rights.

In summary, for an efficient provision of public goods, it may be appropriate to exploit the efficiency-promoting impact of private property rights if exclusion costs are reasonably low. In fact casual empirical observations reveal that many public goods are privately supplied. But the above discussion also implies that the property-rights doctrine cannot claim to have shown that the market process with private property rights is uniformly more efficient as an allocative scheme for public goods than any other scheme, in particular non-exclusive political provision.

4.2 Economic institutions and comparative efficiency

The main effort of modern economic theory of institutions is to study and compare economic institutions for resource allocation under efficiency aspects (cf. Bössmann 1981, 1982; Williamson 1981). An important part of this research program is to focus on transaction costs associated with these institutions. In contrast to our analysis in the preceding section, transaction costs are investigated in contractual terms. An economic institution is said to be "transaction-cost efficient" if the associated "running" costs are not greater than those of all other institutions, if one regards other things as being equal. The factors which determine transaction costs in economic institutions are, according to Williamson (1981), "(1) the frequency with which transactions recur, (2) the uncertainty to which transactions are subject, and (3) the degree to which transactions are supported by durable transaction-specific investments" (p. 1546). As a result, autonomous market contracting is the more efficient the more transactions occur occasionally (Williamson 1979), the more standardized goods are exchanged (Hauser 1981), and the more special capabilities (e.g. knowledge, experience, and skills) are required for certain activities (Richardson 1972). Conversely, internal organization is the more efficient the more transactions are recurring, bilateral, and asset-specific (Williamson 1981), and the more similar capabilities are involved (Richardson 1972).

Although initially this concept aims at explaining the relative advantages of markets and internal organization, it is, in principle, applicable to all conceivable economic institutions (cf. Bössmann 1983, Dugger 1983). However, the theory of institution does not explicitly consider public goods. After having incorporated public goods in the framework of institution theory, the results with regard to transaction costs and comparative merits are quite analogous to those derived in section 3(2) above. Thus, this issue needs no further elaboration. However, for comparative purposes, some important observations can be made if the quality aspects of public goods are analyzed within the framework of institution theory.

The theory of information characterizes all goods by one of the following three quality aspects: search or inspection quality, experience quality, and credence quality (cf. Hauser 1979). In the order of this listing each quality makes it increasingly complex for consumers to evaluate the associated good. Consumers are confronted with rising informational deficits and uncertainty. While goods with inspection qualitites can be evaluated by careful observation (inspection) before the purchase, experience qualities cannot be perceived except through the purchase and the usage of that good. Goods with credence qualities are not accessible for complete inspection neither before nor after the usage, so that some non-measureability and risk remain even after the usage. Apparently it is not clear how ro classify public goods accordingly. Since, however, there is no easy way to measure practically public goods with regard to its quantity and quality aspects, we have a good reason for classifying them as goods with experience and credence qualities. But it is somewhat open how to distinguish between these two categories. In the former case, the attributes of a public good, though very difficult, may be individually assessable during and/or at the end of its production process like, for example, an opera play. In the latter case the individual assesssment is generally impossible (e.g. national defence, environmental quality). In the end, some lack of conceptual clarity remains between these categories. Nonetheless, we are able to make the following two observations.

(1) In the case of experience qualities, informational frictions may completely impede private activities from coming into existence while political provision is maintained. To see this, consider an example given by Akerlof (1970). He shows that a market (e.g. for second-hand cars) is bound to break down if individuals behave myopically. This failure arises from asymmetric quality information about the good. If only price-competition is feasible and if the lowest quality is sold the most cheaply, then the market tends to shrink to the lowest quality level. In certain cases the market will break down. If, on the other hand, political intervention can guarantee a certain above-minimum quality level at reasonable costs, then the asymmetry of information is reduced and an allocative improvement is achieved. However, the situation differs when non-myopic behavior is assumed. In this case, producers can select between several marketing activities such as "good will" [38], for example, in order to persist in competition. Over time, consumers gain some experience on product quality, and the level of information obtained in the long run may render an efficient market outcome more probable (e.g. private theatrical performances).

(2) Consider now the private provision of a public good with credence qualities like national defence, for example. Individuals cannot be sure that a sufficient quality will be maintained by private suppliers. Since it is difficult or impossible to measure external security (unless in case of war) one is confronted with problems such as free riding, moral hazard, and adverse selection. These defects may be overcome by the government's coercive power guaranteeing a sufficient quality level of the public good "national defence". To evaluate the political performance, however, one must look at the process of the public activity by means of established standards or rules (cf. Frey/Pommerehne 1983). Since these are usual performance criteria in the political sector, public provision is said to be superior to private provision of such public goods. Of course, public provision does not necessarily imply public production. In the case of submission to the private

38) The mechanism of "good will" is analyzed in a different context though by von Ungern-Sternberg/Weizsäcker (1982), von Ungern-Sternberg (1984).

sector, a contractual arrangement has to be settled between the public demander of the public good and the private producer. However, external procurement may be too costly due to various contracting costs as compared to costs of internal public direction (cf. Blankart 1980, Williamson 1981). Thus, even political production may be justified on the basis of comparative advantages in transaction costs.

To summarize this section, recent developments in the theory of economic institutions put forward various arguments for the comparative "transaction-cost efficiency" of publicly provided public goods as compared to private (market) provision. In particular, political provision is the more advantageous the more informational deficits and uncertainty arise for consumers about the quality properties of public goods. In order to further develop this approach, however, the concept of transaction costs needs to be clarified both theoretically and empirically to achieve operational and more meaningful comparative studies (cf. Williamson 1981, North 1984).

5. Concluding Remarks

The literature on comparing alternative allocation procedures for public goods, be it the "old-fashioned" efficiency concept or the "newer" multiple-criteria approach, is incapable of diagnosing an unambiguous superiority of any resource allocation scheme. However, it should be conceded that, in some respect, this research is still in its infancy. Thus, it is not surprising that a fairly general comparative analysis which succeeds in ascertaining performance differentials for privately and publicly provided public goods is lacking. These shortcomings are somewhat compensated by recent developments in comparative economics, namely the property-rights approach and the theory of economic institutions.

However, in general, we know little about the disposition of determinants affecting the performance of allocative schemes with public goods and, in particular, the comparable net effect arising from it. Thus, in order to answer the question raised at the beginning of this paper, a well-founded and comprehensive comparative analysis of alternative allocation procedures for public goods suitable as a guide for decision-making in public allocation policy does not exist, in our view. Moreover, it is unlikely that such an encompassing cost-benefit analysis of allocation schemes is feasible on a fairly general level of analysis. It seems that only comparative studies on a case-by-case basis are capable of offering some conclusive proposals for public allocation policy.

References

Akerlof, George A. (1970), "The market for 'lemmons': quality uncertainty and the market mechanism", *Quarterly Journal of Economics* 84(3), August, 488-500

DeAlessi, Louis (1983), "Property rights, transaction costs, and X-efficiency: an essay in econmic theory", *American Economic Review* 73(1), March, 64-81

Alchian, Armen A. (1979), "Some implications of recognition of property right transactions costs", in: Brunner, Karl (ed.), *Economics and Social Institutions*, Nijhoff, Boston, 233-254

Alchian, Armen A., and Demsetz, Harold (1972), "Production, information costs, and economic organization",*American Economic Review* 62(5), December, 777-795

Anderson, Terry L., and Hill, Paul J. (1984), "Privatizing the commons: an improvement?" *Southern Economic Journal* 50(2), October, 438-450

Arrow, Kenneth J. (1962), "Economic welfare and the allocation of resources for invention", in: National Bureau of Economic Research. *The Rate and Direction of Inventive Activity: Economic and Social Factors*, Princton University Press, 609-626

Arrow, Kenneth J. (1969), "The organization of economic acitivity: issues pertinent to the choice of market vs. non-market allocation", in: Joint Economic Committee (ed.). *The Analysis and Evaluation of Public Expenditures: The PPB system 1*, U.S. Government Printing Office, Washington D.C., 47-64

Atkinson, Anthony B., and Stiglitz, Joseph E. (1980), *Lectures on Public Economics*, McGraw-Hill, Maidenhead

Bator, Francis M. (1958), "The anatomy of market failure", *Quarterly Journal of Economics* 72(3), August, 351-379

Bergstrom, Theodore C. (1979), "When does majority rule supply public goods efficiently?", *Scandinavian Journal of Economics* 81(2), 216-226

Bernholz, Peter, and Breyer, Friedrich (1984), *Grundlagen der Politischen Ökonomie*, 2nd ed., Mohr, Tübingen

Blankart, Charles B. (1975), "Zur ökonomischen Theorie der Bürokratie", *Public Finance* 30(2), 166-185

Blankart, Charles B. (1980), "Über die relative Effizienz von Markt und Bürokratie aus der Sicht der Vertragstheorie", in: Boetcher, Erik, Herder-Dorneich, Peter, and Schenk, Karl-Ernst (eds.). *Neue Politische Ökonomie als Ordnungstheorie*, Mohr, Tübingen, 200-206

Blankart, Charles B., Pommerehne, Werner W., and Schneider, Friedrich (1984), "Warum nicht reprivatisieren?" in: Neuman, Manfred (ed.). *Ansprüche, Eigentums- und Verfügungsrechte*, Duncker & Humblot, Berlin, 221-246

Blümel, Wolfgang (1983), "Politikversagen" versus "Marktversagen" bei der Allokation öffentlicher Güter - Ein Überblick, Universität Oldenburg, Wirtschaftswissenschaftliche Diskussionsbeiträge Nr. 36-82, revised version

Blümel, Wolfgang, Pethig, Rüdiger, and von dem Hagen, Oskar (1984), Theory of public goods: a survey of recent issues, Universität Oldenburg, Wirtschaftswissenschaftliche Diskussionsbeiträge Nr. 80-84

Borcherding, Ted E., Pommerehne, Werner W., and Schneider, Friedrich (1982), "Comparing the efficiency of private and public production: the evidence from five countries", *Zeitschrift für Nationalökonomie*, Supplement 2, 127-156

Bössmann, Eva (1981), "Weshalb gibt es Unternehmungen? Der Erklärungsansatz von Ronald H. Coase", *Zeitschrift für die gesamte Staatswissenschaft* 137(4), Dezember, 667-674

Bössmann, Eva (1982), "Volkswirtschaftliche Probleme der Transaktionskosten", *Zeitschrift für die gesamte Staatawissenschaft* 138(4), Dezember, 664-679

Bössmann, Eva (1983), "Unternehmen, Märkte, Transaktionskosten: Die Koordination ökonomischer Aktivitäten, *WiSt* Heft 3, März, 105-111

Brennan, Goeffrey, and Buchanan, James M. (1983), "Predictive power and the choice among regimes", *Economic Journal* 93, March, 89-105

Buchanan, James M. (1968), *Demand and Supply of Public Goods*, Rand McNally, Chicago

Buchanan, James M. (1983), "The achievement and the limits of public choice in diagnosing government failure and in offering bases for constructive reform", in: Hanusch, Horst (ed.). *Anatomy of Government Deficiencies*, Springer, Berlin, 15-25

Buchanan, James M. (1984), "Rights, efficiency, and exchange: the irrelevance of transaction cost", in: Neumann, Manfred (ed.). *Ansprüche, Eigentums- und Verfügungsrechte*, Duncker & Humblot, Berlin, 9-24

Buhbe, Matthes (1980), *Ökonomische Analyse von Eigentumsrechten*, Lang, Frankfurt

Caves, Douglas W., and Christensen, Laurits R. (1980), "The relative efficiency of public and private firms in a competitive environment: the case of canadian railroads", *Journal of Political Economy* 88(5), October, 958-976

Coase, Ronald H. (1960), "The problem of social cost", *Journal of Law and Economics* 3, October, 1-44

Coase, Ronald H. (1964), "Discussion", *American Economic Review, Papers and Proceedings* 54(3), May, 194-197

Cooter, Robert (1982), "The cost of Coase", *Journal of Legal Studies* 11, January, 1-34

Cornes, Richard, and Sandler, Todd (1984), "The theory of public goods: non-Nash behaviour", *Journal of Public Economics* 23(3), April, 376-379

Culyer Anthony J. (1984), "The quest for efficiency in the public sector: economists versus Dr. Pangloss", (or why conservative economists are not nearly conservative enough), in: Hanusch, Horst (ed.). *Public Finance and the Quest for Efficiency*, Wayne State University Press, Detroit, 39-48

Dahlman, Carl J. (1979), "The problem of externality", *Journal of Law and Economics* 22(1), April, 141-162

Demsetz, Harold (1969), "Information and efficiency: another viewpoint", *Journal of Law and Economics* 12(1), April, 1-22

Demsetz, Harold (1970), "The private production of public goods", *Journal of Law and Economics* 13(2), October, 293-306

Dobra, John L. (1983), "Property rights in bureaucracies and bureaucratic efficiency", *Public Choice* 40(1), 95-99

Dugger, William M. (1983), "The transaction cost analysis of Oliver E. Williamson: a new synthesis?" *Journal of Economic Issues* 17(1), March, 95-114

Endres, Alfred (1980), "Second hand markets and the private supply of excludable public goods", *Public Finance* 35(2), 227-238

Endres, Alfred (1981), "Neuere Entwicklungen in der Theorie öffentlicher Güter", *Zeitschrift für die gesamte Staaatswissenschaft* 137(1), März, 134-149

Feldman, Allan M. (1979), "Manipulating voting procedures", *Economic Inquiry* 17, July, 452-474

Frey, Bruno S. (1981), "Braucht es eine Neuorientierung der wirtschaftswissenschaftlichen Forschung?" in: Timmerman, Manfred (ed.) *Nationalökonomie morgen*, Kohlhammer, Stuttgart, 3-23

Frey, Bruno S. (1983), *Democratic Economic Policy*, Martin Robertson, Oxford

Frey, Bruno S., and Pommerehne, Werner W. (1983), Public vs. private production: Misplaced emphasis?, Universität Zürich, mimeo

Furobotn, Erik G., and Pejovich, Svetozar (1972), "Property rights and economic theory: a survey of recent literature", *Journal of Economic Literature* 10(4), December, 1137-1162

Gaertner, Wulf (1978), "Über Kenneth Arrows Allgemeines Unmöglichkeitstheorem und einige Auswege aus dem Dilemma", *Jahrbuch für Sozialwissenschaft* 29(3), 288-310

Gibbard, Alan (1973), "Manipulation of voting schemes: a general result", *Econometrica* 41(4), July, 587-601

Green, Jerry R., and Laffont, Jean-Jacques (1979), *Incentives in Public Decision Making*, North-Holland, Amsterdam

Greenberg, Joseph (1979) "Consistent majority rules over compact sets of alternatives, *Econometrica* 47(3), May, 627-636

Hanusch, Horst (1981), "Äquivalenzprinzip und kollektive Güter - Allokationstheoretische Aspekte", in: Pohmer, Dieter (ed.). *Beiträge zum Äquivalenzprinzip und zur Zweckbindung öffentlicher Einnahmen*, Duncker & Humblot, Berlin, 37-91

Hanusch, Horst (1982), "Markt- und Bürokratieversagen als Probleme der Selbsthilfeförderung", in: Dülfer, Eberhard, and Hamm, Walter (eds.). *Die Genossenchaften zwischen Mitgliederpartizipation, Verbundbildung und Bürokratietendenz*, Vandenhoeck & Ruprecht, Göttingen, 57-72

Hanusch, Horst (1983), "Inefficiencies in the public sector: aspects of demand and supply", in: Hanusch, Horst (ed.). *Anatomy of Government Deficiencies*, Springer, Berlin, 1-14

Hauser, Heinz (1979), "Qualitätsinformationen und Marktstrukturen, *Kyklos* 32(4), 739-763

Hauser, Heinz (1981), "Zur ökonomischen Theorie der Institutionen", in: Timmermann, Manfred (ed.). *Nationalökonomie morgen*, Kohlhammer, Stuttgart, 59-84

Haveman, Robert H. (1980), "Public choice and public economics: the case of collective failure in US water quality policy", in: Roskamp, Karl W. (ed.). *Public Choice and Public Finance*, Cujas, Paris, 137-154

Head, John G. (1977), "Misleading analogies in public goods analysis", *Finanzarchiv* 36(1), 1-18

Hurwicz, Leonid (1972), "On informationally decentralized systems", in: Radner, Roy and McGuire, C.B. (eds.). *Decision and Organization*, North-Holland, Amsterdam, 297-336

Kapp, Karl W. (1965), "Economic development in a new perspective: existential minima and substantive rationality", *Kyklos* 18, 48-79

Kramer, Gerald H. (1977), "Theories of political processes", in: Intriligator, Michael D. (ed.). *Frontiers of Quantitative Economics* IIIB, North-Holland, Amsterdam, 687-702

Ledyard, John, and Roberts, Donald J. (1974), On the incentive problem with public goods, Center for Mathematical Studies in Economics and Management Science, Northwestern University, Evanston, Working Paper # 116, November

Little, Ian M.D. (1957), *A Critique of Welfare Economics*, Oxford

Malinvaud, Edmond (1972), *Lectures on Microeconomic Theory*, North-Holland, Amsterdam

Manne, Henry G. (1981), "The publicly held corporation as a market creation, *Zeitschrift für die gesamte Staatswissenschaft* 137(4), December, 689-693

Marris, Robin, and Mueller, Dennis C. (1980), "The corporation, competition, and the invisible hand", *Journal of Economic Literature* 18(1), March, 32-63

McCaleb, Thomas S. (1983), "Economic paradigms of government and the market: a further look at the Lindahl model", *Public Finance* 38(2), 332-337

McKean, Ronald N. (1965), "The unseen hand in government", *American Economic Review* 55, June, 496-506

McKean, Ronald N., and Browning, James M. (1975), "Externalities from government and non-profit sectors", *Canadian Journal of Economics* 8,(4), November, 574-590

Migué, Jean-Luc, and Bélanger, Gérard (1974), "Torward a general theory of managerial discretion", *Public Choice* 17, Spring, 27-43

Mueller, Dennis C. (1979), *Public Choice*, Cambridge University Press, Cambridge

Musgrave, Richard A. (1959), *The Theory of Public Finance*, McGraw-Hill, New York

Niskanen, William (1971), *Bureaucracy and Representative Government*, Aldine-Atherton, Chicago

North, Douglas C. (1984), "Transaction costs, institutions and economic history", *Zeitschrift für die gesamte Staatswissenschaft* 140(1), März, 7-17

Oakland, William H. (1974), "Public goods, perfect competition, and underproduction", *Journal of Political Economy* 82(5), September /October, 927-939

Olson, Mancur (1965), *The Logic of Collective Action*, Harvard University Press, Cambrige (Mass.)

Orzechowsky, William (1977), "Economic models of bureaucracy: survey, extensions, and evidence", in: Borcherding, Thomas E. (ed.). *Budgets and Bureaucrats: The Source of Government Growth*, Duke University Press, Durham, 229-259

Peacock, Alan (1980), "On the anatomy of collective failure", *Public Finance* 35(1), 33-43

Pethig, Rüdiger (1978), "Das Freifahrerproblem in der Theorie der öffentlichen Güter", in: Helmstädter, Ernst (ed.). *Neuere Entwicklungen in den Wirtschaftswissenschaften*, Duncker & Humblot, Berlin, 75-100

Pethig, Rüdiger (1979), *Umweltökonomische Allokation mit Emissionssteuern*, Mohr, Tübingen

Pethig, Rüdiger (1984a), "Öffentliche Güter, Verfügungsrechte und Ausschließungskosten", in: Neumann, Manfred (ed.). *Ansprüche, Eigentums- und Verfügungsreche*, Duncker & Humblot, Berlin, 539-554

Pethig, Rüdiger (1984b), "Zur intertemporalen Allokationseffizenz nicht erneuerbarer Allmendegüter", in: Siebert, Horst (ed.). *Intertemporale Allokation*, Lang, Frankfurt, 453-492

Pommerehne, Werner W. (1983), Private versus öffentliche Müllabfuhr - nochmals betrachtet, *Finanzarchiv* 41(2), 466-475

Recktenwald, Horst C. (1978), "Ursachen für Unwirtschaftlichkeit im Staatsbereich. Elemente einer Theorie des ökonomischen Staatsversagens'", in: Hanusch, Horst (ed.). *Reform öffentlicher Leistungen*, Nomos, Baden-Baden, 15-41

Recktenwald, Horst C. (1983), "Potential welfare losses in the public sector - anatomy of the nature and causes", in: Hanusch, Horst (ed.). *Anatomy of Government Deficiencies*, Springer, Berlin, 43-58

Reiter, Stanley (1977), "Information and performance in the (new)^2 welfare economics", *American Economic Review, Papers and Proceedings* 67(1), February, 226-234

Richardson, G. B. (1972), "The organization of industry", *Economic Journal* 82 (327), September, 883-896

Roberts, Donald J. (1976), "Incentives for correct revelation of preferences and the number of consumers", *Journal of Public Economics* 6(4), November, 359-374

Roberts, Donald J., and Postlewaite, Andrew (1976), "The incentives for price-taking behavior in large economies", *Econometrica* 44(1), January, 115-128

Roppel, Ulrich (1979), *Ökonomische Theorie der Bürokratie*, Haufe, Freiburg

Rosenschon, Astrid (1980), *Verschwendung in Staat und Markt. Eine vergleichende Analyse*, Vandenhoeck & Ruprecht, Göttingen

Rowley, Charles K. (1978), "Market 'failure' and government 'failure' ", in: Institute of Economic Affairs (ed.). *The Economics of Politics*, Goron Pro-Print, Lancing, West Sussex, 29-43

Samuelson, Paul A. (1954), "The pure theory of public expenditure", *Review of Economics and Statistics* 36(4), November, 387-389

Samuelson, Paul A. (1967a), "Indeterminancy of governmental role in public good theory", *Papers on Non-Market Decision Making* 3, 47

Samuelson, Paul A. (1967b),"Arrow's mathematical politics", in: Hook, Sidney (ed.). *Human Values and Economic Policy, A Symposium*, New York University Press, New York, 41-51

Sato, Fumitaka (1981), "On the informational size of message spaces for resources allocation process in economics with public goods", *Journal of Economic Theory* 24(1), February, 48-69

Satterthwaite, Mark A. (1975), "Strategy-proofness and Arrow's conditions: existence and correspondence theorems of voting procedures and social welfare functions", *Journal of Economic Theory* 10(2), April, 187-217

Schüller, Alfred (ed.) (1983), *Property Rights und ökonomische Theorie*, Vahlen, München

Seidl, Christian (1978), "Allokationsmechanismen - Ein Überblick über dynamische mikroökonomische Totalmodelle", in: Schenk, Karl-Ernst (ed.). *Ökonomische Verfügungsrechte und Allokationsmechanismen in Wirtschaftssystemen*, Duncker & Humblot, Berlin, 123-2O5

Shubik, Martin (1968), "A two party system, general equilibrium and voter's paradox", *Zeitschrift für Nationalökonomie* 28, 341-354

Slutsky, Steven (1977), "A voting model for the allocation of public goods: existence of an equilibrium", *Journal of Economic Theory* 14(2), April, 299-325

Spencer, Barbara (1980), "Outside information and the degree of monopoly power of a public bureau", *Southern Economic Journal* 47(1), July, 228-233

Stigler, George J. (1975), *The Citizen and the State. Essays on Regulation*, University of Chicago Press, Chicago

Thompson, Earl A. (1968), "The perfectly competitive production of public goods", *Review of Economics and Statistics* 50(1), February, 1-12

Tullock, Gordon (1970), *Private Wants, Public Means: An Economic Analysis of the Desirable Scope of Government*, Basic Books, New York

von Ungern-Sternberg, Thomas (1984), "Marktschutz und legaler Schutz auf Märkten mit Qualitätsunsicherheit", in: Neumann, Manfred (ed.) *Ansprüche, Eigentums- und Verfügungsrechte*, Duncker & Humblot, Berlin, 725-737 von Ungern-Sternberg, and von Weizsäcker, Christian C. (1982), "Marktstruktur und Marktverhalten bei Qualitätsunsicherheit", *Zeitschrift für Wirtschafts- und Sozialwissenschaften* 101(6), 609-626

Vogelsang, Ingo (1983), "Comment to Recktenwald", in: Hanusch, Horst (ed.). *Anatomy of Government Deficiencies*, Springer, Berlin, 59-60

Weisbrod, Burton A. (1978), "Problems of enhancing the public interest: toward a model of governmental failures", in: Weisbrod, Burton A., Handler, J.F., and Komesar, N.K. (eds.). *Public Interest Law. An Economic and Institutional Analysis*, University of California Press, Berkeley, 30-41

Wellisz, Stanislaw, and Wilson, John D. (1984), Public sector inefficiency: a general equilibriuim analysis, Columbia University (International Economic Research Center), Working paper # 254

White, Ron D. (1976), "The anatomy of nonmarket failure: an examination of environmental policies", *American Economic Review, Papers and Proceedings* 66(2), May, 454-458

Wicksell, Knut (1896), *Finanztheoretische Untersuchungen nebst Darstellung und Kritik des Steuerwesens Schwedens*, Jena, reprint Aalen 1969

Wille, Eberhard (1983), "Gesamtwirtschaftliche Allokation zwischen "Markt- und Staatsversagen" - ein ordnungspolitischer Überblick", in: Wille, Eberhard (ed.). *Beiträge zur gesamtwirtschaftlichen Allokation*, Lang, Frankfurt, 1-28

Williamson, Oliver E. (1963), "Managerial discretion and business behavior", *American Economic Review* 53(5), December, 1032-1057

Williamson, Oliver E. (1979), "Transaction-cost economics: the governance of contractional relations", *Journal of Law and Economics* 22(2), October, 233-261

Williamson, Oliver E. (1981), "The modern corporation: origins, evolution, attributes", *Journal of Economic Literature* 19(4), December, 1537-1568

Windisch, Rupert (1980), "Staatseingriffe in marktwirtschaftlichen Ordnungen", in: Streißler, Erich/Watrin, Christian (eds.). *Zur Theorie marktwirtschaftlicher Ordnungen*, Mohr, Tübingen, 297-339

Wolf, Charles (1979), "A theory of nonmarket failure: framework for implementation analysis", *Journal of Law and Economics* 22(1), April, 107-139

STAATLICHE ALLOKATIONSPOLITIK IM MARKTWIRTSCHAFTLICHEN SYSTEM

Band 1 Horst Siebert (Hrsg.): Umweltallokation im Raum. 1982.

Band 2 Horst Siebert (Hrsg.): Global Environmental Resources. The Ozone Problem. 1982.

Band 3 Hans-Joachim Schulz: Steuerwirkungen in einem dynamischen Unternehmensmodell. Ein Beitrag zur Dynamisierung der Steuerüberwälzungsanalyse. 1981.

Band 4 Eberhard Wille (Hrsg.): Beiträge zur gesamtwirtschaftlichen Allokation. Allokationsprobleme im intermediären Bereich zwischen öffentlichem und privatem Wirtschaftssektor. 1983.

Band 5 Heinz König (Hrsg.): Ausbildung und Arbeitsmarkt. 1983.

Band 6 Horst Siebert (Hrsg.): Reaktionen auf Energiepreissteigerungen. 1982.

Band 7 Eberhard Wille (Hrsg.): Konzeptionelle Probleme öffentlicher Planung. 1983.

Band 8 Ingeborg Kiesewetter-Wrana: Exporterlösinstabilität. Kritische Analyse eines entwicklungspolitischen Problems. 1982.

Band 9 Ferdinand Dudenhöffer: Mehrheitswahl-Entscheidungen über Umweltnutzungen. Eine Untersuchung von Gleichgewichtszuständen in einem mikroökonomischen Markt- und Abstimmungsmodell. 1983.

Band 10 Horst Siebert (Hrsg.): Intertemporale Allokation. 1984.

Band 11 Helmut Meder: Die intertemporale Allokation erschöpfbarer Naturressourcen bei fehlenden Zukunftsmärkten und institutionalisierten Marktsubstituten. 1984.

Band 12 Ulrich Ring: Öffentliche Planungsziele und staatliche Budgets. Zur Erfüllung öffentlicher Aufgaben durch nicht-staatliche Entscheidungseinheiten. 1985.

Band 13 Ehrentraud Graw: Informationseffizienz von Terminkontraktmärkten für Währungen. Eine empirische Untersuchung. 1984.

Band 14 Rüdiger Pethig (Ed.): Public Goods and Public Allocation Policy. 1985.

Band 15 In Vorbereitung.

Band 16 Helga Gebauer: Regionale Umweltnutzungen in der Zeit. Eine intertemporale Zwei-Regionen-Analyse. 1985.

Band 17 Christine Pfitzer: Integrierte Entwicklungsplanung als Allokationsinstrument auf Landesebene. Eine Analyse der öffentlichen Planung der Länder Hessen, Bayern und Niedersachsen. 1985.

Band 18 Heinz König (Hrsg.): Kontrolltheoretische Ansätze in makroökonometrischen Modellen. 1985.

Band 19 Theo Kempf: Theorie und Empirie betrieblicher Ausbildungsplatzangebote. 1985.

FSC
www.fsc.org
MIX
Papier | Fördert
gute Waldnutzung
FSC® C083411

Kolibri 360 GmbH
Ferdinand-Jühlke-Straße 7
99095 Erfurt, Deutschland
produktsicherheit@kolibri360.de

Druck:
CPI Druckdienstleistungen GmbH
im Auftrag der
Kolibri 360 GmbH
Ferdinand-Jühlke-Str. 7
99095 Erfurt